Writer's Choice

GRAMMAR
WORKBOOK

9

GLENCOE
McGraw-Hill

New York, New York   Columbus, Ohio   Woodland Hills, California   Peoria, Illinois

Glencoe/McGraw-Hill

A Division of The McGraw-Hill Companies

Send all inquiries to:
Glencoe/McGraw-Hill
8787 Orion Place
Columbus, OH 43240

ISBN 0-02-635152-8 (Student Edition)
Writer's Choice Grammar Workbook 9

10 11 12   024   03 02

Contents

*H*andbook of Definitions and Rules

PARTS OF SPEECH

Nouns

1. A **singular noun** is a word that names one person, place, thing, or idea: brother, classroom, piglet, and joy. A **plural noun** names more than one person, place, thing, or idea: brothers, classrooms, piglets, and joys.

2. To help you determine whether a word in a sentence is a noun, try adding it to the following sentences. Nouns will fit in at least one of these sentences:
I know something about _____.   I know something about a(n) _____.
I know something about **brothers**.   I know something about a **classroom**.

3. A **collective noun** names a group. When the collective noun refers to the group as a whole, it is singular. When it refers to the individual group members, the collective noun is plural.
The class meets two days a week. (singular)
The board of trustees come from all walks of life. (plural)

4. A **common noun** names a general class of people, places, things, or ideas: soldier, country, month, or theory. A **proper noun** specifies a particular person, place, thing, event, or idea. Proper nouns are always capitalized: **G**eneral **S**chwartzkopf, **A**merica, **J**uly, or **B**ig **B**ang.

5. A **concrete noun** names an object that occupies space or that can be recognized by any of the senses: tuba, music, potato, and aroma. An **abstract noun** names an idea, a quality, or a characteristic: courage, sanity, power, and memory.

6. A **possessive noun** shows possession, ownership, or the relationship between two nouns: Raul's house, the cat's fur, and the girls' soccer ball.

Pronouns

1. A **pronoun** takes the place of a noun, a group of words acting as a noun, or another pronoun.

2. A **personal pronoun** refers to a specific person or thing. **First person** personal pronouns refer to the speaker, **second person** pronouns refer to the one spoken to, and **third person** pronouns refer to the one spoken about.

	Nominative Case	Possessive Case	Objective Case
First Person, Singular	I	my, mine	me
First Person, Plural	we	our, ours	us
Second Person, Singular	you	your, yours	you
Second Person, Plural	you	your, yours	you
Third Person, Singular	he, she, it	his, her, hers, its	him, her, it
Third Person, Plural	they	their, theirs	them

3. A **reflexive pronoun** refers to the subject of the sentence. An **intensive pronoun** adds emphasis to a noun or another pronoun. A **demonstrative pronoun** points out specific persons, places, things, or ideas.
Reflexive: **They** psyched **themselves** up for the football game.
Intensive: **Freddie himself** asked Julie out.
Demonstrative: **That** is a good idea!   **Those** are my friends.

4. An **interrogative pronoun** is used to form questions. A **relative pronoun** is used to introduce a subordinate clause. An **indefinite pronoun** refers to persons, places, or things in a more general way than a noun does.
Interrogative: **Which** is your choice?   With **whom** were you playing video games?

Relative:	The cake **that** we baked was delicious.
Indefinite:	**Everyone** has already voted. **No one** should enter without knocking.

5. The antecedent of a pronoun is the word or group of words referred to by the pronoun.
   Ben rode **his** bike to school. (*Ben* is the antecedent of *his*.)

Verbs

1. A verb is a word that expresses action or a state of being and is necessary to make a statement. Most verbs will fit one or more of these sentences:
   We _____.   We _____ loyal.   We _____ it.   It _____.
   We **sleep**.   We **remain** loyal.   We **love** it!   It **snowed**.

2. An action verb tells what someone or something does. The two types of action verbs are transitive and intransitive. A transitive verb is followed by a word or words that answer the question *what?* or *whom?* An intransitive verb is not followed by a word that answers *what?* or *whom?*
   Transitive: Children **trust** their parents.   The puppy **carried** the bone away.
   Intransitive: The team **played** poorly.   The light **burned** brightly.

3. A linking verb links, or joins, the subject of a sentence with an adjective, a noun, or a pronoun.
   The concert **was** loud. (adjective)   I **am** a good card player. (noun)

4. A verb phrase consists of a main verb and all its auxiliary, or helping, verbs.
   My stomach **has been growling** all morning.   I **am waiting** for a letter.

5. Verbs have four principal parts or forms: base, past, present participle, and past participle.
   Base: I **eat**.   Present Participle: I am **eating**.
   Past: I **ate**.   Past Participle: I have **eaten**.

6. The principal parts are used to form six verb tenses. The tense of a verb expresses time.

Simple Tenses
   Present Tense: She **eats**. (present or habitual action)
   Past Tense: She **ate**. (action completed in the past)
   Future Tense: She **will eat**. (action to be done in the future)

Perfect Tenses
   Present Perfect Tense: She **has eaten**. (action done at some indefinite time or still in effect)
   Past Perfect Tense: She **had eaten**. (action completed before some other past action)
   Future Perfect Tense: She **will have eaten**. (action to be completed before some future time)

7. Irregular verbs form their past and past participle without adding -ed to the base form.

PRINCIPAL PARTS OF IRREGULAR VERBS

Base	Past	Past Participle	Base	Past	Past Participle
be	was, were	been	catch	caught	caught
beat	beat	beaten	choose	chose	chosen
become	became	become	come	came	come
begin	began	begun	do	did	done
bite	bit	bitten *or* bit	draw	drew	drawn
blow	blew	blown	drink	drank	drunk
break	broke	broken	drive	drove	driven
bring	brought	brought	eat	ate	eaten

Base Form	Past Form	Past Participle	Base Form	Past Form	Past Participle
fall	fell	fallen	run	ran	run
feel	felt	felt	say	said	said
find	found	found	see	saw	seen
fly	flew	flown	set	set	set
freeze	froze	frozen	shrink	shrank *or*	shrunk *or*
get	got	got *or* gotten		shrunk	shrunken
give	gave	given	sing	sang	sung
go	went	gone	sit	sat	sat
grow	grew	grown	speak	spoke	spoken
hang	hung *or*	hung *or*	spring	sprang *or*	sprung
	hanged	hanged		sprung	
have	had	had	steal	stole	stolen
know	knew	known	swim	swam	swum
lay	laid	laid	take	took	taken
lead	led	led	tear	tore	torn
lend	lent	lent	tell	told	told
lie	lay	lain	think	thought	thought
lose	lost	lost	throw	threw	thrown
put	put	put	wear	wore	worn
ride	rode	ridden	win	won	won
ring	rang	rung	write	wrote	written
rise	rose	risen			

8. **Progressive forms** of verbs, combined with a form of *be,* express a continuing action. **Emphatic forms**, combined with a form of *do,* add emphasis or form questions.
   Kari **is scratching** the cat.   Loni **has been washing** the walls.
   We **do support** our hometown heroes. (present)   He **did want** that dinner. (past)

9. The **voice** of a verb shows whether the subject performs the action or receives the action of the verb. The **active voice** occurs when the subject performs the action. The **passive voice** occurs when the action of the verb is performed on the subject.
   The owl **swooped** upon its prey. (active)   The ice cream **was scooped** by the cashier. (passive)

10. A verb can express one of three moods. The **indicative mood** makes a statement or asks a question. The **imperative mood** expresses a command or request. The **subjunctive mood** indirectly expresses a demand, recommendation, suggestion, statement of necessity, or a condition contrary to fact.
    I **am** overjoyed. (indicative)   **Stop** the car. (imperative)
    If I **were** angry, I would not have let you in. (subjunctive)

Adjectives

1. An **adjective** modifies a noun or pronoun by giving a descriptive or specific detail. Adjectives can usually show comparisons. (See Using Modifiers Correctly on pages 9 and 10.)
   cold winter   **colder** winter   **coldest** winter

2. Most adjectives will fit this sentence:
   The _____ one looks very _____.
   The **dusty** one looks very **old.**

3. Articles are the adjectives *a, an,* and *the.* Articles do not meet the above test for adjectives.

4. A **proper adjective** is formed from a proper noun and begins with a capital letter.
   Marijka wore a **Ukrainian** costume.   He was a **Danish** prince.

5. An adjective used as an **object complement** follows and describes a direct object.
   My aunt considers me **funny.**

Adverbs

1. An **adverb** modifies a verb, an adjective, or another adverb. Most adverbs can show comparisons. (See Using Modifiers Correctly on pages 9 and 10.)

   a. Adverbs that tell how, where, when, or to what degree modify verbs or verbals.
   The band stepped **lively.** (how)   Maria writes **frequently.** (when)
   Put the piano **here.** (where)   We were **thoroughly** entertained. (to what degree)

   b. Adverbs of degree strengthen or weaken the adjectives or other adverbs that they modify.
   A **very** happy fan cheered. (modifies adjective)   She spoke **too** fast. (modifies adverb)

2. Many adverbs fit these sentences:
   She thinks _____.   She thinks _____ fast.   She _____ thinks fast.
   She thinks **quickly.**   She thinks **unusually** fast.   She **seldom** thinks fast.

Prepositions, Conjunctions, and Interjections

1. A **preposition** shows the relationship of a noun or a pronoun to some other word. A **compound preposition** is made up of more than one word.
   The first group **of** students arrived.   They skated **in spite of** the cold weather.

2. Some common prepositions include these: *about, above, across, after, against, along, among, around, at, before, behind, below, beneath, beside, besides, between, beyond, but, by, concerning, down, during, except, for, from, into, like, near, of, off, on, out, outside, over, past, round, since, through, till, to, toward, under, underneath, until, up, upon, with, within, without.*

3. A **conjunction** is a word that joins single words or groups of words. A **coordinating conjunction** joins words or groups of words that have equal grammatical weight. **Correlative conjunctions** work in pairs to join words and groups of words of equal weight. A **subordinating conjunction** joins two clauses in such a way as to make one grammatically dependent on the other.
   Coordinating conjunction: He **and** I talked for hours.
   Correlative conjunctions: Russ wants **either** a cat **or** a dog.
   Subordinating conjunction: We ate lunch **when** it was ready.

4. A **conjunctive adverb** clarifies a relationship.
   He did not like cold weather; **nevertheless,** he shoveled the snow.

5. An **interjection** is an unrelated word or phrase that expresses emotion or exclamation.
   Wow, that was cool!   **Aha!** You fell right into my trap!

PARTS OF THE SENTENCE

Subjects and Predicates

1. The **simple subject** is the key noun or pronoun that tells what the sentence is about. A **compound subject** is made up of two or more simple subjects that are joined by a conjunction and have the same verb.
   My **father** snores.   My **mother** and **I** can't sleep.

2. The simple predicate is the verb or verb phrase that expresses the essential thought about the subject of the sentence. A compound predicate is made up of two or more verbs or verb phrases that are joined by a conjunction and have the same subject.
The night **was** cold.   The guests **sang** and **danced** in the flower garden.

3. The complete subject consists of the simple subject and all the words that modify it.
The bright lights of the city burned intensely.   **The cheerful, soothing fire** kept us warm.

4. The complete predicate consists of the simple predicate and all the words that modify it or complete its meaning.
Dinosaurs **died out 65 million years ago.**   The sun **provides heat for the earth.**

5. Usually the subject comes before the predicate in a sentence. In inverted sentences, all or part of the predicate precedes the subject.
There **are** two **muffins** on the plate.   Over the field **soared** the **glider.**

Complements

1. A complement is a word or a group of words that complete the meaning of the verb. There are four kinds of complements: direct objects, indirect objects, object complements, and subject complements.

2. A direct object answers *what?* or *whom?* after an action verb.
Sammi ate the **turkey.** (Sammi ate what?)
Carlos watched his **sister** in the school play. (Carlos watched whom?)

3. An indirect object receives what the direct object names.
Marie wrote **June** a letter.   George Washington gave his **troops** orders.

4. A subject complement follows a subject and a linking verb and identifies or describes the subject. A predicate nominative is a noun or pronoun that follows a linking verb and further identifies the subject. A predicate adjective follows a linking verb and further describes the subject.
Predicate Nominative: The best football player is **Jacob.**
Predicate Adjective: The people have been very **patient.**

5. An object complement describes or renames a direct object.
Object Complement: Ami found the man **handsome.**
Object Complement: Carlo thought the woman a **genius.**

PHRASES

1. A phrase is a group of words that acts in a sentence as a single part of speech.

2. A prepositional phrase is a group of words that begins with a preposition and usually ends with a noun or a pronoun called the object of the preposition. A prepositional phrase can modify a noun or a pronoun, a verb, an adjective, or an adverb.
One of my favorite meals is pigs **in a blanket.** (modifies the noun *pigs*)
The supersonic jet soared **into the sky.** (modifies the verb *soared*)
The love of a household pet can be valuable **for a family.** (modifies the adjective *valuable*)
The child reads well **for a six-year-old.** (modifies the adverb *well*)

3. An appositive is a noun or a pronoun that is placed next to another noun or pronoun to identify it or give more information about it. An appositive phrase is an appositive plus its modifiers.
My grandfather **Géza** takes me fishing.   C.S. Lewis, **my favorite author,** lived in England.

4. A **verbal** is a verb form that functions in a sentence as a noun, an adjective, or an adverb. A **verbal phrase** is a verbal plus any complements and modifiers.

   a. A **participle** is a verbal that functions as an adjective: Gary comforted the **crying** baby.

   b. A **participial phrase** contains a participle plus any complements or modifiers: **Thanking everyone,** my uncle began to carve the turkey.

   c. A **gerund** is a verbal that ends with *-ing*. It is used in the same way a noun is used: **Skiing** is a popular sport.

   d. A **gerund phrase** is a gerund plus any complements or modifiers: **Singing the national anthem** is traditional at many sports events.

   e. An **infinitive** is a verbal that is usually preceded by the word *to*. It is used as a noun, an adjective, or an adverb: I never learned **to dance.** (noun) She has an errand **to run.** (adjective) I will be happy **to help.** (adverb)

   f. An **infinitive phrase** contains an infinitive plus any complements or modifiers: My father woke up **to watch the news on television.**

5. An **absolute phrase** consists of a noun or a pronoun that is modified by a participle or a participial phrase but has no grammatical relation to the sentence.
   His legs terribly tired, Honori sat down.

CLAUSES AND SENTENCE STRUCTURE

1. A **clause** is a group of words that has a subject and a predicate and is used as a sentence or part of a sentence. There are two types of clauses: main and subordinate. A **main clause** has a subject and a predicate and can stand alone as a sentence. A **subordinate clause** has a subject and a predicate, but it cannot stand alone as a sentence.

          main   sub.
   The book bored me until I read Chapter 5.

2. There are three types of subordinate clauses: adjective, adverb, and noun.

   a. An **adjective clause** is a subordinate clause that modifies a noun or a pronoun.
   The students **who stayed after school for help** did well on the test.

   b. An **adverb clause** is a subordinate clause that modifies a verb, an adjective, or an adverb. It tells *when, where, how, why, to what extent,* or *under what conditions.*
   When the sun set, everyone watched from the window. (modifies a verb)
   Today is warmer **than yesterday was.** (modifies an adjective)

   c. A **noun clause** is a subordinate clause used as a noun.
   Who will become president has been declared.   I now remember **what I need to buy.**

3. Main and subordinate clauses can form four types of sentences. A **simple sentence** has only one main clause and no subordinate clauses. A **compound sentence** has two or more main clauses. A **complex sentence** has one main clause and one or more subordinate clauses. A **compound-complex sentence** has more than one main clause and at least one subordinate clause.

                                  main
   Simple: The stars fill the sky.
                           main   main
   Compound: The plane landed,   and the passengers left.
                             sub.   main
   Complex: Although the children found the letter,   they couldn't read it.
                           main   main   sub.
   Compound-Complex: The earth is bountiful;   we may destroy it   if we abuse it.

4. A sentence that makes a statement is classified as a declarative sentence: The Cleveland Browns are my favorite team. An imperative sentence gives a command or makes a request: Please go to the dance with me. An interrogative sentence asks a question: Who would abandon a family pet? An exclamatory sentence expresses strong emotion: Look out!

SUBJECT-VERB AGREEMENT

1. A verb must agree with its subject in person and number.
Doli **runs.** (singular)   Doli and Abay **run.** (plural)
He **is** singing. (singular) They **are** singing. (plural)

2. In inverted sentences the subject follows the verb. The sentence may begin with a prepositional phrase, the words *there* or *here,* or the verb form of *do.*
Out of the bushes **sprang** the *leopard.*   There **is** never enough *time.*
Do those *pigs* **eat** leftover food?

3. Do not mistake a word in a prepositional phrase for the subject.
The **boss** of the employees **works** very hard. (The verb *works* tells the action of the boss.)

4. Make the verb in a sentence agree with the subject, not with the predicate nominative.
Her problem **was** the twins.   The twins **were** her problem.

5. A title is always singular, even if nouns in the title are plural.
***The War of the Worlds* was** a radio broadcast that caused widespread panic.

6. Subjects combined with *and* or *both* use plural verbs unless the parts are of a whole unit. When compound subjects are joined with *or* or *nor,* the verb agrees with the subject listed last.
Chocolate, strawberry, and vanilla are common ice cream flavors.
Peanut butter and jelly is a good snack.   Neither **books nor a briefcase is** needed.

7. Use a singular verb if the compound subject is preceded by the words *many a, every,* or *each.*
Every **dog and cat** needs to be cared for.   Many a **young man** has stood here.

8. A subject remains singular or plural regardless of any intervening expressions.
Gloria, as well as the rest of her family, **was** late.
The **players,** accompanied by the coach, **enter** the field.

9. A verb must agree in number with an indefinite pronoun subject.
Always singular: *each, either, neither, one, everyone, everybody, everything, no one, nobody, nothing, anyone, anybody, anything, someone, somebody,* and *something.*
Always plural: *several, few, both,* and *many.*
Either singular or plural: *some, all, any, most,* and *none.*
Is any of the **lemonade** left?   **Are** any of the **biscuits** burnt?

10. When the subject of an adjective clause is a relative pronoun, the verb in the clause must agree with the antecedent of the relative pronoun.
He is one of the singers who dance. (The antecedent of *who* is *singers,* plural: singers dance.)

USING PRONOUNS CORRECTLY

1. Use the nominative case when the pronoun is a subject or a predicate nominative.
She eats cake.   Is **he** here?   That is **I.** (predicate nominative)

2. Use the objective case when the pronoun is an object.
   Clarence invited **us**. (direct object)   Chapa gave **me** a gift. (indirect object)
   Spot! Don't run around **me**! (object of preposition)

3. Use the possessive case to replace possessive nouns and precede gerunds. Never use an apostrophe in a possessive pronoun.
   That new car is **hers**.   They were thrilled at **his** playing the violin.

4. Use the nominative case when the pronoun is a subject or a predicate nominative.
   We three—Marijian, his sister, and I—went to camp.

5. Use the objective case to rename an object.
   The teacher acknowledged **us**, Burny and **me**.

6. When a pronoun is followed by an appositive, choose the case of the pronoun that would be correct if the appositive were omitted.
   We the jury find the defendant guilty.   That building was erected by **us** workers.

7. In elliptical adverb clauses using *than* and *as*, choose the case of the pronoun that you would use if the missing words were fully expressed.
   Kareem is a better sprinter than **I**. (I am)   It helped you more than **me**. (it helped me)

8. Use a reflexive pronoun when it refers to the person who is the subject of the sentence. Avoid using *hisself* or *theirselves.*
   Jerry found **himself** in a mess.   The candidates questioned **themselves** about their tactics.

9. In questions, use *who* for subjects and *whom* for objects. Use *who* and *whoever* for subjects and predicate nominatives in subordinate clauses. Use the objective pronouns *whom* and *whomever* for objects of subordinate clauses.
   Who roasted these marshmallows?   **Whom** will you hire next?
   This medal is for **whoever** finishes first.
   The newspaper will interview **whomever** the editor chooses.

10. An antecedent is the word or group of words to which a pronoun refers or that a pronoun replaces. All pronouns must agree with their antecedents in number, gender, and person.
    Colleen's **friends** gave up **their** free time to help.   The **Senate** passed **its** first bill of the year.

11. Make sure that the antecedent of a pronoun is clearly stated.
    VAGUE: The people who lost their dogs stayed in their yards, hoping **they** would return.
    CLEAR: The people who lost their dogs stayed in their yards, hoping **the dogs** would return.

    INDEFINITE: If you park the car under the sign **it** will be towed away.
    CLEAR: If you park the car under the sign **the car** will be towed away.

USING MODIFIERS CORRECTLY

1. Most adjectives and adverbs have three degrees of form. The positive form of a modifier cannot be used to make a comparison. The comparative form of a modifier shows two things being compared. The superlative form of a modifier shows three or more things being compared.
   The year went by **fast**.   This year went by **faster** than last year.
   I expect next year to go by the **fastest** of all.

2. One- and two-syllable adjectives add -*er* to form comparative and -*est* to form superlative.

POSITIVE:	bold	happy	strong
COMPARATIVE:	bolder	happier	stronger
SUPERLATIVE:	boldest	happiest	strongest

3. For adverbs ending in -*ly* and modifiers with three or more syllables, use *more* and *most* or *less* and *least* to form the comparative and superlative degrees.

He was the **least** exhausted of the group.　　She spoke **more** caringly than some others.

4. Some modifiers have irregular forms.

POSITIVE:	good, well	badly, ill	far	many, much	little
COMPARATIVE:	better	worse	farther	more	less
SUPERLATIVE:	best	worst	farthest	most	least

5. Do not make a double comparison using both -*er* or -*est* and *more* or *most*.

INCORRECT:　That musical was the **most funniest** I have ever seen.
CORRECT:　　That musical was the **funniest** I have ever seen.

6. Do not make an incomplete or unclear comparison by omitting *other* or *else* when you compare one member of a group with another.

UNCLEAR:　Joey has missed more school than any kid in the ninth grade.
CLEAR:　　Joey has missed more school than any **other** kid in the ninth grade.

7. Avoid **double negatives**, which are two negative words in the same clause.

INCORRECT:　I have **not** seen **no** stray cats.
CORRECT:　　I have **not** seen **any** stray cats.

8. For clarity, place modifiers as close as possible to the words they modify.

MISPLACED: The fire was snuffed out by the storm **that we accidentally started**.

CLEAR: The fire **that we accidentally started** was snuffed out by the storm.

DANGLING: **To avoid the long walk,** a friend drove us.

CLEAR: **To avoid the long walk,** we were driven by a friend.

9. Place the adverb *only* immediately before the word or group of words it modifies.

Only Afi wants choir rehearsal next week. (No one but Afi wants rehearsal.)
Afi wants **only** choir rehearsal next week. (She wants no other rehearsal.)
Afi wants choir rehearsal **only** next week. (She does not want rehearsal any other week.)

USAGE GLOSSARY

a, an　Use the article *a* when the following word begins with a consonant sound. Use *an* when the following word begins with a vowel sound.

a house　　**an** understudy　　**an** hour　　**a** united front

a lot, alot　Always write this expression, meaning "a large amount," as two words.

With his help, we will learn **a lot** about photography.

a while, awhile　*In* or *for* often precedes *a while*, forming a prepositional phrase. *Awhile* is used only as an adverb.

Let us listen to the forest for **a while**.　　The students listened **awhile**.

accept, except *Accept,* a verb, means "to receive" or "to agree to." *Except* may be a preposition or a verb. As a preposition it means "but." As a verb it means "to leave out."
I will **accept** all of your terms **except** the last one.

adapt, adopt *Adapt* means "to adjust." *Adopt* means "to take something for one's own."
Species survive because they **adapt** to new situations. My church will **adopt** a needy family.

advice, advise *Advice,* a noun, means "helpful opinion." *Advise,* a verb, means "to give advice."
I must **advise** you to never take Jakel's **advice**.

affect, effect *Affect,* a verb, means "to cause a change in, to influence." *Effect* may be a noun or a verb. As a noun it means "result." As a verb it means "to bring about."
Is it true that the observer can **affect** the results? (verb)
I have no idea what **effect** that may have. (noun)
How can the president **effect** a good approval rating? (verb)

ain't *Ain't* is unacceptable in speaking and writing. Use only in exact quotations.

all ready, already *All ready* means "completely ready." *Already* means "before or by this time."
We had **already** purchased our plane tickets, and we were **all ready** to board.

all right, alright Always write this expression as two words. *Alright* is unacceptable.
Because she is your friend, she is **all right** with me.

all together, altogether The two words *all together* mean "in a group." The single word *altogether* is an adverb meaning "completely" or "on the whole."
The hikers gathered **all together** for lunch, and they were **altogether** exhausted.

allusion, illusion *Allusion* means "an indirect reference." *Illusion* refers to something false.
Mr. Lee made an **allusion** to *The Grapes of Wrath*.   The magician performed **illusions**.

anyways, anywheres, everywheres, somewheres Write these words and others like them without a final *-s: anyway, anywhere, everywhere, somewhere.*

bad, badly Use *bad* as an adjective and *badly* as an adverb.
We watched a **bad** movie.   He sang the national anthem quite **badly**.

being as, being that Use these only informally. In formal writing and speech, use *because* or *since.*

beside, besides *Beside* means "next to." *Besides* means "moreover" or "in addition to."
Who, **besides** Antonio, will offer to sit **beside** the window?

between, among Use *between* to refer to or to compare two separate nouns. Use *among* to show a relationship in a group.
I could not choose **between** Harvard and Princeton.   Who **among** the class knows me?

borrow, lend, loan *Borrow* is a verb meaning "to take something that must be returned." *Lend* is a verb meaning "to give something that must be returned." *Loan* is a noun.
People **borrow** money from banks.   Banks will **lend** money to approved customers.
People always must apply for a **loan**.

bring, take Use *bring* to show movement from a distant place to a closer one. Use *take* to show movement from a nearby place to a more distant one.
Bring in the paper, and **take** out the trash.

can, may *Can* indicates the ability to do something. *May* indicates permission to do something.
Anyone **can** use a credit card, but only the cardholder **may** authorize it.

can't hardly, can't scarcely These terms are considered double negatives. Do not use them. Use *can hardly* and *can scarcely.*

continual, continuous *Continual* describes repetitive action with pauses between occurrences. *Continuous* describes an action that continues with no interruption in space or time.

We make **continual** trips to the grocery.   **Continuous** energy from our sun lights the sky.

could of, might of, must of, should of, would of Do not use *of* after *could, might, must, should,* or *would.* Instead, use the helping verb *have.*

That **must have been** the longest play ever!

different from, different than The expression *different from* is preferred to *different than.*

Baseball is **different from** the English sport of cricket.

doesn't, don't *Doesn't* is the contraction of *does not* and should be used with all singular nouns. *Don't* is the contraction of *do not* and should be used with *I, you,* and all plural nouns.

My dog **doesn't** like the mail carrier.   Bobsled riders **don't** take their job lightly.

emigrate, immigrate Use *emigrate* to mean "to move from one country to another." Use *immigrate* to mean "to enter a country to settle there." Use *from* with *emigrate* and *to* with *immigrate.*

Refugees **emigrate** from war-torn countries.   My great-grandfather **immigrated** to America.

farther, further *Farther* refers to physical distance. *Further* refers to time or degree.

Traveling **farther** from your home may **further** your understanding of different places.

fewer, less Use *fewer* to refer to nouns that can be counted. Use *less* to refer to nouns that cannot be counted. Also use *less* to refer to figures used as a single amount or quantity.

If **fewer** crimes were committed, there would be **less** misery in the world.
The box measured **less** than 100 cm^2.

good, well *Good* is an adjective, and *well* is an adverb.

That spot is a **good** place for a picnic.   We dined **well** that day.

had of Do not use *of* between *had* and a past participle.

I wish I **had eaten** my sundae when I had the chance.

hanged, hung Use *hanged* to mean "put to death by hanging." Use *hung* in all other cases.

In the Old West, many were convicted and **hanged**.   I **hung** my coat on the hook.

in, into, in to Use *in* to mean "inside" or "within" and *into* to indicate movement or direction from outside to a point within. *In to* is made up of an adverb *(in)* followed by a preposition *(to)*.

The fish swim **in** the sea.   We moved **into** a new house last year.
The student walked **in to** see the principal for a meeting.

irregardless, regardless Always use *regardless. Irregardless* is a double negative.

Root beer tastes great **regardless** of the brand.

this kind, these kinds Because *kind* is singular, it is modified by the singular form *this* or *that.* Because *kinds* is plural, it is modified by the plural form *these* or *those.*

I love **these kinds** of desserts!   I do not feel comfortable with **this kind** of situation.

lay, lie *Lay* means "to put" or "to place," and it takes a direct object. *Lie* means "to recline" or "to be positioned," and it never takes an object.

I taught my dog to **lay** the paper at my feet and then **lie** on the ground.

learn, teach *Learn* means "to receive knowledge." *Teach* means "to impart knowledge."

I want to **learn** a new language and later **teach** it to others.

leave, let *Leave* means "to go away." *Let* means "to allow" or "to permit."

My guest had to **leave** because his parents do not **let** him stay up too late.

like, as *Like* is a preposition and introduces a prepositional phrase. *As* and *as if* are subordinating

conjunctions and introduce subordinate clauses. Never use *like* before a clause.
I felt **like** a stuffed crab after the feast.   The pigeons flew away, **as** they always do when scared.

loose, lose Use *loose* to mean "not firmly attached" and *lose* to mean "to misplace" or "to fail to win."
You don't want to **lose** your nice pair of **loose** jeans.

passed, past *Passed* is the past tense and the past participle of the verb *to pass*. *Past* can be an adjective, a preposition, an adverb, or a noun.
He **passed** the exit ramp because he could not see the sign **past** the bushes.

precede, proceed *Precede* means "to go or come before." *Proceed* means "to continue."
We can **proceed** with the plans.   From a distance, lightning appears to **precede** thunder.

raise, rise *Raise* means "to cause to move upward," and it always takes an object. *Rise* means "to get up"; it is intransitive and never takes an object.
Raise the drawbridge!   For some, it is difficult to **rise** in the morning.

reason is because Use either *reason is that* or *because*.
The **reason** he left **is that** he was bored.   He left **because** he was bored.

respectfully, respectively *Respectfully* means "with respect." *Respectively* means "in the order named."
We **respectfully** bowed to the audience.
Abla, Héctor, and Shelly, **respectively,** play first, second, and third base.

says, said *Says* is the third-person singular of *say*. *Said* is the past tense of *say*.
Listen carefully to what she **says**.   I love what the keynote speaker **said**.

sit, set *Sit* means "to place oneself in a sitting position." It rarely takes an object. *Set* means "to place" or "to put" and usually takes an object. *Set* can also refer to the sun's going down.
Sit anywhere you would like.   **Set** the nozzle back in its slot before paying for the gas.
Today the sun will **set** at seven o'clock.

than, then *Than* is a conjunction that is used to introduce the second element in a comparison; it also shows exception. *Then* is an adverb.
Julio hit more home runs **than** Jacob this year.   Call for help first, and **then** start CPR.

this here, that there Avoid using *here* and *there* after *this* and *that*.
This bunk is yours.

who, whom *Who* is a subject, and *whom* is an object.
Who first sang the song "Memories"?   To **whom** should I throw the ball now?

CAPITALIZATION

1. Capitalize the first word in a sentence, including direct quotes and sentences in parentheses unless they are contained within another sentence.
Shakespeare asked, "**W**hat's in a name?" (**T**his is from *Romeo and Juliet*.)

2. Always capitalize the pronoun *I* no matter where it appears in a sentence.
Because **I** woke up late, **I** had to race to school.

3. Capitalize the following proper nouns.
   a. Names of individuals, titles used in direct address or preceding a name, and titles describing a family relationship used with a name or in place of a name
   President Nixon   **George Burns**   **Sis**   **Sir Anthony Hopkins**   **Uncle Jay**

 b. Names of ethnic groups, national groups, political parties and their members, and languages
  African Americans   **Mexicans**   **Republican party**   **Hebrew**

 c. Names of organizations, institutions, firms, monuments, bridges, buildings, and other structures
  National Honor Society **Vietnam War Memorial** **Brooklyn Bridge** **Parliament**

 d. Trade names and names of documents, awards, and laws
  Kleenex tissues **Declaration of Independence** **Academy Award** **Bill of Rights**

 e. Geographical terms and regions or localities
  North Carolina **Arctic Ocean** **Nile River** **West Street** the **South** **Central Park**

 f. Names of planets and other heavenly bodies
  Jupiter   **Horsehead Nebula**   the **Milky Way**

 g. Names of ships, planes, trains, and spacecraft
  Challenger   *Spirit of St. Louis*   **USS** *George Washington*

 h. Names of most historical events, eras, calendar items, and religious terms
  Fourth of July **Jurassic** **Gulf War** **Friday** **Yom Kippur** **Protestant**

 i. Titles of literary works, works of art, and musical compositions
  "**The Road Less Traveled**" (poem) *The Old Man and the Sea* [book]
  Venus de Milo (statue)   *The Magic Flute* (opera)

4. Capitalize proper adjectives (adjectives formed from proper nouns).
  Socratic method **Jungian theory** **Chinese food** **Georgia clay** **Colombian coffee**

PUNCTUATION, ABBREVIATIONS, AND NUMBERS

1. Use a period at the end of a declarative sentence and at the end of a polite command.
  Robin Hood was a medieval hero. Pass the papers to the front.

2. Use an exclamation point to show strong feeling or to give a forceful command.
  What a surprise that is! Watch out! That's just what I need!

3. Use a question mark to indicate a direct question. Use a period to indicate an indirect question.
  DIRECT: Who ruled France in 1821?
  INDIRECT: Gamal wanted to know how much time was left before lunch.

4. Use a colon to introduce a list or to illustrate or restate previous material.
  For my team, I choose the following people: Zina, Ming, and Sue.
  In light of the data, the conclusion was not hard to obtain: Earth is not flat.

5. Use a colon for precise time measurements, biblical chapter and verse references, and business letter salutations.
  10:02 A.M.   John 3:16   Dear Ms. Delgado:

6. Use a semicolon in the following situations:

 a. To separate main clauses not joined by a coordinating conjunction
  My computer isn't working; perhaps I need to call a technician.

 b. To separate main clauses joined by a conjunctive adverb or by *for example* or *that is*
  Cancer is a serious disease; however, heart disease kills more people.

 c. To separate items in a series when those items contain commas
  I have done oral reports on Maya Angelou, a poet; Billy Joel, a singer; and Mario van Peebles, a director and actor.

d. To separate two main clauses joined by a coordinating conjunction when such clauses already contain several commas
According to Bruce, he spent his vacation in Naples, Florida; but he said it was a business, not a pleasure, trip.

7. Use a comma in the following situations:

a. To separate the main clauses of compound sentences
She was a slow eater, but she always finished her meal first.

b. To separate three or more words, phrases, or clauses in a series
Apples, oranges, grapefruit, and cherries are delicious.

c. To separate coordinate modifiers
The prom was a happy, exciting occasion.

d. To set off parenthetical expressions
He will, of course, stay for dinner.   Mary, on the other hand, is very pleasant.

e. To set off nonessential clauses and phrases; to set off introductory adverbial clauses, participial phrases, and long prepositional phrases
Adjective clause: The bride, who is a chemist, looked lovely.
Appositive phrase: The parade, the longest I've ever seen, featured twelve bands.
Adverbial clause: After we had eaten, I realized my wallet was still in the car.
Participial phrase: Laughing heartily, Milan quickly left the room.
Prepositional phrase: At the sound of the final buzzer, the ball slid through the hoop.

f. To separate parts of an address, a geographical term, or a date
1640 Chartwell Avenue, Edina, Minnesota   September 11, 1982

g. To set off parts of a reference
Read *Slaughterhouse-Five*, pages 15–20.   Perform a scene from *Hamlet*, Act II.

h. To set off words or phrases of direct address and tag questions
Sherri, please pass the butter.   How are you, my friend?   We try hard, don't we?

i. After the salutation and close of a friendly letter and after the close of a business letter
Dear Richard,   Sincerely,   Yours,   Dear Mother,

8. Use dashes to signal a change in thought or to emphasize parenthetical matter.
"Remember to turn off the alarm—oh, don't touch that!"

9. Use parentheses to set off supplemental material. Punctuate within the parentheses only if the punctuation is part of the parenthetical expression.
I saw Bill Cosby (he is my favorite comedian) last night.

10. Use brackets to enclose information inserted by someone besides the original writer.
The paper continues, "The company knows he [Watson] is impressed."

11. Ellipsis points, a series of three spaced points, indicate an omission of material.
The film critic said, "The show was great . . . a must see!"

12. Use quotation marks to enclose a direct quotation. When a quotation is interrupted, use two sets of quotation marks. Use single quotation marks for a quotation within a quotation.
"This day," the general said, "will live on in infamy."
"Yes," the commander replied. "The headlines today read, 'Allies Retreat.'"

13. Use quotation marks to indicate titles of short works, unusual expressions, and definitions.
"The Gift of the Magi" (short story)   "Ave Maria" (song)
Large speakers are called "woofers," and small speakers are called "tweeters."

14. Always place commas and periods *inside* closing quotation marks. Place colons and semicolons *outside* closing quotation marks. Place question marks and exclamation points *inside* closing quotation marks only when those marks are part of the quotation.
"Rafi told me," John said, "that he could not go."
Let me tell you about "Piano Man": it is a narrative song.
He yelled, "Who are you?"
Did she say "Wait for me"?

15. Italicize (underline) titles of books, lengthy poems, plays, films, television series, paintings and sculptures, long musical compositions, court cases, names of newspapers and magazines, ships, trains, airplanes, and spacecraft.

The Last Supper (painting) *Bang the Drum Slowly* (film) *Roe v. Wade* (court case)
Titanic (ship) *Time* (magazine) *Boston Globe* (newspaper)

16. Italicize (underline) foreign words and expressions that are not used frequently in English and words, letters, and numerals used to represent themselves.
Please discuss the phrase *caveat emptor.*
Today, *Sesame Street* was sponsored by the letters *t* and *m* and the number *6*.

17. Add an apostrophe and *-s* to all singular indefinite pronouns, singular nouns, plural nouns not ending in *-s,* and compound nouns to make them possessive. Add only an apostrophe to plural nouns ending in *-s* to make them possessive.

anyone's guess the dog's leash the women's club
students' teacher singers' microphones runners' shoes

18. If two or more people possess something jointly, use the possessive form for the last person's name. If they possess things individually, use the possessive form for both names.
mom and dad's checkbook Carmen's and Sumil's projects

19. Use a possessive form to express amounts of money or time that modify a noun.
a day's pay fifty dollars' worth a block's walk

20. Use an apostrophe in place of omitted letters or numerals. Use an apostrophe and *-s* to form the plural of letters, numerals, and symbols.
cannot is *can't* *do not* is *don't* 1978 is '78
Mind your p's and q's.

21. Use a hyphen after any prefix joined to a proper noun or a proper adjective. Use a hyphen after the prefixes *all-, ex-,* and *self-* joined to a noun or an adjective, the prefix *anti-* joined to a word beginning with *i-,* the prefix *vice-* (except in *vice president*), and the prefix *re-* to avoid confusion between words that are spelled the same but have different meanings.
all-inclusive ex-wife self-reliance
anti-immigrant vice-principal re-call *instead of* recall

22. Use a hyphen in a compound adjective that precedes a noun. Use a hyphen in compound numbers and in fractions used as adjectives.
a green-yellow jersey a red-hot poker jet-black hair
ninety-nine one-fifth cup of sugar

23. Use a hyphen to divide words at the end of a line.
daz-zle terri-tory Mediter-ranean

24. Use one period at the end of an abbreviation. If punctuation other than a period ends the sentence, use both the period and the other punctuation.
Bring me the books, papers, pencils, etc. Could you be ready at 2:00 P.M.?

25. Capitalize the abbreviations of proper nouns and some personal titles.

    U.K. C.E.O. R. F. Kennedy B.C. A.D. Ph.D.

26. Abbreviate numerical measurements in scientific writing but not in ordinary prose.

    Measure 89 g into the crucible.   Jim ran ten yards when he heard that dog barking!

27. Spell out cardinal and ordinal numbers that can be written in one or two words and those that appear at the beginning of a sentence.

    Five hundred people attended.   I look forward to my **eighteenth** birthday.

28. Use numerals for dates; for decimals; for house, apartment, and room numbers; for street and avenue numbers greater than ten; for sums of money involving both dollars and cents; and to emphasize the exact time of day and with A.M. and P.M.

    April **1, 1996**   Room **251**   **$2.51**   **2:51** P.M.

29. Express all related numbers in a sentence as numerals if any one should be a numeral.

    The subscriptions gradually rose from **10** to **116**.

30. Spell out numbers that express decades, amounts of money that can be written in one or two words, streets and avenues less than ten, and the approximate time of day.

    the **seventies**   **fifty** cents   **Fifth** Avenue   half past **five**

VOCABULARY AND SPELLING

1. Clues to the meaning of an unfamiliar word can be found in its context. Context clues include definition, the meaning stated; example, the meaning explained through one familiar case; comparison, similarity to a familiar word; contrast, opposite of a familiar word; and cause and effect, a cause described by its effects.

2. Clues to the meaning of a word can be obtained from its base word, its prefix, or its suffix.

    telegram **gram** = writing   psychology **psych** = soul, mind
    antibacterial **anti** = against   biology **-logy** = study

3. The *i* comes before the *e*, except when both letters follow a *c* or when both letters are pronounced together as an $\overline{a}$ sound. However, many exceptions exist to this rule.

    f**ie**ld (*i* before *e*)   dec**ei**ve (*ei* after *c*)   r**ei**gn ($\overline{a}$ sound)   w**ei**rd (exception)

4. Most word endings pronounced *sēd* are spelled *-cede*. In one word, *supersede*, the ending is spelled *-sede*. In *proceed, exceed,* and *succeed*, the ending is spelled *-ceed*.

    pre**cede**   re**cede**   con**cede**

5. An unstressed vowel sound is not emphasized when a word is pronounced. Determine the spelling of this sound by comparing it to a known word.

    hesitant (Compare to *hesitate*.)   *fantasy* (Compare to *fantastic*.)

6. When adding a suffix that begins with a consonant to a word that ends in silent *e*, generally keep the *e*. If the suffix begins with a vowel or *y*, generally drop the *e*. If the suffix begins with *a* or *o* and the word ends in *ce* or *ge*, keep the *e*. If the suffix begins with a vowel and the word ends in *ee* or *oe*, keep the *e*.

    encourag**ement**   scar**y**   chang**eable**   fle**eing**

7. When adding a suffix to a word ending in a consonant +*y*, change the *y* to *i* unless the suffix begins with *i*. If the word ends in a vowel +*y*, keep the *y*.

    hearti**ness**   readi**ness**   spy**ing**   stray**ing**

8. Double the final consonant before adding a suffix that begins with a vowel to a word that ends in a single consonant preceded by a single vowel if the accent is on the root's last syllable.

plan**ned**   fin**ned**   misfit**ted**

9. When adding *-ly* to a word that ends in a single *l*, keep the *l*. If it ends in a double *l*, drop one *l*. If it ends in a consonant +*le*, drop the *le*.

real becomes real**ly**   dull becomes dul**ly**   inexplicable becomes inexplica**bly**

10. When adding *-ness* to a word that ends in *n*, keep the *n*.

lean**ness**   mean**ness**   green**ness**

11. When joining a word or prefix that ends in a consonant to a suffix or word that begins with a consonant, keep both consonants.

quiet**ness**   great**ly**   red**ness**

12. Most nouns form their plurals by adding *-s*. However, nouns that end in *-ch, -s, -sh, -x,* or *-z* form plurals by adding *-es*. If the noun ends in a consonant +*y*, change *y* to *i* and add *-es*. If the noun ends in *-lf*, change *f* to *v* and add *-es*. If the noun ends in *-fe*, change *f* to *v* and add *-s*.

can**s**   chur**ches**   fax**es**   sp**ies**   hal**ves**   loa**ves**

11. To form the plural of proper names and one-word compound nouns, follow the general rules for plurals. To form the plural of hyphenated compound nouns or compound nouns of more than one word, make the most important word plural.

Shatner**s**   Stockholder**s**   brother**s**-in-law   Master Sergeant**s**

12. Some nouns have the same singular and plural forms.

sheep   species

COMPOSITION

Writing Themes and Paragraphs

1. Use **prewriting** to find ideas to write about. One form of prewriting, **freewriting**, starts with a subject or topic and branches off into related ideas. Another way to find a topic is to ask and answer questions about your starting subject, helping you to gain a deeper understanding of your chosen topic. Also part of the prewriting stage is determining who your readers or **audience** will be and deciding your **purpose** for writing. Your purpose—as varied as writing to persuade, to explain, to describe something, or to narrate—is partially shaped by who your audience will be, and vice versa.

2. To complete your first **draft**, organize your prewriting into an introduction, body, and conclusion. Concentrate on unity and coherence of the overall piece. Experiment with different paragraph orders: **chronological order** places events in the order in which they happened; **spatial order** places objects in the order in which they appear; and **compare/contrast order** shows similarities and differences in objects or events.

3. **Revise** your composition if necessary. Read through your draft, looking for places to improve content and structure. Remember that varying your sentence patterns and lengths will make your writing easier and more enjoyable to read.

4. In the **editing** stage, check your grammar, spelling, and punctuation. Focus on expressing your ideas clearly and concisely.

5. Finally, prepare your writing for **presentation**. Sharing your composition, or ideas, with others may take many forms: printed, oral, or graphic.

Outlining

1. The two common forms of outlines are sentence outlines and topic outlines. Choose one type of outline and keep it uniform throughout.

2. A period follows the number or letter of each division. Each point in a sentence outline ends with a period; the points in a topic outline do not.

3. Each point begins with a capital letter.

4. A point may have no fewer than two subpoints.

SENTENCE OUTLINE	TOPIC OUTLINE

I. This is the main point.
  A. This is a subpoint of *I*.
    1. This is a detail of *A*.
      a. This is a detail of *1*.
      b. This is a detail of *1*.
    2. This is a detail of *A*.
  B. This is a subpoint of *I*.
II. This is another main point.
	I. Main point
	  A. Subpoint of *I*
	    1. Detail of *A*
	      a. Detail of *1*
	      b. Detail of *1*
	    2. Detail of *A*
	  B. Subpoint of *I*
	II. Main point

Writing letters

1. Personal letters are usually handwritten in indented form (the first line of paragraphs, each line of the heading, the complimentary close, and the signature are indented). Business letters are usually typewritten in block or semiblock form. Block form contains no indents; semiblock form indents the heading, the complimentary close, and the signature.

2. The five parts of a personal letter are the heading (the writer's address and the date), the salutation (greeting), the body (message), the complimentary close (such as "Yours truly"), and the signature (the writer's name). The business letter has the same parts and also includes an inside address (the recipient's address).

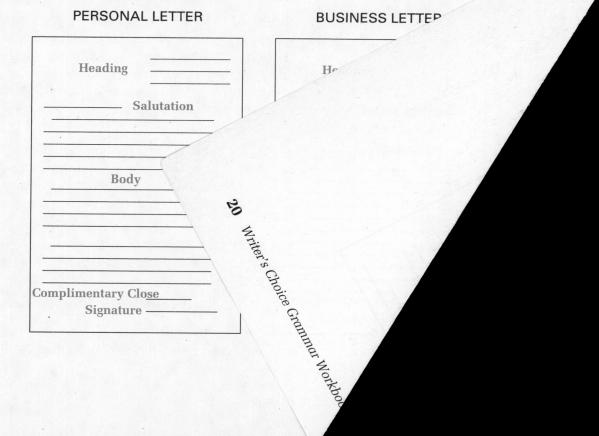

PERSONAL LETTER

BUSINESS LETTER

3. Reveal your personality and imagination in colorful personal letters. Keep business letters brief, clear, and courteous.

4. **Personal letters** include letters to friends and family members. **Thank-you notes** and **invitations** are personal letters that may be either formal or informal in style.

5. Use a **letter of complaint** to convey a concern. Begin the letter by telling what happened. Then use supporting details as evidence. Complete the letter by explaining what you want done. Avoid insults and threats, and make reasonable requests. Use a **letter of request** to ask for information or to place an order of purchase. Be concise, yet give all the details necessary for your request to be fulfilled. Keep the tone of your letter courteous and be generous in allotting time for a response.

6. Use an **opinion letter** to take a firm stand on an issue. Make the letter clear, firm, rational, and purposeful. Be aware of your audience, their attitude, how informed they are, and their possible reactions to your opinion. Support your statements of opinion with facts.

7. Use a **résumé** to summarize your work experience, school experience, talents, and interests. Be clear, concise, and expressive. Use a consistent form. You do not need to write in complete sentences, but use as many action verbs as possible.

8. Use a **cover letter** as a brief introduction accompanying your résumé.

*T*roubleshooter

Sentence Fragments

PROBLEM 1

Fragment that lacks a subject

frag   Ali baked a chocolate cake. (Took it to the party.)

frag   Maria thought the comedian was funny. (Laughed at his jokes.)

SOLUTION

Ali baked a chocolate cake. He took it to the party.

Maria thought the comedian was funny. She laughed at his jokes.

Make a complete sentence by adding a subject to the fragment.

PROBLEM 2

Fragment that lacks a complete verb

frag   Helen is a photographer. (She becoming well-known for her work.)

frag   Alicia has a new computer. (It very powerful.)

SOLUTION A

Helen is a photographer. She is becoming well-known for her work.

Alicia has a new computer. It is very powerful.

Make a complete sentence by adding a complete verb or a helping verb.

SOLUTION B

Helen is a photographer and is becoming well-known for her work.

Alicia has a new computer, which is very powerful.

Combine the fragment with another sentence.

PROBLEM 3

Fragment that is a subordinate clause

| frag | Akira repaired the old boat. Because it was beautiful. |
| frag | Jennifer has two race car magazines. Which she bought at the store. |

SOLUTION A

Akira repaired the old boat because it was beautiful.
Jennifer has two race car magazines, which she bought at the store.

Combine the fragment with another sentence.

SOLUTION B

Akira repaired the old boat. It was beautiful.
Jennifer has two race car magazines. She bought them at the store.

Make the fragment a complete sentence by removing the subordinating conjunction or the relative pronoun and adding a subject or other words necessary to make a complete thought.

PROBLEM 4

Fragment that lacks both subject and verb

| frag | The soft rustle of the trees makes me sleepy. In the afternoon. |
| frag | The next morning. We talked about our adventure. |

SOLUTION

The soft rustle of the trees makes me sleepy in the afternoon.
The next morning, we talked about our adventure.

Make the fragment part of a sentence.

More help in avoiding sentence fragments is available in Lesson 31.

Run-on Sentences

PROBLEM 1

Comma splice—two main clauses separated only by a comma

run-on   I don't know where the oil paints are, they were over by the easel.

SOLUTION A

I don't know where the oil paints are. They were over by the easel.

Make two sentences by separating the first clause from the second with end punctuation, such as a period or a question mark, and start the second sentence with a capital letter.

SOLUTION B

I don't know where the oil paints are; they were over by the easel.

Place a semicolon between the main clauses of the sentence.

SOLUTION C

I don't know where the oil paints are, but they were over by the easel.

Add a coordinating conjunction after the comma.

PROBLEM 2

No punctuation between two main clauses

run-on   Deelra ran the hurdles in record time Shawna placed second.

SOLUTION A

Deelra ran the hurdles in record time. Shawna placed second.

Make two sentences out of the run-on sentence.

SOLUTION B

Deelra ran the hurdles in record time; Shawna placed second.

Separate the main clauses with a semicolon.

SOLUTION C

Deelra ran the hurdles in record time, but Shawna placed second.

Add a comma and a coordinating conjunction between the main clauses.

PROBLEM 3

Two main clauses without a comma before the coordinating conjunction

run-on The robins usually arrive in the spring and they start building nests at once.

run-on Emily won the scholarship last year but she decided not to accept it.

SOLUTION

The robins usually arrive in the spring, and they start building nests at once.

Emily won the scholarship last year, but she decided not to accept it.

Separate the main clauses by adding a comma before the coordinating conjunction.

More help in avoiding run-on sentences is available in Lesson 32.

Lack of Subject-Verb Agreement

PROBLEM 1

A prepositional phrase between a subject and its verb

agr   The arrangement of those colorful pictures (make) a vivid, exciting combination.

agr   One of those big, gray sea gulls (have perched) on the roof.

SOLUTION

The arrangement of those colorful pictures makes a vivid, exciting combination.

One of those big, gray sea gulls has perched on the roof.

Make the verb agree with the subject, not with the object of the preposition.

PROBLEM 2

A predicate nominative differing in number from the subject

agr   Fast-paced adventure movies (was) always Jenny's choice.

SOLUTION

Fast-paced adventure movies were always Jenny's choice.

Make the verb agree with the subject, not with the predicate nominative.

PROBLEM 3

A subject following the verb

agr   On the sun deck there (was) several chairs and a table.

agr   Here (comes) the rain clouds and the heavy, slanting rain.

SOLUTION

On the sun deck there were several chairs and a table.
Here come the rain clouds and the heavy, slanting rain.

Look for the subject after the verb in an inverted sentence. Make sure that the verb agrees with the subject.

PROBLEM 4

Collective nouns as subjects

agr   The crowd really (like) the music, doesn't it?

agr   Margaret's company (arrives) tomorrow by bus and by train.

SOLUTION A

The crowd really likes the music, doesn't it?

Use a singular verb if the collective noun refers to a group as a whole.

SOLUTION B

Margaret's company arrive tomorrow by bus and by train.

Use a plural verb if the collective noun refers to each member of a group individually.

PROBLEM 5

A noun of amount as the subject

agr   The past two days (seems) like a week.

agr   One thousand millimeters (equal) a meter.

SOLUTION

The past two days seem like a week.
One thousand millimeters equals a meter.

A noun of amount that refers to one unit is singular. A noun of amount that refers to a number of individual units is plural.

PROBLEM 6

Compound subject joined by and

agr	A clear day and a light breeze (brightens) a summer afternoon.
agr	Pop and pizza (are) a common meal.

SOLUTION A

A clear day and a light breeze brighten a summer afternoon.

Use a plural verb if the parts of the compound subject do not belong to one unit or if they refer to different people or things.

SOLUTION B

Pop and pizza is a common meal.

Use a singular verb if the parts of the compound subject belong to one unit or if they refer to the same person or thing.

PROBLEM 7

Compound subject joined by or *or* nor

agr	Neither Yuri nor Sarah (like) the menu.

SOLUTION

Neither Yuri nor Sarah likes the menu.

Make your verb agree with the subject closer to it.

PROBLEM 8

Compound subject preceded by many a, every, *or* each

agr	Many a brush and tube of paint (were scattered) around the studio.

SOLUTION

Many a brush and tube of paint was scattered across the studio.

The subject is considered singular when *many a, each,* or *every* precedes a compound subject.

PROBLEM 9

Subjects separated from the verb by an intervening expression

agr   Jamal's new sculpture, in addition to his other recent works, (reflect) his abiding love of nature.

SOLUTION

Jamal's new sculpture, in addition to his other recent works, reflects his abiding love of nature.

Expressions that begin with *as well as, in addition to,* and *together with* do not change the number of the subject. Make the verb agree with its subject, not with the intervening expression.

PROBLEM 10

Indefinite pronouns as subjects

agr   Each of the trees along the old canal (have) different colors in the fall.

SOLUTION

Each of the trees along the old canal has different colors in the fall.

Some indefinite pronouns are singular, some are plural, and some can be either singular or plural depending on the noun to which they refer. (A list of indefinite pronouns is on page 53.)

More help with subject-verb agreement is available in Lessons 44–51.

Lack of Agreement Between Pronoun and Antecedent

PROBLEM 1

A singular antecedent that can be either male or female

> ant   A great coach inspires (his) athletes to be their best on or off the field.

Traditionally, masculine pronouns referred to antecedents that might have been either male or female.

SOLUTION A

A great coach inspires his or her athletes to be their best on or off the field.

Use *he* or *she, him* or *her,* and so on, to reword the sentence.

SOLUTION B

Great coaches inspire their athletes to be their best on or off the field.

Make both the antecedent and the pronoun plural.

SOLUTION C

Great coaches inspire athletes to be their best on or off the field.

Eliminate the pronoun.

PROBLEM 2

A second-person pronoun that refers to a third-person antecedent

> ant   Mary and Jodi prefer the new bridle trail because (you) get long
>   stretches for galloping.

Do not use the second-person pronoun *you* to refer to an antecedent in the third person.

SOLUTION A

Mary and Jodi prefer the new bridle trail because they get long stretches for galloping.

Replace *you* with the appropriate third-person pronoun.

SOLUTION B

Mary and Jodi prefer the new bridle trail because the horses have long stretches for galloping.

Replace *you* with an appropriate noun.

PROBLEM 3

Singular indefinite pronouns as antecedents

> ant   Each of the women in the boat received a rowing medal for (their) victory.

SOLUTION

Each of the women in the boat received a rowing medal for her victory.

Determine whether the antecedent is singular or plural, and make the personal pronoun agree with it.

More help with pronoun-antecedent agreement is available in Lessons 55–57.

PROBLEM 1

Unclear antecedent

> ref   The wind was fair and the water calm, and (that) made sailing across the bay an absolute pleasure.
>
> ref   The traffic was snarled, (which) was caused by an accident.

SOLUTION A

The wind was fair and the water calm, and those conditions made sailing across the bay an absolute pleasure.

Substitute a noun for the pronoun.

SOLUTION B

The traffic was snarled in a massive tie-up, which was caused by an accident.

Rewrite the sentence, adding a clear antecedent for the pronoun.

PROBLEM 2

A pronoun that refers to more than one antecedent

> ref   The team captain told Karen to take (her) guard position.
>
> ref   The buses came early for the students, but (they) were not ready.

SOLUTION A

The team captain told Karen to take the captain's guard position.

Substitute a noun for the pronoun.

SOLUTION B

Because the buses came early, the students were not ready.

Rewrite the sentence, eliminating the pronoun.

PROBLEM 3

Indefinite uses of you *or* they

ref   In those hills you rarely see mountain lions.

ref   In some movies they have too much violence.

SOLUTION A

In those hills hikers rarely see mountain lions.

Substitute a noun for the pronoun.

SOLUTION B

Some movies have too much violence.

Eliminate the pronoun entirely.

More help in making clear pronoun references is available in Lesson 58.

Shifts in Pronouns

PROBLEM 1

Incorrect shift in person between two pronouns

pro	They went to the stadium for the game, but(you)could not find a place to park.
pro	One needs to keep(their)study time free from other commitments.
pro	We were on the hill at dawn, and(you)could see the most wondrous sunrise.

Incorrect pronoun shifts occur when a writer or a speaker uses a pronoun in one person and then illogically shifts to a pronoun in another person.

SOLUTION A

They went to the stadium for the game, but they could not find a place to park.

One needs to keep one's study time free from other commitments.

Replace the incorrect pronoun with a pronoun that agrees with its antecedent.

SOLUTION B

We were on the hill at dawn, and Mary and I could see the most wondrous sunrise.

Replace the incorrect pronoun with an appropriate noun.

Shift in Verb Tenses

PROBLEM 1

Unnecessary shifts in tense

> shift t   Akira waits for the bus and (worked) on the computer.
>
> shift t   Jenny hit the home run and (runs) around the bases.

Two or more events occurring at the same time must have the same verb tense.

> ### SOLUTION
>
> **Akira waits for the bus and works on the computer.**
>
> **Jenny hit the home run and ran around the bases.**
>
> Use the same tense for both verbs.

PROBLEM 2

Tenses do not indicate that one event precedes or succeeds another

> shift t   By the time the movie finally started, we (waited) impatiently through ten minutes of commercials.

If events being described occurred at different times, shift tenses to show that one event precedes or follows another.

> ### SOLUTION
>
> **By the time the movie finally started, we had waited impatiently through ten minutes of commercials.**
>
> Use the past perfect tense for the earlier of two actions to indicate that one action began and ended before another action began.

 More help with shifts in verb tenses is available in Lesson 42.

Incorrect Verb Tenses or Forms

PROBLEM 1

Incorrect or missing verb endings

tense   Ricardo said it (snow) last night.

tense   Karen and her family (travel) to Costa Rica last year.

SOLUTION

Ricardo said it snowed last night.

Karen and her family traveled to Costa Rica last year.

Regular verbs form the past tense and the past participle by adding *-ed*.

PROBLEM 2

Improper formation of irregular verbs

tense   The sun (rised) out of scarlet clouds into a clear, blue sky.

SOLUTION

The sun rose out of scarlet clouds into a clear, blue sky.

An irregular verb forms its past tense and past participle in some way other than by adding *-ed*.

PROBLEM 3

Confusion between the past form of the verb and the past participle

tense   The horses (have ate) their feed already.

tense   The coach (has wore) the old team jacket to every graduation.

PROBLEM 4

Improper use of the past participle

tense   Deemee ⟨drawn⟩ the winning ticket for the door prize at the dance.

tense   The old rowboat ⟨sunk⟩ just below the surface of the lake.

Past participles of irregular verbs cannot stand alone as verbs. They must be used in conjunction with a form of the auxiliary verb *have.*

SOLUTION A

Deemee had drawn the winning ticket for the door prize at the dance.

The old rowboat had sunk just below the surface of the lake.

Form a complete verb by adding a form of the auxiliary verb *have* to the past participle.

SOLUTION B

Deemee drew the winning ticket for the door prize at the dance.

The old rowboat sank just below the surface of the lake.

Use the simple past form of the verb instead of the past participle.

More help with correct verb forms is available in Lessons 36, 37, and 41.

Misplaced or Dangling Modifiers

PROBLEM 1

Misplaced modifier

mod	(Untended and overgrown since last summer,)Marlene helped Keshia in her garden.
mod	Sarah won the jumping contest with her mother's horse, (wearing western riding gear.)

A misplaced modifier appears to modify the wrong word or group of words.

SOLUTION

Marlene helped Keshia in her garden, untended and overgrown since last summer.

Wearing western riding gear, Sarah won the jumping contest with her mother's horse.

Place the modifying phrase as close as possible to the word or words it modifies.

PROBLEM 2

Misplacing the adverb only

mod	Akiko (only) runs hurdles in track.

SOLUTION

Only Akiko runs hurdles in track.
Akiko runs only hurdles in track.
Akiko runs hurdles only in track.

Each time *only* is moved in the sentence, the meaning of the sentence changes. Place the adverb immediately before the word or group of words it is to modify.

PROBLEM 3

Dangling modifiers

mod   (Branches swaying in the breeze,) we rested in the shade.

mod   (Trying out the new exercise equipment,) the new gym is a great
       improvement over the old one.

A dangling modifier does not modify any word in the sentence.

SOLUTION

Branches swaying in the breeze, the tree provided us with shade.

**Trying out the new exercise equipment, Mary said the new gym is a
great improvement over the old one.**

Add a noun to which the dangling phrase clearly refers. You might have
to add or change other words, as well.

*More help with misplaced or
dangling modifiers is available
in Lesson 64.*

Misplaced or Missing Possessive Apostrophes

PROBLEM 1

Singular nouns

> poss   (Charles) car is the white one, but (Jamals) is the red convertible.

SOLUTION

Charles's car is the white one, but Jamal's is the red convertible.

To form the possessive of a singular noun, even one that ends in *-s*, use an apostrophe and an *-s* at the end of the word.

PROBLEM 2

Plural nouns that end in -s

> poss   The seven maple (trees) cool, delicious shade is the best in the park.

SOLUTION

The seven maple trees' cool, delicious shade is the best in the park.

To form the possessive of a plural noun that ends in *-s*, use an apostrophe by itself after the final *-s*.

PROBLEM 3

Plural nouns that do not end in -s

> poss   The (childrens) movies are on that rack next to the nature films.

SOLUTION

The children's movies are on that rack next to the nature films.

Form the possessive of a plural noun that does not end in *-s* by using an apostrophe and *-s* at the end of the word.

PROBLEM 4

Pronouns

poss	That painting cannot be just (anybodys) work.
poss	(Their's) is the trophy in the center of the display case.

SOLUTION A

That painting cannot be just anybody's work.

Form the possessive of a singular indefinite pronoun by adding an apostrophe and -*s* to it.

SOLUTION B

Theirs is the trophy in the center of the display case.

With any of the possessive personal pronouns, do not use an apostrophe.

PROBLEM 5

Confusing its *with* it's

poss	The computer is booting up; I see (it's) power light blinking.
poss	(Its) going to be a great victory party.

SOLUTION

**The computer is booting up; I see its power light blinking.
It's going to be a great victory party.**

It's is the contraction of *it is,* not the possessive of *it.*

More help with apostrophes and possessives is available in Lesson 89.

Missing Commas with Nonessential Elements

PROBLEM 1

Missing commas with nonessential participles, infinitives, and their phrases

com	Lois scowling fiercely turned her back on Clark.
com	The detective mystified by the fresh clue scratched his head in bewilderment.
com	Television to tell the truth just doesn't interest me.

SOLUTION

Lois, scowling fiercely, turned her back on Clark.

The detective, mystified by the fresh clue, scratched his head in bewilderment.

Television, to tell the truth, just doesn't interest me.

If the participle, infinitive, or phrase is not essential to the meaning of the sentence, set off the phrase with commas.

PROBLEM 2

Missing commas with nonessential adjective clauses

com	The sailboat which looked like a toy in the storm rounded the point into the breakwater.

SOLUTION

The sailboat, which looked like a toy in the storm, rounded the point into the breakwater.

If the clause is not essential to the meaning of the sentence, set it off with commas.

PROBLEM 3

Missing commas with nonessential appositives

com   The palomino a beautiful horse with almost golden hair is often seen in parades.

SOLUTION

The palomino, a beautiful horse with almost golden hair, is often seen in parades.

If the appositive is not essential to the meaning of the sentence, set it off with commas.

PROBLEM 4

Missing commas with interjections and parenthetical expressions

com   Wow did you see that falling star?

com   I would have told you by the way but you weren't home.

SOLUTION

Wow, did you see that falling star?
I would have told you, by the way, but you weren't home.

Set off the interjection or parenthetical expression with commas.

Need More Help?

More help with commas and nonessential elements is available in Lesson 78.

Missing Commas in a Series

PROBLEM 1

Commas missing in a series of words, phrases, or clauses

s com   Mona said that Amy Tan James Baldwin and Charles Dickens were her favorite authors.

s com   Sailing on the Great Lakes can be as challenging adventurous and rewarding as sailing on the ocean.

s com   Our forensics team practiced hard did their research and used all their wit and intelligence to win the championship.

s com   The wind shifted the clouds parted and the sunlight streamed down.

SOLUTION

Mona said that Amy Tan, James Baldwin, and Charles Dickens were her favorite authors.

Sailing on the Great Lakes can be as challenging, adventurous, and rewarding as sailing on the ocean.

Our forensics team practiced hard, did their research, and used all their wit and intelligence to win the championship.

The wind shifted, the clouds parted, and the sunlight streamed down.

Use a comma after each item in a series except the last.

More help with commas is available in Lessons 76–82.

Grammar

Unit 1: Parts of Speech

Lesson 1
Nouns: Singular, Plural, and Collective

A **noun** is a word that names a person, place, thing, or idea. A **singular noun** names one person, place, thing, or idea, and a **plural noun** names more than one. Most plural nouns are formed by adding -s to the singular form. Words that end in *ch, sh, s, x,* or *z* form the plural by adding *-es*. Words that end in a consonant and *y* form the plural by changing *y* to *i* and adding *-es*. Some plurals are formed irregularly, for example, *child, children; foot, feet; mouse, mice*. Some singular and plural forms are the same, for example, *sheep, deer, series*.

	SINGULAR	PLURAL		SINGULAR	PLURAL
Person:	child	children	**Thing:**	piano	pianos
Place:	corner	corners	**Idea:**	religion	religions

A **collective noun** names a group. A collective noun is singular when it refers to the group as a whole. It is plural when it refers to the individual members of a group.

The **jury** is still deliberating. (singular)   The **jury** are arguing loudly. (plural)

▶ **Exercise 1** Write *S* above each singular noun and *P* above each plural noun.

      S   S   S   P
Congress debated the issue and approved the bill defining consumer rights.

1. My parents expect us children to help with the housework.

2. The film followed a herd of cows through a typical day.

3. She probably has more self-confidence than any of my other friends.

4. The returning astronauts waved to the cheering crowd.

5. The principal congratulated the class on its performance.

6. The dodo is an extinct bird.

7. Her favorite team lost in the playoffs.

8. My grandmother always used to say that pride went before a fall.

9. The paintings were in the new section of the museum.

10. This particular book contains both stories and poems.

11. Before we could paint the house, we had to scrape off the old paint.

Grammar

12. Frankly, your dog is not the smartest creature I've ever seen.

13. The eerie music during the play added to the atmosphere of mystery.

14. Every time he went to the mall he saw the same group of kids.

15. The awful smell from the laboratory reached to the gym.

16. When the chain fell off her bicycle, she heard a terrible grating sound.

17. One panel gave a presentation about democracy.

18. I usually don't like spicy food.

19. That girl works at the store on the corner.

20. The audience gasped in disbelief when the senators appeared.

▶ **Exercise 2** **Choose 30 singular nouns you identified above. On the lines below, write the plural form for each of those nouns.**

congresses   issues   bills

_____   _____   _____
_____   _____   _____
_____   _____   _____
_____   _____   _____
_____   _____   _____
_____   _____   _____
_____   _____   _____
_____   _____   _____
_____   _____   _____

▶ **Writing Link** **Write three sentences about a concert or other performance you have seen. Use at least three collective nouns in your sentences.**

_____
_____
_____
_____

Lesson 2
Nouns: Proper and Common; Concrete and Abstract

A **proper noun** is a noun that names a particular person, place, thing, or idea. A proper noun begins with a capital letter. A **common noun** is the general name of a person, place, thing, or idea.

	PROPER	COMMON
Person:	Uncle Al	uncle
Place:	Dominican Republic	country
Thing:	*Schindler's List*	movie
Idea:	(the) Renaissance	era

▶ **Exercise 1** Write *P* above each proper noun and *C* above each common noun.

   P   C   P   C

Pedro is taking his little brother to Wrigley Field to see a baseball game.

1. The World Cup is the most popular sporting event in the world.

2. Every four years, soccer teams from continents such as Europe, Africa, and

    South America battle for first place.

3. In 1994, the tournament was held in the United States.

4. Teams from 24 nations took part in the 1994 World Cup.

5. In every city where a game was played, fans of each country cheered their players.

6. Thousands of soccer fans from Italy and Ireland invaded New Jersey .

7. Soldier Field in Chicago rocked to the cheers of Germans and Bolivians.

8. Brazilians backed their team by singing samba songs in Portuguese.

9. Fans of Nigeria, champions of Africa, pounded drums to spur their team to victory.

10. Supporters of the home team enthusiastically waved the Stars and Stripes.

11. Only 16 teams advanced to the second round of the World Cup.

12. These teams then met to decide who would become world champion.

13. Several games were decided by a "shoot-out," in which a single player

    challenges the goalkeeper.

14. One of the best games in the second round was Holland against Brazil.

15. The United States put up a good fight against Brazil but lost by a score of 1–0.

16. When the smoke had cleared, only four teams were left.

17. Brazil, led by goalscorers Romario and Bebeto, advanced to the final by edging Sweden.

18. In the other semifinal, Italy and its star Roberto Baggio crushed Bulgaria.

19. More than two billion soccer fans around the world watched the final game on television.

20. They saw the Brazilians edge a tough Italian team to become world champions.

A **concrete noun** names an object that occupies space or can be recognized by any of the senses. An **abstract noun** names an idea, quality, or characteristic.

Concrete: sneeze, star, explosion, hedgehog, chimney
Abstract: politeness, ability, honesty, love, beauty

▶ **Exercise 2 Write** *con.* **above each concrete noun and** *abs.* **above each abstract noun.**

con.　　　　con.　　　　　　abs.
Bob admires people who practice modesty.

1. Sheila likes to plant and care for flowers.

2. Daniel's integrity cannot be questioned.

3. Ruth and Joe have shown their devotion to this company.

4. Kindness and sincerity dominate my list of important qualities.

5. Claire's new bicycle impressed her neighbors.

6. Uncle Rico will give you the recipe.

7. The coach reminded his players of the necessity for good sportsmanship.

8. The bakery on the corner sells the best chocolate chip cookies.

9. Thoughtfulness is always appreciated.

10. Rashida wants us to make compassion a priority.

11. Mr. Fernandez is teaching us about great world leaders.

12. Jealousy can be extremely destructive.

13. Sunee has empathy for Roger because she has gone through a similar experience.

14. Brad and Caroline hosted a reception for the new exchange student.

15. I always enjoy visiting Mexico and Canada, although they have few similarities.

Lesson 3
Pronouns: Personal and Possessive; Reflexive and Intensive

A **pronoun** is a word that takes the place of a noun, a group of words acting as a noun, or another pronoun. A **personal pronoun** refers to a specific person or thing and can be either singular or plural. The **first person** indicates the person speaking. The **second person** indicates the person being addressed. The **third person** indicates the person or thing being discussed.

	SINGULAR	PLURAL
First Person	I, me	we, us
Second Person	you	you
Third Person	he, him	they, them
	she, her, it	

We are aware that **you** will be bringing **them** to the party.

A **possessive pronoun** indicates possession or ownership. It takes the place of the possessive form of a noun.

	SINGULAR	PLURAL
First Person	my, mine	our, ours
Second Person	your, yours	your, yours
Third Person	his	their, theirs
	her, hers, its	

My coat and **your** bookbag are in **her** locker.

A **reflexive pronoun** refers to a noun or another pronoun and indicates that the same person or thing is involved. An **intensive pronoun** adds emphasis to a noun or another pronoun.

	SINGULAR	PLURAL
First Person	myself	ourselves
Second Person	yourself	yourselves
Third Person	himself, herself, itself	themselves

Reflexive: I bought **myself** a pair of jeans. Intensive: I **myself** bought a pair of jeans.

▶ **Exercise 1 Underline each pronoun.**

<u>She</u> glanced in the mirror and saw <u>him</u> behind <u>her</u>.

1. I could tell it made no sense at all to her.

2. His father runs the cafe by himself.

3. Can you imagine how they felt when they saw them?

4. Their burrito is a meal in itself!

Grammar

Grammar

5. We told her we wanted to do it ourselves.

6. The telephone was ringing off its hook.

7. Randall couldn't tell theirs from yours.

8. She told him skipping breakfast was a bad idea.

9. Did you double-check your answers as they did?

10. Give them enough time, and they will reveal their secret.

11. I myself will perform the leading role in the play.

12. You have only yourselves to blame.

13. Its shine and softness make the material very popular.

14. Their crowd spends a lot of time at the swimming pool.

15. They still had one difficult task in front of them.

16. She had been studying to become a lawyer.

17. Jason forgot to bring his volleyball, so we had to use hers.

18. You mean you found your report in the recycling bin?

19. Cars are a lot smaller than they used to be.

20. He was shocked when he learned the congresswoman herself would be attending.

▶ **Exercise 2 Identify what type of pronoun is in italics. Write *per.*—personal, *pos.*—possessive, *ref.*—reflexive, and *int.*—intensive. Then write S if the pronoun is singular and *Pl.* if it is plural.**

_____per., S_____ I'm not sure *she* understands how important it is.

_____ 1. The large book about Alaska is *hers.*

_____ 2. *I* had never seen anything so amazing!

_____ 3. The coach gave the speech *herself.*

_____ 4. Did that girl ask *you* to dance?

_____ 5. We planned to build it *ourselves.*

_____ 6. She took *his* order after the song stopped.

_____ 7. What did he think *they* were doing?

_____ 8. She watched *herself* in the mirror as she practiced.

_____ 9. Nikki and I agreed *their* project was the best.

_____ 10. You *yourselves* will have to decide.

_____ 11. That silly dog followed *them* all the way home.

_____ 12. Customers serve *themselves* from the smorgasbord.

Lesson 4
Pronouns: Interrogative, Relative, Demonstrative, Indefinite

A pronoun is a word that takes the place of a noun, a group of words acting as a noun, or another pronoun. An interrogative pronoun is used to form a question.

who   whom   whose   what   which

Which is the correct answer?

A relative pronoun is used to begin some subject-verb word groups called subordinate clauses.

who	whom	whose	whoever	whomever	which
whichever	that	what	whosoever	whatever	

Maya is the student **who** wrote the article.

A demonstrative pronoun points out specific persons, places, things, or ideas.

this   these   that   those

These are the most interesting videodiscs.

An indefinite pronoun refers to persons, places, or things in a more general way than a noun does.

all	both	everything	none	several
another	each	few	no one	some
any	either	many	nothing	somebody
anybody	enough	most	one	someone
anyone	everybody	neither	other	something
anything	everyone	nobody	others	

Few are ever found again.

▶ **Exercise 1** Underline each pronoun. In the blank, write *int.* if the pronoun is interrogative, *rel.* if it is relative, *dem.* if it is demonstrative, and *ind.* if it is indefinite.

___int.___ Who can answer this question?

_____ **1.** What is the longest river in the United States?

_____ **2.** The Missouri, which flows 2,540 miles, is the longest river.

_____ **3.** In fact, the Missouri is one of the longest rivers in the world.

_____ **4.** How many of the world's rivers are longer than the Missouri?

Grammar

_____ 5. The Ohio River and the Missouri River, which are tributaries of the Mississippi River, flow into the Mississippi at Cairo, Illinois, and St. Louis, Missouri.

_____ 6. Both are vital transportation routes.

_____ 7. These, along with other smaller rivers, help make up the Mississippi River Basin.

_____ 8. Statistics show that the Mississippi River carries almost two thirds of the country's inland freight.

_____ 9. St. Louis, Memphis, and New Orleans are several of the cities on the river.

_____ 10. Which is the largest state bordering the Mississippi River?

_____ 11. A famous writer who is associated with the Mississippi is Mark Twain.

_____ 12. Twain wrote about whatever was around his hometown of Hannibal, Missouri.

_____ 13. The bustling life of the river was something Twain described in book after book.

_____ 14. Nothing was closer to the writer's heart.

_____ 15. Three books that are set on the river are *Life on the Mississippi, Tom Sawyer,* and *Pudd'nhead Wilson.*

_____ 16. Twain's most famous book is one many people love.

_____ 17. Many literary critics believe that *Huckleberry Finn* is the finest American novel.

_____ 18. What makes the story so popular?

_____ 19. Perhaps there is a little bit of Huck Finn in everybody.

_____ 20. Anybody interested in America's greatest river should read Mark Twain's books.

▶ **Exercise 2 Complete each sentence by filling in an appropriate pronoun of the type indicated.**

_____ This *or* That _____ is a subject open for discussion. (demonstrative)

1. The Zaire River, _____ was known as the Congo River until 1971, flows through west-central Africa. (relative)

2. _____ is the river that drains an area of the African continent known as the Congo Basin. (demonstrative)

3. The area, _____ is fed annually by as much as 100 inches of rainfall, covers 1.5 million square miles. (relative)

4. The Zaire River, _____ is 2,900 miles long, is of great importance to the people of the area. (relative)

5. _____ of the rivers in Africa is the longest? (interrogative)

Lesson 5
Verbs: Action (Transitive/Intransitive)

A **verb** is a word that expresses action or a state of being and is necessary to make a statement. An **action verb** tells what someone or something does. Some action verbs express physical action. Other action verbs express mental action. A **transitive verb** is an action verb that is followed by a word or words that answer the question *what?* or *whom?*

The dancer **performed** the most difficult movements. (The action verb *performed* is followed by the noun *movements,* which answers the question *what?*)

An **intransitive verb** is an action verb that is not followed by words that answer the question *what?* or *whom?*

The dancer **performed** gracefully. (The action verb *performed* is followed by a word that tells how.)

▶ **Exercise 1** Underline the verb in each sentence. In the blank, write *T* if the verb is transitive. Write *I* if the verb is intransitive.

___T___   Jaelyn <u>followed</u> the recipe carefully.

_____ **1.** Kathleen Battle, the opera star, sings amazingly well.

_____ **2.** The red ants fought the black ants.

_____ **3.** My aunt plays rugby every Sunday.

_____ **4.** The hawk flew slowly over the forest.

_____ **5.** Everyone saw the horse with the beautiful saddle.

_____ **6.** Twenty-thousand people watched in amazement.

_____ **7.** Beth finally heard that new song by the Ooglies.

_____ **8.** The members of the chess club elected Janelle president.

_____ **9.** The sound engineer recorded the bass and guitars first.

_____ **10.** Dogs hear much better than humans.

_____ **11.** I never watch game shows on television.

_____ **12.** Robin finished early.

_____ **13.** The dolphin turned quickly and smoothly.

_____ **14.** I finished my homework during study hall.

_____ **15.** I turned the pages of the old book with care.

_____ **16.** Hummingbirds eat almost constantly.

_____ **17.** Salmon actually swim up rivers.

_____ **18.** The plan succeeded in spite of his strong opposition.

_____ **19.** Carson's dog eats almost anything.

_____ **20.** Raeanne tasted my bagel.

_____ **21.** My dad never drinks coffee with his meals.

_____ **22.** The beavers built the dam in less than a day.

_____ **23.** Luis stayed at his grandmother's house for three weeks in the spring.

_____ **24.** The parakeet died of pneumonia.

_____ **25.** The outfielder caught the ball near the wall.

_____ **26.** The crow looked at the scarecrow without the slightest trace of fear.

_____ **27.** Aleksandr Solzhenitsyn returned to Russia in 1994.

_____ **28.** Quentin conducted the school jazz band during one number.

_____ **29.** Chen ran faster than anyone else in the entire school.

_____ **30.** He returned her calculator with a big scratch on it.

_____ **31.** Good detectives never reveal their theories.

_____ **32.** The tour director made all the reservations.

_____ **33.** The bloodhound smelled something on the old, dirty jacket.

_____ **34.** The bell rang at exactly midnight.

_____ **35.** Mr. Rossi ran the shop with an iron hand.

_____ **36.** She opened the window in the kitchen.

_____ **37.** People called often during the holidays.

_____ **38.** In *Casablanca* Bogart and Bergman meet for the last time at an airport.

_____ **39.** The mayor called just before dinner.

_____ **40.** Uncle Roscoe met me at the bus station.

▶ **Writing Link** **Write three sentences describing your favorite movie. Use both transitive and intransitive verbs in your description.**

_____

_____

_____

_____

Lesson 6
Verbs: Linking

A linking verb links, or joins, the subject of a sentence (often a noun or a pronoun) with a word or expression that identifies or describes the subject. *Be* in all its forms (*am, is, are, was, were, been, being*) is the most common linking verb. Other linking verbs include *look, sound, feel, grow, remain, stay, seem, appear, become,* and *taste.*

I **am** a soldier.	Bananas **were** plentiful.
The opera **sounded** wonderful.	She **felt** sad.

▶ **Exercise 1 Place a check in the blank next to each sentence whose main verb is a linking verb.**

___✔___   Fiona is Irish.

_____ **1.** Irish Americans are one of this country's largest immigrant groups.

_____ **2.** About 40 million Americans claim Irish ancestry.

_____ **3.** This total is almost ten times the number of people in the country of Ireland today.

_____ **4.** Among the states with the largest number of Irish Americans are Massachusetts, Delaware, New Hampshire, and Rhode Island.

_____ **5.** Irish immigrants came to this country very early in its history.

_____ **6.** Ireland was a country with a large population.

_____ **7.** The large number of people caused a rise in the poverty level.

_____ **8.** Many Irish felt hopeful about the endless job opportunities in America.

_____ **9.** In 1845 a terrible potato famine struck Ireland.

_____ **10.** The first big wave of Irish immigrants started in the 1840s.

_____ **11.** Most Irish immigrants settled in the large cities of the Northeast.

_____ **12.** Irish immigrants were important in building the famous Erie Canal and many highways, railroads, and cities.

_____ **13.** The Irish had an advantage over other immigrants because they could speak English.

_____ **14.** In spite of this, however, many Irish suffered discrimination.

_____ **15.** Irish Americans have made important contributions in many areas of American life and society.

_____ **16.** One well-known Irish American was President John F. Kennedy.

_____ **17.** Irish American Eugene O'Neill, an outstanding dramatist, won the Nobel Prize in literature for his plays.

_____ 18. John L. Sullivan, America's first sports superstar, reigned as world heavyweight boxing champion in the late 1800s.

_____ 19. Other famous Irish Americans are actor John Wayne, singer Bing Crosby, and Ronald Reagan, the former president.

_____ 20. March 17, St. Patrick's Day, is the day when Irish Americans celebrate their heritage.

▶ **Exercise 2** **Underline the linking verb (or verbs) in each sentence. Then circle the word or words after the linking verb that identify or describe the subject.**

This is the (story) of an American hero.

1. John Fitzgerald Kennedy was the thirty-fifth president of the United States.

2. When he was a child, his life seemed easy.

3. Joseph and Rose Kennedy appeared eager to give their children every opportunity to succeed.

4. John became an author when an expanded version of his senior thesis was published as a book.

5. *Why England Slept* is an account of Great Britain's difficulty in trying to react to military events.

6. Events grew bleaker in Europe as World War II advanced.

7. The United States stayed neutral for a time but eventually sent troops to Europe and Asia.

8. John Kennedy felt confident that he could command a Navy motor torpedo boat.

9. His mission grew dangerous when a Japanese destroyer sank his boat.

10. He became a hero when he led his men back to safety.

11. After the war ended, Kennedy became a politician.

12. He was first a congressman and then a senator.

13. In Congress, he was responsive to his constituents' concerns.

14. Though often ill, he looked vigorous and strong.

15. He became a strong supporter of civil rights legislation.

16. In 1960, Kennedy was the Democratic party's candidate for president.

17. He remains the youngest person ever elected President of the United States.

18. His inaugural address sounded eloquent to the citizens.

19. His ideas were new and exciting.

20. His influence on young people was great.

Lesson 7
Verb Phrases

The **verb** in a sentence may consist of more than one word. The words that accompany the main verb are called **auxiliary**, or helping, **verbs**. A **verb phrase** consists of a main verb and all its auxiliary verbs.

forms of *be*	am, is, are, was, were, being, been
forms of *have*	has, have, had
other auxiliaries	can, could, may, might, shall, will, do, does, did, must, should, would

The most common auxiliary verbs are the forms of *be* and *have*.

They **are going**.   They **have gone**.   They **had been going**.

The other auxiliary verbs are not used primarily to express time.

She **should be arriving**.   **Could** she **have arrived?**
She **could** already **be sitting** there.

▶ **Exercise 1** **Place a check next to each sentence that contains an auxiliary verb. In the sentences that contain an auxiliary verb, underline the verb phrase. Then circle the auxiliary verb.**

_____✔_____   Stock car racing (has) been popular for years.

_____   **1.** No one has been more successful in auto races than Richard Petty.

_____   **2.** The stock car race driver was known to millions of fans as "King Richard."

_____   **3.** Stock cars are quite different from the sleek cars in the Indianapolis 500.

_____   **4.** On the outside, stock cars may appear normal.

_____   **5.** But under the hood, stock cars have always had special, powerful engines.

_____   **6.** The cars also have additional safety features.

_____   **7.** From 1960 to 1984, Richard Petty was winning in his trademark blue car.

_____   **8.** He had crossed the finish line first more than two hundred times.

_____   **9.** Did Richard Petty ever crash his race car?

_____   **10.** The King was involved in many crashes, including a nasty one at the 1976 Daytona 500.

_____   **11.** Richard Petty won his last race on July 4, 1984.

_____   **12.** Did Richard Petty's great success go to his head?

_____   **13.** No, he remained a favorite with fans because of his friendliness.

_____ **14.** Thousands of fans have visited his headquarters in Level Cross, North Carolina.

_____ **15.** For many fans, stock car racing is a family affair.

_____ **16.** Men and women, boys and girls, and people of all ages enjoy watching the races.

_____ **17.** For drivers, racing can also be a family affair.

_____ **18.** Richard Petty's father, Lee, had been one of the first great stock car drivers.

_____ **19.** Not surprisingly, Richard's son is following in his father's footsteps.

_____ **20.** Any interested people should attend a stock car race.

▶ **Exercise 2 Complete each sentence by writing a verb phrase (main verb and auxiliary verbs) using the verb indicated.**

Myra _____was reading_____ about race car drivers. (read)

1. Janet Guthrie _____ cars for thirteen years before she first competed in the Indianapolis 500. (race)

2. Many famous auto racing drivers _____ about the sport at a young age. (think)

3. However, Janet Guthrie _____ in flying airplanes. (interest)

4. She _____ a famous pilot. (be)

5. In fact, by age nineteen she _____ a commercial pilot's license. (obtain)

6. Five years later, she _____ tests for a competition license in auto racing. (take)

7. She _____ third in her Sports Car Club of America class the following year. (finish)

8. Racing _____ her primary interest. (become)

9. When she _____ for her graduate school finals in physics, she was racing somewhere instead. (study)

10. That is when she decided she _____ a professional race car driver. (be)

11. She used all the money she _____ to pursue her dream. (save)

12. She _____ race car owners and ask them to hire her. (stop)

13. Finally, Janet decided she _____ to build her own car. (try)

14. After building a good record, she _____ an opportunity to qualify for the Indianapolis 500. (offer)

15. In 1978, Janet Guthrie _____ history by finishing in ninth place. (make)

Grammar

Lesson 8
Adjectives

An **adjective** is a word that modifies a noun or pronoun by limiting its meaning.

shiny toaster   **friendly** neighbor   **horrible** accident   **green** bird   **that** book

Articles are the adjectives *a, an,* and *the. A* and *an* are indefinite articles. *The* is the definite article.

Possessive pronouns, such as *my* and *our,* can be considered adjectives because they modify nouns. Similarly, possessive forms of nouns, such as *Roger's* and *the captain's,* can also be considered adjectives.

A **proper adjective** is formed from a proper noun and begins with a capital letter.

Cervantes was a **Spanish** writer.   The **Korean** restaurant is very popular.

▶ **Exercise 1** **Underline the adjectives, including articles, possessive pronouns, possessive forms of nouns, and proper adjectives in each sentence.**

The weary rebels climbed the hill to the fort.

1. The weight lifter grunted and groaned trying to lift the heavy barbell.

2. The hungry boy ate a juicy hamburger and a tossed salad.

3. My little brother loves Chinese food.

4. Where did you get that beautiful coat?

5. The designers changed the basic design of the popular model.

6. A good hiking boot needs a sturdy sole.

7. We watched the little silvery fish jump completely out of the water.

8. His mother watched the new sitcom on Monday night.

9. This music is putting me in a relaxed mood.

10. Wooden tent stakes have been replaced by plastic or metal ones.

11. Whose car is parked in front of your apartment?

12. Because of the dense fog, the nervous detective could see only a dim outline of the figure.

13. Michael's new puppy loves to chew on things.

14. Probably the hottest new sport in town is in-line skating.

15. All the excited fans cheered on their favorite tennis star.

16. Kristin brought some Norwegian cookies her grandmother made to the club's last party.

Grammar

17. Trevor really wanted the lead role in the play, but his tryout was a disaster.

18. Juwan's sister donated her old computer to the new club.

19. Please take off that awful mask!

20. The international student in our class is a Brazilian.

▶ **Exercise 2** **Complete each sentence by adding an appropriate adjective in the space provided.**

That was the most _____interesting_____ book I've ever read.

1. Sylvia unpacked her _____ jacket.

2. The actor gave a _____ portrayal of the downtrodden farmer.

3. The _____ traveler stared at the icy glass of water.

4. The women entered the _____ store.

5. We gave the _____ server a generous tip.

6. Samantha bit into the ripe, _____ peach.

7. The _____ knife cut the roast easily.

8. People consider Lucas a very _____ boy.

9. The teacher seems to like _____ paintings.

10. My brother's _____ motorcycle is in the garage.

11. _____ food can be really tasty.

12. The _____ girl is the captain of the volleyball team.

13. The inspector confiscated the _____ diamonds.

14. My aunt and uncle's vacation in Colorado was a _____ experience.

15. Her best friend moved to a town in the _____ part of the state.

16. Tracy's favorite class was the one on _____ literature.

17. It's _____ to climb on the bridge.

18. I like any kind of _____ music.

19. The _____ person who came around the corner was a police officer.

20. The _____ article about the school's dress code was written by the assistant editor.

Lesson 9
Adverbs

An **adverb** is a word that modifies a verb, an adjective, or another adverb by making its meaning more specific. Adverbs modify by answering the questions *when? where? how?* and *to what degree?*

We left **early** for the soccer game. (The adverb *early* modifies the verb *left* by answering the question *when?*)

Janine waited **there** for the bus. (The adverb *there* modifies the verb *waited* by answering the question *where?*)

The nurse **quietly** shut the door of the hospital room. (The adverb *quietly* modifies the verb *shut* by answering the question *how?*)

Very few things in life are **completely** perfect. (The adverb *completely* modifies the adjective *perfect* by answering the question *to what degree?*)

Negative words, such as *not* and its contraction *-n't,* are also considered adverbs. Other negative words such as *nowhere, hardly,* and *never* can also function as adverbs.

The boat has **not** arrived.   I have **never** eaten squid.

▶ **Exercise 1** **Circle the word or words modified by the adverb in italics. On the blank, write *v* if the adverb modifies a verb. Write *adj.* if the adverb modifies an adjective. Write *adv.* if the adverb modifies another adverb.**

___*v*___   Whitney *almost* (cleared) the hurdle.

_____ **1.** I've seen Alison at the nursing home *very* often.

_____ **2.** Ben *easily* made the cross-country team.

_____ **3.** Our class had a *really* fantastic time on the field trip to the science museum.

_____ **4.** Two hundred people had *already* ordered tickets.

_____ **5.** *Sometimes* nice guys do finish first.

_____ **6.** Shannon had a *very* difficult time after the accident.

_____ **7.** Late in the afternoon storm clouds gathered *overhead*.

_____ **8.** Farrah's purse was *nowhere* in the room.

_____ **9.** *Now* and *then,* I wish for something impossible.

_____ **10.** England had not *yet* prepared for war.

_____ **11.** Don't stay out in the sun too *long*.

_____ **12.** Zach would *never* understand his sister and her friends.

Grammar

_____ **13.** *Almost* every person at the meeting was angry about the decision.

_____ **14.** I'll talk to you *later*.

_____ **15.** Tuyen was *completely* calm when we jumped out and yelled "Happy Birthday!"

_____ **16.** Birds migrate alone *very* infrequently.

_____ **17.** Hand in your paper *today*.

_____ **18.** I don't think she was *entirely* sure what she had said.

_____ **19.** *Only* rarely can gorillas breed in captivity.

_____ **20.** We have*n't* succeeded yet, but we'll keep on trying.

▶ Exercise 2 **Underline the adverb or adverbs in each sentence.**

<u>Slowly</u>, Marcus made his way to the front of the train.

1. Nicholas timidly thanked me for the birthday gift.

2. Your business with Carol is altogether private.

3. We had scarcely arrived at the park when the storm began.

4. The visiting team arrived late for the big game.

5. Kwan came here looking for you.

6. Louis had not considered that alternative.

7. Mr. Wilson usually hires students during the summer.

8. Gillian is the player who most frequently scores.

9. The votes cast in the third precinct were counted early.

10. Surprisingly, the plane was nearly empty.

11. Janice often runs through the field to the track.

12. The frightened rabbit never knew I only wanted to take its picture.

13. The rink will soon be filled with skaters.

14. Mr. Hernandez caught some bass and perch today in Silver Lake.

15. The referee blew his whistle loudly.

16. The runaway colt has not been seen lately.

17. I really must leave now.

18. We went back to the very dark cave.

19. Cooper was startled enough to scream.

20. Next, our class wholeheartedly applauded the speaker.

▶ **Exercise 3** **Underline the adverb or adverbs in each sentence. Then draw an arrow from each adverb to the word or words it modifies.**

The results of the experiment were clearly shown.

1. Fry these Chinese vegetables quickly.

2. The woman in the movie seemed truly sorry for her behavior.

3. I'll probably never get this chance again.

4. Aunt Polly was quite surprised by the thoughtful gift.

5. We heard the foghorn twice.

6. There was a yellow ribbon on almost every tree.

7. I have not seen that show yet.

8. Reluctantly, the old man closed the gate.

9. Ms. Rustagi seemed very glad about the results of the election.

10. Mortimer always talks foolishly at these editorial meetings.

11. Put your coats and hats here.

12. They asked us so politely.

13. The rank of Eagle Scout is not easily achieved.

14. The last contestant finally raised her hand.

15. Somewhat unhappily, the basketball team left the court.

16. That package should arrive tomorrow.

17. The baby looked everywhere for the rattle.

18. My mother recently got a job in an insurance office.

19. LaShon hasn't called lately.

20. Very often, the best team doesn't win the tournament.

Grammar

▶ **Exercise 4** **Complete each sentence by adding an adverb that answers the question indicated.**

The Beatles became _____ *extremely* _____ popular in America. (to what degree?)

1. You can read your book _____. (when?)

2. Put the soccer ball _____, where no one will trip over it. (where?)

3. The woodpecker _____ plucked the insect out of the hole. (how?)

4. James understood _____ well what he needed to do. (to what degree?)

5. In spite of the sandbag wall, the river _____ flooded its banks. (how?)

6. I saw prairie dogs _____ I looked. (where?)

7. Darcie's campaign for student council wasn't going _____. (how?)

8. We were _____ paid back out of the club treasury. (to what degree?)

9. The children behaved _____ when the teacher left the room. (how?)

10. Mr. Li promised we would work on the algebra _____. (when?)

11. I've never seen anyone eat so _____. (how?)

12. The butler looked _____ nervous as the detective asked questions. (to what degree?)

13. Lisa's family moved into their new apartment _____. (when?)

14. They had been staying _____ at a motel on Broad Street. (how?)

15. If you enter this contest, you are _____ registered for all others. (how?)

16. Lea was _____ lucky to win the contest. (to what degree?)

17. The veterinarian said there was nothing _____ wrong with their hamster. (how?)

18. The woman at the desk asked us to wait _____ for the mayor. (where?)

19. Hawks and eagles fly _____ than almost any other birds. (how?)

20. If the patient doesn't receive the medicine _____, he will be in great danger. (when?)

▶ **Writing Link** **Write three or four sentences about sledding. Use adverbs in your sentences.**

_____

_____

_____

_____

_____

Some adverbs have different forms to indicate degree of comparison.

POSITIVE	COMPARATIVE	SUPERLATIVE
walks **fast**	walks **faster**	walks **fastest**
writes **neatly**	writes **more neatly**	writes **most neatly**
hears **well**	hears **better**	hears **best**
behaves **badly**	behaves **worse**	behaves **worst**

▶ **Exercise 5** **Complete each sentence by adding the adverb in the form indicated.**

Kayla swam _____*more frequently*_____ than her sister. (frequently, comparative)

1. Stephanie seemed _____ grateful for all the gifts she received. (truly, positive)

2. I've never seen anyone walk _____ than my younger brother. (slow *or* slowly, comparative)

3. The liquid in the third beaker bubbled _____ of all. (rapidly, superlative)

4. He will probably sing _____ in a rock band. (well, positive)

5. It was obvious that Josh had copied the drawing _____ than Reese did. (accurately, comparative)

6. The A group performed badly, but the E group did _____ of all. (badly, superlative)

7. If you trained harder, you could ride _____. (fast, comparative)

8. She changed from subject to subject _____ than I could follow. (quickly, comparative)

9. He knew the material in the chapter _____ than anyone else. (well, comparative)

10. The green car was moving _____. (slow *or* slowly, superlative)

11. The black and white kitten behaved _____ than the ginger-colored one. (shyly, comparative)

12. Tony wore his letter jacket _____ of all the team members. (proudly, superlative)

13. All the students handed in their reports _____ than I did. (early, comparative)

14. Your brother Chris did really _____ on his college entrance tests, didn't he? (well, positive)

15. The young woman in the melodrama sat _____ by the riverbank and sang a melancholy tune. (forlornly, positive)

16. The bells seemed to peal _____ than ever before. (joyfully, comparative)

17. Jessica handled the difficult situation _____. (tactfully, superlative)

18. The doctor said she will see you as _____ as possible. (soon, positive)

19. Our school's team played badly, but luckily for us, Lincoln County played _____.
(badly, comparative)

20. Unfortunately, the team from Vernon played _____. (well, superlative)

When an adverb modifies a *verb,* it may be placed in various positions in relation to the
verb. When an adverb modifies an *adjective* or *another adverb,* it comes immediately
before the modified word.

Modifying a verb	Danielle is **probably** eating lunch. Danielle **probably** is eating lunch. **Probably** Danielle is eating lunch.
Modifying an adjective	The ground was **very** dry.
Modifying an adverb	We **almost** always take our dog.

▶ **Exercise 6** **Place a check next to each sentence in which the adverb is positioned correctly.**

___✔___   Owning a bike probably requires some knowledge of repair.

_____ **1.** Bikes work much more efficiently when all their systems are adjusted properly.

_____ **2.** If you learn to repair your own bike, you'll never have to take it to a bike shop almost.

_____ **3.** Generally, a person who is handy can repair most things on a bike.

_____ **4.** There are, however, quite some difficult jobs that are best left to a professional.

_____ **5.** Probably the most important safety feature on a bicycle is the brakes.

_____ **6.** You can adjust the brakes more easily with a simple tool called a third hand.

_____ **7.** A third hand simply holds the yokes apart so that you can adjust the rubber brake pads.

_____ **8.** It's time to adjust the brake pads when they start making an unpleasant screeching
sound somewhat.

_____ **9.** The brake pads should press smoothly against the metal wheel rims.

_____ **10.** Another occasionally repair that bike owners attempt is cleaning or replacing an old
chain.

_____ **11.** Scrubbing a dirty chain with kerosene and an old toothbrush will usually do the trick.

_____ **12.** Rarely only does a chain or other part need to be completely replaced.

Lesson 10
Prepositions

A **preposition** is a word that shows the relationship of a noun or a pronoun to some other word in a sentence.

The cat food is **inside** the cupboard.   We'll go to the movie **after** lunch.

These are some commonly used prepositions:

aboard	as	but (except)	in	out	toward
about	at	by	inside	outside	under
above	before	concerning	into	over	underneath
across	behind	despite	like	past	until
after	below	down	near	pending	unto
against	beneath	during	of	regarding	up
along	beside	except	off	since	upon
amid	besides	excepting	on	through	with
among	between	for	onto	throughout	within
around	beyond	from	opposite	to	out

A **compound preposition** is a preposition made up of more than one word.

according to	apart from	because of	in front of	next to	out of
ahead of	aside from	by means of	in spite of	on account of	owing to
along with	as to	in addition to	instead of	on top of	

Prepositions begin phrases that generally end with a noun or a pronoun called the **object of the preposition**

The horses jumped **over the fence**.   They showered the king **with gifts**.

▶ **Exercise 1** Circle the prepositions in each sentence. Sentences can have more than one preposition. If the sentence has no prepositions, circle nothing.

Keith visited the island (during) the rainy season.

1. Roberto Clemente was one of the greatest baseball players of all time.

2. Roberto Walker Clemente was born on August 18, 1934, in Carolina, Puerto Rico.

3. He is a member of the Baseball Hall of Fame in Cooperstown, New York.

4. Clemente began his career playing softball for the Santruce Cangrejeros.

5. He played with them until 1953, when he signed with the Brooklyn Dodgers.

6. Clemente played his entire major league career as an outfielder with the Pittsburgh Pirates.

7. He batted and threw right-handed throughout his career.

8. Although he weighed only 175 pounds, Clemente used one of the heaviest bats in the big leagues.

9. Clemente could hit with power, averaging seventeen home runs in a season.

10. In 1967 Clemente achieved his highest batting average of .357.

11. He batted .362 in the 1960 and the 1971 World Series.

12. He was named Most Valuable Player at the end of the 1966 season.

13. Roberto Clemente was also the most feared defensive outfielder of his time.

14. His powerful throwing arm was legendary.

15. He led the league in throwing out base runners five times.

16. His acrobatic fielding often took fans' breath away.

17. Sandy Koufax's advice for pitching to Clemente was "Roll the ball."

18. The manager of the New York Yankees called Clemente the best rightfielder he had ever seen.

19. Clemente played on twelve National League All-Star teams during his career.

20. On the last day of the regular 1972 season, Roberto got his three-thousandth hit.

21. Clemente was a superstar on the baseball field, but he is also remembered for other things.

22. When the Puerto Rican-born Clemente played his first game in 1955, fewer than twenty-five Hispanic players were on the rosters.

23. Hispanic players faced prejudice from both teammates and fans.

24. In fact Roberto Clemente was called "Bob" in his first few seasons because many Americans were still uncomfortable with foreign-sounding names.

25. Major league baseball had been allowing African American players for less than ten years.

26. Like Jackie Robinson, the first African American in the major leagues, Roberto Clemente changed the attitudes of baseball fans across the country.

27. When the Pirates won the 1960 World Series, Clemente skipped the team party.

28. Instead, he walked around the neighborhoods of Pittsburgh thanking fans for their support.

29. Clemente often helped people in trouble.

30. Clemente's concern for others cost him his life.

31. When an airplane carrying supplies for earthquake victims in Nicaragua crashed into the Caribbean Sea on December 31, 1972, Roberto Clemente was aboard that plane.

32. His loss was felt by Puerto Rico, the city of Pittsburgh, and baseball fans everywhere.

33. Roberto Clemente helped make a difference in the lives of many people.

Lesson 11
Conjunctions: Coordinating, Correlative, and Subordinating; Interjections

A conjunction is a word that joins single words or groups of words. A coordinating conjunction joins words or groups of words that have equal grammatical weight in a sentence. *And*, *but*, *or*, *nor*, *for*, *so*, and *yet* are coordinating conjunctions.

Germaine washed the dishes **and** dried them.
The squirrel buried the nut, **but** the dog dug it up.

Correlative conjunctions work in pairs to join words and groups of words of equal weight in a sentence.

both...and	just as...so	not only...but also
either...or	neither...nor	whether...or

Both whales **and** dolphins are mammals.
Whether I fail **or** succeed, my parents will still support me.

A subordinating conjunction joins two ideas, or clauses, so that one is grammatically dependent on the other.

after	as long as	if	than	whenever
although	as soon as	in order that	though	where
as	as though	since	unless	whereas
as far as	because	so	until	wherever
as if	before	so that	when	while

He listened to music **until** he fell asleep.
Whenever I see a mountain, I want to climb it.

▶ **Exercise 1** Circle the conjunctions. In the blank write *coord.* if the conjunction is coordinating. Write *corr.* if the conjunction is correlative. Write *sub.* if the conjunction is subordinate.

__sub.__ We will leave for vacation (as soon as) the tickets arrive.

_____ **1.** While many people have watched a marathon race, few have ever competed in one.

_____ **2.** It's Friday night, and I have to stay home to clean my room.

_____ **3.** Neither Sasha nor her brother could locate the car.

_____ **4.** We will visit Washington, D.C., or Williamsburg, Virginia, in June.

_____ **5.** Although I prefer apples, I also like strawberries.

_____ **6.** Both Jason and Eric made the basketball team.

_____ **7.** Whenever the parents leave for work, the children throw a temper tantrum.

_____ **8.** The fans were quiet until the golfer putted.

_____ 9. The deadline for our science project is in two weeks, so you still have time.

_____ 10. Not only did Maria win, but she also broke her record.

_____ 11. Patrick overslept and missed the bus.

_____ 12. In soccer, as long as you head the ball properly, it will not hurt you.

_____ 13. Coach Ramirez debated whether to kick or to run.

_____ 14. When the verdict came in, the defendant sobbed.

_____ 15. Is Dad cooking dinner tonight or ordering pizza?

_____ 16. Wherever the divers went, they found a treasure.

_____ 17. Either your assignments are in on time or you fail the course.

_____ 18. The Jacksons lock their doors every night because thefts occur frequently in their town.

_____ 19. The storm intensified, but the hikers continued their journey.

_____ 20. Just as radar works by sending out signals, so does sonar.

An **interjection** is a word that expresses emotion or exclamation. An interjection has no grammatical connection to other words.

| oh | wow | oops | ouch | well | whew | ah | yipes | uh-oh |
| gee | ow | hey | hooray | alas | why | man | my | uh-huh |

Why, I didn't realize that.   **Oops,** sorry about that.   **Uh-oh,** she'd better watch out.

▶ **Exercise 2** **Complete each sentence by choosing an interjection from the list above.**

_____ , I forgot my jacket.

1. _____ ! That hurt!

2. _____ ! We won!

3. _____ , I'm going. Will I see you there?

4. _____ , that was a close call.

5. _____ , I didn't know you wanted to come.

6. _____ , that tastes great!

7. _____ , if you don't want to play, don't play.

8. _____ ! You stepped on my foot.

9. _____ , what did you think it meant?

10. _____ , how you've grown.

☑ Unit 1 **Review**

▶ **Exercise 1** **In the blank, identify the part of speech of the words in italics. Write *n* for a noun and *p* for a pronoun. Write *adj.* for an adjective and *adv.* for an adverb. Write *v* for a verb, *prep.* for a preposition, *c* for a conjunction, and *i* for an interjection.**

_____ 1. The United States has hundreds of important *historical* sites, many of which have been designated national monuments.

_____ 2. Our national monuments include *both* natural wonders *and* structures built by people.

_____ 3. Millions of tourists *visit* these monuments every year.

_____ 4. Some of the monuments, such as the Statue of Liberty, are located *in* urban areas.

_____ 5. *Others,* including Yellowstone, the first national park, are located far from big cities.

_____ 6. One of the *most* popular national monuments is the Vietnam Veterans Memorial.

_____ 7. On the wall are the *names* of more than fifty-eight thousand Americans who died in the Vietnam War from 1960 to 1975.

_____ 8. The nation's capital *is* also the site of memorials to many outstanding Americans.

_____ 9. High points *of* a visit to Washington, D.C., are the Washington Monument, the Lincoln Memorial, and the Jefferson Memorial.

_____ 10. Massive *images* of these three presidents, along with one of Theodore Roosevelt, are included in the Mount Rushmore National Monument in South Dakota.

_____ 11. Not all of our national monuments *honor* famous people.

_____ 12. If you visited southwestern Colorado, you would find *there* Mesa Verde National Park.

_____ 13. *Mesa Verde* is a collection of Native American cliff dwellings.

_____ 14. Here is an ancient apartment building with 217 rooms—*all* under one roof!

_____ 15. The country's *highest* mountain, Mount McKinley, is in Denali National Park in Alaska.

_____ 16. *Surprisingly,* the lowest point in the United States is also a national monument.

_____ 17. In fact California's Death Valley is the lowest *point* in the Western Hemisphere.

_____ 18. Other national monuments honor groups of Americans, *among* them the Women's Rights National Historic Park and the Civil Rights Memorial.

_____ 19. Seneca Falls, New York, is the site of the first large meeting held in 1848 to plan a campaign to bring *equal* rights to women.

_____ 20. The Civil Rights Memorial was built in Montgomery, Alabama, where Martin Luther King Jr. led a boycott of the city bus system to protest *racial* discrimination.

Cumulative Review: Unit 1

▶ **Exercise 1** In the blank write *n* if the italicized word is used as a noun. Write *p* if it is used as a pronoun. Write *v* if it is used as a verb. Write *adj.* if it is used as an adjective. Write *adv.* if it is used as an adverb. Write *c* if it is used as a conjunction. Write *prep.* if it is used as a preposition. Write *i* if it is used as an interjection.

_____ 1. He *cut* six slices of bread and put them on the plate.

_____ 2. Her letter came *back* stamped "Return to Sender."

_____ 3. In all fairness, I haven't heard his *side* of the story yet.

_____ 4. The freight train pulled off onto a *side* track to let the passenger train pass.

_____ 5. The hero rode off into the sunset, and the townspeople haven't seen him *since.*

_____ 6. *Since* you're so sure you're right, why don't you raise your hand?

_____ 7. You probably drove *past* the school building on your way here.

_____ 8. A person who can't dance very well is sometimes said to have two *left* feet.

_____ 9. The problem is they turned right when they should have turned *left.*

_____ 10. Whenever she insists on going *up* the down staircase, it causes a massive traffic jam.

_____ 11. *Why,* you're the news anchor for the Channel 10 news!

_____ 12. I do *not* want that rusty old bicycle.

_____ 13. It was fascinating to watch the border collies *corner* the runaway sheep.

_____ 14. If you ask me, the best thing about winter is that it's always followed by *spring.*

_____ 15. *Before* you go, be sure to turn off all the lights and close the curtains.

_____ 16. I told her I would call her *before* next Monday.

_____ 17. The fans cheered wildly when the American women won the *shot put* at the track meet.

_____ 18. The sales clerk at the department store said I could choose *either* blouse.

_____ 19. Richard said he didn't really care for *either.*

_____ 20. *Well,* don't say I didn't warn you.

_____ 21. If you don't *clean* your car's carburetor, the engine won't run smoothly.

_____ 22. *When* I found out about the concert, I was really upset.

Unit 2: Parts of the Sentence

Lesson 12
Simple Subjects and Simple Predicates

Every sentence has two main parts, a subject and a predicate. The simple subject is the main noun or pronoun that tells what the sentence is about.

The **batter** swung at the third ball. (main noun as simple subject)
She hit a high pop foul. (main pronoun as simple subject)

A simple predicate is the verb or verb phrase that expresses action or being about the subject.

The crowd **cheered** after the touchdown. (main verb as simple predicate)
The team **will practice** on Saturday. (main verb phrase as simple predicate)

You can find a simple subject by asking *Who?* or *What?* about the verb.

My **grandmother** lived in Poland as a girl. (Who lived in Poland?)
Her **quilts** have won many prizes at state fairs. (What won many prizes?)

▶ **Exercise 1** **Draw one line under the simple subject and two lines under the simple predicate of each sentence below.**

I am ready for a vacation.

1. Our family traveled through Africa last summer.

2. At the airport we joined a sightseeing tour.

3. The guide loaded us into a huge old van.

4. He drove the van to a nearby game preserve.

5. Unfortunately, the ancient vehicle lacked good shock absorbers.

6. Our bodies were jolted with every turn of the wheels.

7. Clouds of dust around the van obscured our vision.

8. The driver slowed the van to a stop.

9. Mom started loading her camera in anticipation.

10. Suddenly, several passengers spotted a giraffe and several lions.

11. Soundlessly, we crept from the van for a closer look.

12. The lions were snoozing in the sun.

13. Two small cubs batted each other with padded paws.

14. A zebra herd cautiously passed the sleeping lions.

15. The driver pointed at a hyena on the lookout for its meal.

16. In the distance an elephant was eating the bark off a tree.

17. I could hardly believe the nearness of so many wild creatures.

18. Mom shot a whole roll of film at just that one location.

19. The day ended too soon with a journey back to the town.

20. Maybe we can return to this serene spot next year.

▶ **Exercise 2 Supply a simple subject for each of the sentences below by writing a noun or a pronoun in the blank. Draw two lines under each simple predicate.**

My _____pets_____ are safe.

1. Earlier today, the weather _____ announced an approaching snowstorm.

2. _____ filled several plastic bottles with fresh water.

3. _____ hung extra tarpaulins over the windows in the family room.

4. My _____ rushed outside to find the animals.

5. My _____ gathered flashlights and candles.

6. Soon the _____ darkened.

7. The _____ in the trees was moaning eerily.

8. _____ heard the sounds of the storm distinctly.

9. After a particularly loud crash _____ told a joke for relief.

10. The _____ were crouching unhappily at our feet.

11. The _____, however, strolled through the house serenely.

12. Shortly after a lightning strike, the _____ flickered out.

13. Luckily _____ had bought a battery-powered radio after the last storm.

14. _____ sat in the dark with the radio as a friendly voice.

15. A _____ had been smashed by high water on the Little River.

16. Thankfully, the _____ had closed it just minutes before.

17. Civil defense _____ were providing shelter in the schools.

18. My _____ worried about their families a few miles upstate.

19. The long _____ passed slowly into daylight.

20. _____ will not forget the storm of July 1994.

Lesson 13
Complete Subjects and Complete Predicates

Most sentences have additional words that tell more about the simple subject and the simple predicate.

The complete subject is made up of the simple subject and all the words that tell about it.

The members of the team voted to buy new uniforms.

The complete predicate is made up of all the words that tell what the subject is or does, including the simple predicate.

The principal of the school **invited us to a board meeting**.

A good way to find the complete subject and complete predicate in a sentence is to find the simple subject and simple predicate first.

The **president** of our class **won** the election by a landslide.

Once you have located the simple subject and predicate, then you can divide the entire sentence into complete subject and complete predicate.

The **president** of our class | **won** the election by a landslide.

▶ **Exercise 1** **Draw one line under the simple subject. Draw two lines under the simple predicate. Draw a vertical line (|) between the complete subject and the complete predicate.**

A <u>box</u> of old letters | <u><u>was found</u></u> in the trunk.

1. Several photos of the fire were in the paper.

2. Gabriella will take her science project to the fair.

3. The nature documentary showed the life of a coral reef.

4. Miguel's bicycle was stolen from the school bike rack.

5. Many people on our block have dogs and cats.

6. We are learning about the Arctic tundra in geography.

7. Rita kicked four goals in her soccer game yesterday.

8. Three of the high-school classes planned a community project.

9. A new video will be my present to my brother.

10. Our local scout troop has hiked up Mount Baldy three times.

11. Jena spoke to me about her birthplace in Bosnia-Herzegovina.

12. The new encyclopedia contains much updated material.

13. A number of farmers formed a credit union.

14. The rescuers chopped through the door.

15. Carla's grandfather writes often to his family in Italy.

16. The beautiful stone in her ring is an opal.

17. That television drama was very unrealistic.

18. A high wall surrounded the large mansion.

19. We will study for the exam next week.

20. The airport is just off Exit 14.

21. The fans in the grandstand cheered the home team.

22. My uncle knows a lot about solar energy.

23. The frisky squirrel leaped for the birdfeeder.

24. Forty Canada geese landed on the lawn.

25. Our families were invited to the school picnic.

26. They dived into the pool.

27. The lovely old oak came down in the storm.

28. Suellen was practicing for the skating contest.

29. My cousin called me long distance last night.

30. The angry drivers were stalled at the accident site.

31. The heavy rain brought many worms to the surface.

32. The pilot landed the stricken jet in a field.

33. My favorite dessert is lemon sherbet.

34. The cooks at school baked a cake for the principal's birthday.

35. Our visitors from the city were listening to the croaking frogs.

36. Hillary's cousins from Seattle will be at the wedding tomorrow.

37. Jan performed the chemistry experiment successfully.

38. You will enjoy the seventh-grade play.

39. The simmering volcano erupted suddenly.

40. Roger slid into third base safely.

Lesson 14
Compound Subjects and Compound Predicates

A **compound subject** consists of two or more simple subjects that share the same verb. The two subjects are joined by a conjunction. (For a list of conjunctions, see Lesson 11, page 71.) The conjunctions in the following sentences are *and, neither ... nor,* and *either ... or.*

Andrea and **Rick** entered the relay race.
Neither the **teachers** nor the **students** favor the new schedule.
Either **cinnamon** or **nutmeg** is used in this recipe.

▶ **Exercise 1** **Draw one line under each compound subject and two lines under the simple predicate they share. Circle the conjunction or conjunctions.**

Misha (and) I saw Lani at the mall.

1. Clubs and sports are two of Lani's favorite hobbies.

2. Neither Chris nor Juan shares her interest.

3. Lani and her other friends belong to the drama club.

4. Either Tuesday or Wednesday is the day of their next meeting.

5. Sets, costumes, and props will be discussed.

6. Scripts and audition forms will be passed out.

7. Lani and Susan will audition for the fall play.

8. Either *Our Town* or *Romeo and Juliet* will be the first production.

9. Neither the drama teacher nor the club president can decide.

10. Either March or April will be the month of the second production.

11. Tessa and Mr. Tanaka will choose a musical for the spring play.

12. *Oklahoma!* and *The Sound of Music* are Lani's favorite shows.

13. Lights and sound could be a problem, though.

14. Neither time nor money is available for the improvement of the auditorium.

15. Mr. Tanaka and the drama club are meeting with the school board this afternoon.

16. Either Ms. Jenkins or Mr. Rodriguez will preside at the meeting.

17. Drama and other extracurricular activities are on the agenda.

18. Mr. Tanaka, Tessa, and Lani will make short speeches.

19. Interest and enthusiasm for drama clubs are their topics.

20. Either Lani or Tessa will speak first.

A **compound predicate** consists of two simple predicates that share the same subject. The two simple predicates are connected by a conjunction.

Harold **picked** the flowers and **arranged** them.
The well-trained dogs **will** neither **bark** nor **bite**.
The angry customer has either **called** or **written** five times.
A flock of birds **swooped** behind the hill but **reappeared** above the trees.

The conjunctions in the sentences above are *and, neither ... nor, either ... or*, and *but*.

▶ **Exercise 2** Draw one line under each simple subject and two lines under each compound predicate in the following sentences.

Audiences admire and enjoy the writer's work.

1. Plays entertain and inform audiences.

2. New plays often open the mind and spark new ideas.

3. Regional theaters either commission new works or read submissions.

4. Playwrights improve and refine their dialogue during rehearsal.

5. Directors can add elements but cannot save a weak script.

6. Actors often try different approaches and choose the most effective one for the character.

7. Set designers create and develop the proper atmosphere for the play.

8. The playwright neither describes nor limits every element of production.

9. Each artist contributes ideas and enhances the show.

10. After the first performance, the playwright will evaluate the script and make improvements.

11. Sometimes audience members complete surveys or offer comments to the writer.

12. The writer can either accept or reject their suggestions.

13. A single play may be produced and revised several times.

14. Broadway producers seek new plays and acquire rights to the best ones.

15. Audiences appreciate new shows but often buy more tickets for familiar works.

16. Producers neither desire nor support unpopular plays.

17. However, interesting new plays excite producers and draw large audiences.

18. The best plays win awards and sometimes become movies.

19. Movies are neither produced nor directed like stage shows.

20. Live theater heightens drama and adds a third dimension for the audience.

Lesson 15
Order of Subject and Predicate

In most sentences that you read and write, the subject comes before the predicate.

SUBJECT   PREDICATE
The red-tailed **hawk** | **soared** high overhead.

For variety or special emphasis, some sentences are written in inverted order. In such cases the predicate comes before the subject.

PREDICATE   SUBJECT
High overhead **soared** | the red-tailed **hawk**.

The subject also follows the verb in any sentence that begins with *there* or *here*.

PREDICATE   SUBJECT
There **sit** | the missing **books**!
Here **is** | your birthday **present**.

▶ **Exercise 1 Draw a vertical line (|) between the complete subject and the complete predicate.**

Here is |a summary of the plot.

1. Behind the hills sank the setting sun.

2. Here are the photographs of the eclipse.

3. Across the lawn crept the stalking cat.

4. Myra watched the baby.

5. Rich took the pie to the Bayers next door.

6. The rainbow appeared after the storm.

7. Over the bridge rumbled the ancient truck.

8. From the broken dam tumbled the floodwaters.

9. Here are several of Grandma's quilts.

10. My friend Helen wants to be a teacher.

11. Here are the corrected test papers.

12. Over the intercom came the principal's announcement.

13. Inside the car sat my baby sister.

14. Behind the bookcase was the entrance to a secret tunnel.

15. There is no excuse for your behavior.

16. Through the storm flew the brave seagull.

17. The weary travelers camped by the river.

18. Beyond the planet Mars lie the asteroids.

19. Here is your baseball glove.

20. Beside the desk was the missing picture.

▶ **Exercise 2** **Rewrite the sentences below by inverting the order of the subjects and predicates.**

Players from both teams were at the meeting. _At the meeting were players from both teams._

1. Up the falls swam the salmon. _____

2. Past the crowd sped the wheelchair racers. _____

3. Across the range flew the fighter plane. _____

4. On the stove bubbled the chocolate pudding. _____

5. Spring comes after winter. _____

6. A grandfather clock stood against the wall. _____

7. Through the woods hiked the weary scouts. _____

8. Tulips and daffodils grew along the fence. _____

9. A pirate ship appeared out of the mist. _____

_____

10. Behind the house stood a pine forest. _____

11. Across the sky twinkled the light of the satellite. _____

_____

12. Down the road trotted a riderless pony. _____

13. My best friend stood beside me. _____

14. Between the jagged cliffs flowed the river. _____

15. Throughout the book appeared colorful illustrations. _____

_____

16. Tiny fish swam beneath the surface of the pond. _____

_____

17. A family of bears lived in the cave. _____

18. From the kitchen came the wonderful smell of challah. _____

_____

Lesson 16
Complements: Direct and Indirect Objects

A **complement** completes the meaning of a verb. It may be one word or a group of words.
One kind of complement is the direct object. A **direct object** answers the question *what?*
or *whom?* after an action verb.

Mario picked some **flowers** for the mantel. (Mario picked what?)
Liu trusts her **sister** completely. (Liu trusts whom?)

A **direct object** may have more than one part.

The farmer carried the **calf** and the **lamb** through the floodwaters.

▶ **Exercise 1** Draw one line under the simple subject and two lines under the simple predicate.
Circle the direct object. At the end of the sentence, write the word *what?* or *whom?* to tell which
question the direct object answers.

Astronomers study celestial (bodies.) _what?_____

1. Early astronomers observed the heavens constantly. _____

2. The movements of the sky fascinated them. _____

3. Often they created myths and stories explaining the stars. _____

4. To learn more, our class visited the planetarium yesterday. _____

5. Mr. Simpson told us about the solar system. _____

6. Then we named the planets in order from the sun. _____

7. All the planets orbit the sun. _____

8. On its surface, tiny Mercury resembles our moon. _____

9. However, Mercury lacks an atmosphere and a moon. _____

10. Venus possesses a poisonous atmosphere. _____

11. The spacecraft photographed the surface of Venus. _____

12. Clouds covered the surface. _____

13. We told Mr. Simpson about our studies. _____

14. First, Earth contains rocky material. _____

15. A moon orbits our home planet. _____

16. Earth's atmosphere supports many forms of life. _____

17. My friend studies Mars and Jupiter. _____

18. Some people plan a trip to Mars. _____

19. Mr. Simpson often studies the moon through a telescope. _____

20. He prefers the moon to everything else in the solar system. _____

Another kind of complement, the indirect object, answers these questions following an action verb: *to whom? for whom? to what?*

The child threw her **father** and **mother** a kiss. (The child threw a kiss to whom?)
Keanu bought **them** some popcorn. (Keanu bought popcorn for whom?)
The crowd gave our **team** a cheer. (The crowd gave a cheer to what?)

▶ **Exercise 2** **Write *D.O.* above the direct objects and *I.O.* above the indirect objects.**

                     I.O.   D.O.

Mr. Stephens read us a legend about the wind.

1. Ms. Bailey gave our class a lecture on weather.

2. She teaches college students weather forecasting.

3. Our science teacher, Mr. Stephens, sent her an invitation.

4. She brought us weather maps and other data.

5. We showed her our ideas for the weather forecasts.

6. She offered the class her opinion.

7. Mr. Stephens showed us pictures of the first thermometers and barometers from the seventeenth century.

8. Weather stations once gave others information on current conditions by telegraph.

9. By the late nineteenth century, organizations were providing forecasters standards for weather records.

10. In turn, these records provide meteorologists statistics.

11. Recent technology gives them more help.

12. Satellites send professional forecasters information from space.

13. Computers offer them numerical models for predictions.

14. These models save meteorologists time.

15. The predictions give people warnings about bad weather.

16. Ms. Bailey drew our class a graph of weather trends.

Lesson 17
Subject Complements and Object Complements

Certain words in sentences complete the meaning of linking verbs. These words are called subject complements because they further identify or describe the subject. The linking verbs used in such sentences include all forms of the verb *be*, as well as the verbs *become, seem, remain, feel, taste, smell, appear, look, grow, stay*, and *sound*.

The two kinds of subject complements are predicate nominatives and predicate adjectives. A predicate nominative is a noun or pronoun that follows a linking verb and identifies or renames the subject.

Harold is our **quarterback.** (What word identifies Harold?)
Reggie Lee remains my **friend.** (What word identifies Reggie Lee?)

A predicate adjective is an adjective that follows a linking verb and describes the subject.

Her paintings look **mysterious.** (What word describes the paintings?)
The swimmer was **powerful.** (What word describes the swimmer?)

▶ **Exercise 1** **Identify the italicized word(s) in the following sentences as either a predicate nominative, *P.N.*, or a predicate adjective, *P.A.***

__P.A.__   The new car was *bright* and *shiny.*

_____ **1.** Mr. Kravitz may become our new science *teacher.*

_____ **2.** That object in the tree is a *pineapple.*

_____ **3.** That train robbery remains an unsolved *mystery.*

_____ **4.** This book on whales is a *gift* from my sister.

_____ **5.** Jayelle and Simon are the best *performers* in the play.

_____ **6.** These old apples smell *rotten.*

_____ **7.** Both Tanya and Rick seemed *cheerful* after the exam.

_____ **8.** Tika's favorite reptiles are *crocodiles, lizards*, and *turtles.*

_____ **9.** These pears don't appear *fresh.*

_____ **10.** The runners look *weary* but *triumphant.*

_____ **11.** Stella became *chairwoman* of the committee.

_____ **12.** The soaked and exhausted scouts looked *miserable.*

_____ **13.** Red, yellow, and blue are primary *colors.*

_____ **14.** The cut flowers looked *dry* and *lifeless.*

_____ **15.** My uncle has been *ill.*

_____ **16.** The sculpture in the park remains his greatest *accomplishment*.

_____ **17.** First prize in the contest will be a *trip* to Grand Canyon.

_____ **18.** The runners felt *jubilant* after the race.

_____ **19.** Her orchard's main crops were *apples* and *cherries*.

_____ **20.** The Conways and the Hopes seem good *friends*.

Object complements are words that identify or describe a direct object in a sentence. They answer the question *what?* after a direct object in order to complete the meaning of the direct object. An object complement may be a noun, a pronoun, or an adjective.

The mayor appointed Ken **treasurer**. (Noun)
The dog considers the sofa **his**. (Pronoun)
Residents think the new structure **ugly**. (Adjective)

▶ **Exercise 2** **Draw one line under the direct object. Draw two lines under the object complement.**

I find school <u>elections</u> good <u>experience</u>.

1. Our science club chose Gayle the chairperson.

2. Gayle considers astronomy the most compelling science.

3. We, on the other hand, consider her starstruck.

4. I, for example, find botany fascinating.

5. I named my science project "Fabulous Flowers."

6. Other club members call me silly.

7. I will make them botanists by next year.

8. My fellow members will never elect me president.

9. However, they may appoint me lowly notetaker.

10. Several scientists in the club make geology a priority.

11. They call earthquakes and volcanoes marvelous.

12. But then, they consider liquid lava an occasion for celebration.

13. Horace declared Mount Saint Helens his favorite volcano.

14. Of course, the chemistry fans think chemistry a treat.

15. They consider all test tubes theirs.

16. Lena and Ty will make chemistry their major.

☑ Unit 2 **Review**

▶ **Exercise 1** **Draw a vertical line between the complete subject and the complete predicate. Label each direct object** *D.O.* **and each indirect object** *I.O.* **Draw one line under each predicate nominative. Draw two lines under each predicate adjective. Circle each object complement.**

             I.O.   **D.O.**
     Fred|gave Dave a baseball.

1. Jason threw Antonio the ball.

2. The club named Moira president.

3. This salsa tastes spicy.

4. Mr. Kotlinski may become our new soccer coach.

5. Wilson and Kurt wrote letters to their friends in Japan.

6. First prize will be a trip to Hong Kong.

7. The conclusion of Noah's paper was a surprise.

8. Corky's dog brought Sally a torn slipper.

9. Giorgio wrote the agenda and gave a copy to each member of the group.

10. The ship's course seemed unusual.

11. At the conference were representatives from forty nations.

12. Hiking and camping are Lee's favorite activities.

13. Juanita considers math her best subject.

14. Hawaii's flowers are breathtaking.

15. My friend Heidi was the leader at the golf tournament.

16. Alex baked the class pumpkin bread.

17. The judges called Colin's science fair project extraordinary.

18. My cousin Jessica wants a new stereo.

19. Across many miles traveled the colorful caravan.

20. Martha bought some lace in Brussels.

Cumulative Review: Units 1–2

▶ **Exercise 1** Underline nouns once and verbs twice. Draw a vertical line between each complete subject and complete predicate. Label adjectives *Adj.*, articles *A.*, adverbs *Adv.*, direct objects *D.O.*, and indirect objects *I.O.*

1. Omar and Alicia took a trip to the museum.

2. Kristy sent Aunt Sue a lovely lamp.

3. Julia wrote and directed the funny play.

4. The supplier accidentally delivered the wrong material.

5. The lawyer carefully asked the witness several questions.

6. Aaron ate the apple and threw the core into the wastebasket.

7. Those students are being honored today.

8. On the counter were handmade boxes of every description.

9. Our swimming team easily won the large trophy.

10. Nora's incredible singing was the best part of the program.

11. Francis scrubbed and waxed the kitchen floor.

12. Someone had been giving Demetrius mysterious gifts.

13. Both Claudia and her brother have been looking tense lately.

14. The rainy weather had severely limited our activity.

15. You offered me a nearly perfect plan.

16. Someone left an unfinished jigsaw puzzle on the table.

17. Dr. Connor, a medical missionary, carefully walked across the barren field.

18. Julio became the best shortstop on the team.

19. The panting racers swiftly turned the corner.

20. Lisa and Jacques made Mrs. O'Brien a pie from the strawberries they picked.

Grammar

Unit 3: Phrases

Lesson 18
Prepositional Phrases

A **prepositional phrase** begins with a preposition and usually ends with a noun or a pronoun, called the **object of the preposition**. (For a list of prepositions, see Unit 1, Lesson 10, page 69.) The object may be compound or may have modifiers.

Our stockpile **of snowballs** was depleted quickly.
This pudding is made **with milk and bread.** (compound object)
I brought back film footage **of the horrible storm.** (object with modifier)

A prepositional phrase acts as an **adjective** when it modifies a noun or a pronoun. A prepositional phrase acts as an **adverb** when it modifies a verb, an adjective, or an adverb.

David tried every pair of skis **in the lodge.** (adjective phrase modifying the noun *skis*)
You can come **to the party.** (adverb phrase modifying the verb phrase *can come*)

▶ **Exercise 1** **Circle each prepositional phrase in the following sentences.**

We met (in the lobby) (after school.)

1. My sister took her books off the table at dinnertime.

2. At the party, we met students who did not go to our school.

3. Which of the movies is your favorite?

4. Tim sat motionless for a long time.

5. We ran toward the water when we reached the beach.

6. Sheila always gets nervous before a performance.

7. Inside the auditorium people talked loudly until the end of the show.

8. I ran around the table and hid beneath the chair.

9. Sue promised me her recipe for stew.

10. Cheers filled the stadium throughout the football game.

11. Would you rather live in Alaska or in Africa?

12. By two o'clock on the day of the bake sale, all the cookies had been sold.

13. Derek looked behind the garage and saw his roller skates.

14. The four of us swam laps in the pool after school.

15. We laughed at the joke, though it wasn't very funny.

16. Marty proved she could compete against any member of the other team.

17. Did you travel by car or by train?

18. The students were encouraged in their efforts.

19. The parking garage below the mall is always full.

20. He studies hard, and his grades are always above the average.

▶ **Exercise 2** **Circle each prepositional phrase in the sentences below and draw an arrow to the word or words it modifies.**

Sarah looked (through the telescope.)

1. The captain slipped on the wet deck.

2. We went to the movie at the last minute.

3. Which of the barbells is heavier?

4. Melissa earned the money for her new dress.

5. When Jo forgot her key, she knocked on the window.

6. The boy in the red jacket plays on my soccer team.

7. The doctor told him that joining the track team would be healthful for him.

8. She was taught table manners at a young age.

9. We found sticky paw prints on the kitchen floor.

10. Let's meet the new coach at four o'clock.

11. Bill hit the ball into the bleachers.

12. Each of the girls wanted some pizza.

13. The computer in the lab was used frequently.

14. The school band performed during the half-time show.

15. Did you pass your driving test with flying colors?

16. At the museum we saw paintings and sculptures.

Lesson 19
Participles and Participial Phrases

A **participle** is a verb form that acts as an adjective. It modifies a noun or pronoun.

The car screeched down the (twisting) road. (The participle *twisting* modifies the noun *road*.)

A participle can be present or past. A present participle ends in *-ing*. A past participle usually ends in *-ed*.

A participle with complements and modifiers is called a **participial phrase**. A participial phrase acts as an adjective. It can be in different positions in a sentence. If a participial phrase falls at the beginning of a sentence, it is usually followed by a comma.

Screeching loudly, the car pulled into the service station.

▶ **Exercise 1 Circle the participle or participial phrase in each sentence.**

(Growing up in an active family,) Carla had acquired many athletic skills.

1. Being a good kicker, Carla tried out for the football team.

2. She wanted to be the team's leading kicker.

3. Playing for her middle school team, she felt ready to compete.

4. However, many other students, having equal experience, also decided to try out for the team.

5. Startled by the number of competitors, Carla grew nervous.

6. Did all of them have a winning record?

7. Glancing at her competitors, she discovered that three of them were female.

8. Considered unique in middle school, Carla was not prepared to meet other female kickers.

9. A girl named Molly introduced herself to Carla.

10. She had been a celebrated middle school kicker, too.

11. Carla, worried about the tryouts, made a nervous joke.

12. Molly's determined pacing showed that she was also nervous.

13. Breathing deeply, Carla began to calm down.

14. The coaches holding the tryouts gave each student a ball.

15. Smiling at Molly, Carla suggested they help each other practice.

16. Molly nodded and gave a relieved sigh.

17. Running after the football, both girls forgot to be nervous.

Grammar

18. They had a contest with the other two girls waiting in the stands.

19. Working together, Carla and Molly kicked more field goals than the other team.

20. A coach watching them insisted they try out first.

▶ **Exercise 2** **Circle the participial phrase and draw an arrow to the noun or pronoun it modifies.**

Donato sat at his desk, listening to a classmate's oral report.

1. Waiting patiently, Donato organized his notes.

2. His oral report, inspired by the World Cup competition, was about a famous soccer player.

3. Reading his first note card, he remembered that soccer is called "football" in many countries.

4. This sport, played around the world, is growing in popularity.

5. Keeping that in mind, he thought his classmates would enjoy his report.

6. The student standing in front of the class finished her report.

7. Clearing his throat, Donato approached the lectern.

8. A friend sitting in the first row smiled at him.

9. His teacher, seated in the back, instructed him to begin.

10. Placing his note cards on the lectern, he introduced his topic.

11. Speaking carefully, he explained that Edson Arantes do Nascimento was known as Pelé.

12. Playing for a minor league "football" club, Pelé tried to earn a place on a major league team.

13. The Brazilian athlete, rejected by several teams, joined the Santos Football Club.

14. This team, led by Pelé, won two world club championships.

15. Pelé, continuing to play, headed the Brazilian national team that won three World Cup titles.

16. Retired from the game in 1975, he decided to play for the New York Cosmos.

17. Aided by his presence, the Cosmos won the North American Soccer League championship in 1977.

18. Retiring again, Pelé received the International Peace Award.

Lesson 20
Gerunds and Gerund Phrases;
Appositives and Appositive Phrases

A **gerund** is a verb form ending in *-ing* that is used as a noun.

Sewing has never interested me.

A **gerund phrase** is a gerund with any complements or modifiers needed to complete its meaning.

Her enthusiastic cheering drew people from yards away.
Moving the chair was not easy.

▶ **Exercise 1 Circle the gerund or gerund phrase in each sentence.**

(Running for class president) requires a lot of work.

1. I like eating healthful foods.

2. Recycling gives our family a sense of accomplishment.

3. Quitting is almost never the best solution.

4. Cheryl's delicious cooking keeps her restaurant popular.

5. Leafing through photos is a good way to remember old times.

6. We enjoyed painting the barn.

7. Doing the yard work made us tired.

8. The whistling of the wind makes the house seem lonely.

9. Constant bickering was making the twins a nuisance.

10. Pacing the floors can relieve tension for some people.

11. Public speaking was the class assignment everyone feared.

12. Skating was Karen's favorite pastime.

13. The dog's loud barking made it difficult to hear the television.

14. Miranda enjoyed exploring new places.

15. His unique singing made him a good candidate for the choir.

16. My hobbies, cycling and reading, keep me busy.

17. We wanted to win, but playing a good game was just as important.

18. Her greatest hope was finding her long-lost sister.

19. Capturing the enemy was the mission in the latest video game.

20. Traveling is a good way to see the world.

An **appositive** is a noun or pronoun placed next to another noun or pronoun to further identify it.

My brother **David** is an engineer.

An **appositive phrase** contains an appositive and any words that modify it. An appositive phrase is usually not essential to the meaning of a sentence. Appositives are often set off by commas.

My brother David, **an engineer in Philadelphia**, enjoys his job.

▶ **Exercise 1 Circle the appositive or appositive phrase in each sentence.**

Dontonio, (my science partner,) helped me write the lab report.

1. Mariel, a dancer in her own right, watched the ballerinas dance.

2. My doctor, Dr. Enriquez, recently moved to our neighborhood.

3. Nancy's dog Molly never barks at anyone.

4. Meagan, a hard-working student, will run for class president.

5. The noise, a piercing wail, made us cover our ears.

6. The Bears, the team in the red jerseys, are going to the playoffs.

7. That museum has several paintings of the French Impressionist painter Monet.

8. Tom, the actor on the left, has performed in many musicals.

9. My friend Rachel came to see me march in the band.

10. The Wright brothers, Orville and Wilbur, are credited with the first flight.

11. She lives in Seattle, the capital of Washington.

12. Our local newspaper, *The Sentinel*, printed a picture of my stepfather with his award.

13. Mrs. Ito, my sixth-grade teacher, was a chaperone at the dance.

14. *Animal Farm* is a book by the acclaimed author George Orwell.

15. Was that Krista, the captain of the drill team?

16. Willie Mays, the famous home run hitter, signed one of my baseball cards.

17. During biology, my first class of the day, we dissected frogs.

18. *Frankenstein,* a novel by Mary Shelley, has been the basis for many films.

Lesson 21
Infinitives and Infinitive Phrases

An **infinitive** is a verb form usually preceded by the word *to*. In this case, *to* is not a preposition, but a part of the infinitive verb form. An infinitive can be used as a noun, an adjective, or an adverb.

I love **to gather** flowers in the spring. (infinitive as a noun)
Our plans **to visit** Civil War battlefields changed drastically. (infinitive as an adjective)
Your address is difficult **to remember**. (infinitive as an adverb)

An **infinitive phrase** includes an infinitive and any complements and modifiers needed to complete its meaning.

Many animals can learn **to recognize people**.

▶ **Exercise 1** Above each infinitive, write *n* if it is used as a noun, *adj.* if it is used as an adjective, and *adv.* if it is used as an adverb.

                                                     adj.
Choosing a setting for a novel is not a decision to make hastily.

1. An author must choose the right setting to make a novel memorable.

2. For some writers, it was easy to find the best setting.

3. To live in London is to have the perfect setting.

4. A novelist can find it interesting to create plots based on the city's rich history.

5. As the center of government, it is the place to witness politics in action.

6. To see a great opera, one would also travel to London.

7. To shop, a character would head for Oxford Street.

8. There are many parks for a hero or heroine to walk through.

9. To visit the oldest royal park, one would go to St. James's.

10. At Regent's Park it is fun to view the Zoological Gardens.

11. At Trafalgar one likes to admire the statue of Lord Nelson, the hero of the battle of Trafalgar.

12. Perhaps the character to write about is Lord Nelson.

13. In his day, the place to be was a London district called Mayfair.

14. The author to read was Jane Austen.

15. To purchase one of Miss Austen's books, one went to Hatchard's on Piccadilly.

16. Later in the nineteenth century, London became the setting to read about in books by

   Charles Dickens.

17. His old house is an interesting place to visit.

18. Dickens liked to stroll through London gathering ideas for characters.

19. Read one of his books to determine what life was like at the time.

20. Think of other authors who chose to place their stories in London.

▶ **Exercise 2** **Circle the infinitive or the infinitive phrase in each sentence.**

Sherlock Holmes is known for his ability (to solve baffling mysteries).

1. Sir Arthur Conan Doyle has come to be well-known as the creator of Sherlock Holmes.

2. Conan Doyle received a degree in medicine and decided to work as an eye specialist.

3. Unfortunately, he was unsuccessful in his attempt to make a good living.

4. He wrote his first book to make money.

5. Conan Doyle used a doctor he knew to be the model for Sherlock Holmes.

6. The time he spent with his friend helped him to develop the characteristics of Holmes.

7. Holmes became known for his ability to observe.

8. Readers were able to appreciate the fictional detective's inquisitive nature.

9. Holmes always used his sharp wit to solve a mystery.

10. Conan Doyle was knighted to recognize his defense of the British in one of his books.

11. That is how he came to be called "Sir."

12. Conan Doyle created the character Dr. Watson to assist Holmes in his mysteries.

13. "My dear Watson" is one of the famous phrases to come from the Sherlock Holmes mysteries.

14. He often chose to write books with odd titles.

15. *The Red-Headed League* is another book title that is hard to forget.

16. At one time, Conan Doyle chose to kill off the legendary detective.

17. Readers called for him to bring Holmes back.

18. Conan Doyle went on to write fifty-nine more books featuring Sherlock Holmes.

19. Holmes's signature pipe and hat are items that readers are likely to remember.

20. To see Sherlock Holmes on television and in movies is not unusual.

Grammar

Lesson 22
Distinguishing Participial, Gerund, and Infinitive Phrases

The three types of verbal phrases, participial, gerund, and infinitive, are closely related to verbs. However, they do not function as verbs, but as nouns, adjectives, and adverbs. The easiest way to distinguish the phrases is by the way they function in a sentence and by their forms.

- An infinitive phrase can function as a noun, an adjective, or an adverb. Infinitives are usually preceded by the word *to*.
- Participial phrases function as adjectives. Present participles end in *-ing*. Most past participles end in *-ed*.
- Gerund phrases function as nouns. Gerunds end in *-ing*.

▶ **Exercise 1** **Identify the phrase in italics as *I* for infinitive, *G* for gerund, or *P* for participial.**

__G__   Harold will never forget *fumbling in the big game.*

_____ **1.** She collects figurines *made in the thirties.*

_____ **2.** *Buying fire extinguishers* is a good way to save lives.

_____ **3.** *Practicing constantly,* Mike improved his tennis game.

_____ **4.** The science lab contains many jars *labeled as dangerous.*

_____ **5.** Jim's goal, *getting elected,* was achieved through hard work.

_____ **6.** Dan has never been one *to complain about his problems.*

_____ **7.** There is no excuse for *reckless driving.*

_____ **8.** My younger sister likes *to slide down the big hill.*

_____ **9.** *Baking brownies* is our favorite activity on a rainy day.

_____ **10.** *Laughing at his jokes,* we nearly fell off our chairs.

_____ **11.** *Putting in extra time,* Ben finished his work.

_____ **12.** The lawyer argued *to set the record straight.*

_____ **13.** *Combining the ingredients* is the easy part.

_____ **14.** Laura was irritated by the wet towels *lying on the carpet.*

_____ **15.** *Using a flashlight,* Julia found her ring in the dark.

_____ **16.** Fines were imposed *to discourage littering.*

_____ **17.** She suggested several books *to read before the test.*

_____ **18.** The admiral wore a jacket *decorated with many medals.*

_____ **19.** *Getting ahead in business* is my uncle's primary goal.

_____ **20.** *To do a tough job well* can be rewarding.

▶ **Exercise 2** **Circle the infinitives and infinitive phrases in each sentence below. Then change each infinitive to a gerund and write the gerund form on the line at the left.**

_____Adding_____   (To add sound effects) to a production is called dubbing.

_____ **1.** According to researchers, to reduce your fat intake can be healthy.

_____ **2.** To install a smoke detector is usually a good idea.

_____ **3.** To burn leaves is against the law in some places.

_____ **4.** Jackie hates to wear long underwear.

_____ **5.** My mother's main concern was to raise healthy children.

_____ **6.** My stepbrother reminded me that to fail was no disgrace.

_____ **7.** To cough during the performance would have been rude, so I walked outside.

_____ **8.** Since we were playing our arch rivals, to lose the game would have been humiliating.

_____ **9.** To bite the apple could have been fatal for Snow White.

_____ **10.** Some people think that to be shy is a pleasant quality.

_____ **11.** To sleep late is a treat for Don, who has a paper route.

_____ **12.** According to my choir director, to perform in the choir is an honor.

_____ **13.** To knock down the toy clowns was the biggest challenge at the school festival.

_____ **14.** My grandfather loves to ride his bicycle.

_____ **15.** To forget the accident was a difficult task for Joanie.

_____ **16.** The children like to play outdoors.

_____ **17.** To play our school song before a game is a band tradition.

_____ **18.** Katie likes to watch her younger brothers.

_____ **19.** To compute the figures will require a calculator.

_____ **20.** To mow the whole lawn took four hours.

✓ Unit 3 **Review**

▶ **Exercise 1 Label each word or phrase in italics using the abbreviations below.**

Pr. - prepositional   *I* - infinitive   *P* - participial   *G* - gerund   *A* - appositive

                   A   G

My cousin *Martin* says *flying* is the only way to travel.

1. Teddy, *a professional*, was not eligible *for the prize*.

2. *Serving his country bravely*, my brother returned home a hero.

3. My friend *Kay* had several assignments *to complete*.

4. *Running* is not necessary, since we have plenty *of time*.

5. Philadelphia, the City *of Brotherly Love*, is a popular place *to visit*.

6. *To learn calculus* is challenging for me.

7. *Dialing* is not necessary now that we have a touch-tone telephone.

8. *For relaxation*, my dad turned to *walking*.

9. *Eating the leftover food*, the pilot survived *for weeks*.

10. *Writing several popular books*, the author became a celebrity.

11. *For technical reasons* the ground crew needed *to delay the flight*.

12. *To identify the alternatives*, the president consulted *with his advisers*.

13. My friend *Paul* is preparing *to study medicine*.

14. *Using my computer*, I typed my term paper *for English class*.

15. Kari, *my best friend*, has lived *near me since first grade*.

16. *At midnight* can you meet me *in the kitchen for a snack?*

17. *Claiming ignorance*, the witness was dismissed.

18. Maya Angelou, *the famous poet*, wrote that particular poem.

19. *Blending two families together* can be difficult *for some people*.

20. *Receiving my tickets*, I packed *for the trip*.

Cumulative Review: Units 1–3

▶ **Exercise 1** Draw a vertical line between the subject and predicate of each sentence. Underline each noun. Circle each verb. Label each participle *P*, each gerund *G*, and each infinitive *I*.

To become a good pianist | requires great concentration.

1. Autumn is her favorite time of the year.

2. She loves to rake leaves.

3. Galloping her horse through fields is another favorite activity.

4. Enjoying the crisp air, Miki rides her horse in the park.

5. She hopes to gather her friends together this week.

6. They enjoy riding, too.

7. Stavros rides the horse trained in Kentucky.

8. His horse, named Whirlwind, was trained to race.

9. Whirlwind prefers ambling.

10. Stavros likes to amble, too.

11. Miki and her horse, Star, are more adventurous.

12. Roaming through the fields, they explore the changes fall brings.

13. Miki wants to watch the leaves turn different colors.

14. Photographing the trees preserves their beautiful appearance.

15. Miki is putting together an album of pictures to show her biology class.

16. She took pictures of budding leaves in the spring.

17. She then took pictures of young flourishing trees.

18. She will take pictures of grown trees during the winter.

19. Placing the photographs in sequence, she will display the life of a leaf.

20. She will describe beneath each photograph what is happening.

Unit 4: Clauses and Sentence Structure

Lesson 23
Main and Subordinate Clauses

There are two types of clauses: main and subordinate. A main clause contains a subject and a predicate. This type of clause is also called independent, because it can stand alone as a sentence.

The baby cried.

A subordinate, or dependent, clause contains a subject and predicate but cannot stand alone. This type of clause must be used with a main clause in order to make sense. It usually begins with a subordinating conjunction, such as *after, although, as, as if, because, if, since, so that, than, unless, until, when, where,* or *while;* a relative pronoun such as *who, whose, whom, which, that,* or *what;* or a relative adverb, such as *when, where,* or *why.*

The baby cried when the dog barked loudly.

▶ **Exercise 1** **Draw one line under the subordinate clause or clauses in each sentence.**

<u>While I hem the skirt,</u> will you finish the blouse?

1. After the storm cleared, the flight took off.

2. You will learn to speak Spanish if you practice.

3. I know a girl who sings in the chorus.

4. Although English is my favorite subject, I also like algebra.

5. We can go to the mall unless you are too busy.

6. Madeline is from a part of France where few people speak English.

7. The judge, who was angered by the outburst, slammed her gavel down.

8. When we arrived at the hotel, we discovered that our reservation had been cancelled.

9. Though many of us stood in line, only a few people bought concert tickets.

10. Maggie, whose birthday is in July, has already decided what she wants.

11. The restaurant where we used to eat dinner went out of business.

12. I peeled the potatoes while mother shredded the carrots.

13. Because the subject was complicated, Brad studied very hard.

14. Whenever we visit the zoo, Emma and I look for the giraffes first.

15. Dawn's letter had a sad tone, as if something had gone wrong.

16. Until Diana learned to trust, she had very few friends.

17. The computer that Jill bought a year ago is already outdated.

18. Because the epidemic had grown worse, the area hospitals were overcrowded.

19. Whenever we go to the dentist, she encourages us to brush.

20. My uncle reads at the dinner table, a habit that I consider rude.

▶ **Exercise 2** **Underline the main clause in each sentence. Then circle the subordinate clause.**

(When you finish your drawing,) you may frame it.

1. The kitten ran when the children came near it.

2. Chad has quit his job so he can devote more time to his studies.

3. If the door is open, you can go right into the house.

4. Players who wish to join the team may sign up today.

5. Dr. Thomas returned to the site where we first saw the unusual rocks.

6. Do you remember the time when we stayed up all night?

7. My cousin who lives in Saudi Arabia came to visit last summer.

8. After I had written the letter, I mailed it.

9. Africa had changed since the last time I was there.

10. When we reached the top of the mountain, we felt tired but proud.

11. Mitch lives in the building where the burglary happened.

12. Although we were worried about Jason, we did not want to show our nervousness.

13. When the list of winners was announced, Kelly ran to claim her prize.

14. We watched as the archaeologists dug up the dinosaur remains.

15. Because Antonio loves water sports, we bought him water skis for Christmas.

16. Before he sat down, Rick took off his jacket.

17. Sarah spun around as if she were an ice skater.

18. When she was given an example, Tessa could do just about any math problem.

19. When the clouds lifted, the sun shone brightly.

20. When the teacher is speaking, we are not supposed to interrupt.

Lesson 24
Simple and Compound Sentences

A **simple sentence** contains one main clause and no subordinate clauses. The simple sentence may not appear to be simple. It may have a compound subject or a compound predicate. It may also contain modifiers. As long as it has only one main clause, it is a simple sentence.

Li-Ching and Maria sang a duet.

A **compound sentence** contains two or more main clauses that are usually joined by a comma and a coordinating conjunction.

Maria sang one of her own songs, **and** Robert danced.
Maria sang, Robert danced, **and** Li-Cheng played the piano.

▶ **Exercise 1** Write *s* if the sentence is simple or *c* if it is compound.

___s___   Marcus and Wolfgang, brothers from Germany, toured the United States and Canada last spring.

_____ **1.** The polio vaccine was developed by Jonas Salk and Albert Sabin.

_____ **2.** My little brother Jake got a toy in his breakfast-cereal box.

_____ **3.** We watched the baseball game, and we went for ice cream afterward.

_____ **4.** A red car pulled up to the house, and a girl climbed out.

_____ **5.** One of the remotes controlled the stereo, and another controlled the television.

_____ **6.** The doctor determined the cause of Gina's health problem.

_____ **7.** Collin played well, but Andrea had the highest score.

_____ **8.** The rescue helicopter landed on top of the hospital.

_____ **9.** Jim didn't take good notes, but Mary helped him study for the test.

_____ **10.** The battery was dead, and the gas tank was almost empty.

_____ **11.** The parade moved from the boulevard to the park.

_____ **12.** Laura's new coat was blue, and her hat was burgundy.

_____ **13.** The library was empty and quiet.

_____ **14.** My grandfather made his fortune in the computer industry.

_____ **15.** Monique is interested in protecting animal rights.

_____ **16.** The change jingled loudly in my pocket.

_____ **17.** Claire worked hard and earned a lot of money.

_____ **18.** Zach and Amanda helped out at the car wash.

_____ **19.** You can help with the dishes, or you can wash the car.

_____ **20.** We helped the neighbors rake leaves, and they helped us wash windows.

▶ Exercise 2 **Write *c* next to each compound sentence.**

__c__ We picked up our lunch, and we ran to the park.

_____ **1.** The Statue of Liberty was created by the French sculptor, Frederic Auguste Bartholdi.

_____ **2.** Bartholdi studied painting and architecture in Paris, and his first sculpture was shown in 1883.

_____ **3.** The original name of the statue was "Liberty Enlightening the World."

_____ **4.** The statue was planned to honor the centennial celebration of 1876, but the statue was not completed until later.

_____ **5.** The statue was given to the United States by France in 1886.

_____ **6.** The statue is often called "Miss Liberty."

_____ **7.** Gustave Eiffel created the statue's internal structure, and his engineering method is used today.

_____ **8.** Eiffel later designed France's Eiffel Tower.

_____ **9.** The statue is hollow to allow visitors inside, but it weighs approximately 450,000 pounds.

_____ **10.** Tremendous fundraising was required for Bartholdi to complete the colossal statue.

_____ **11.** Americans were asked to provide the pedestal for the statue, and they did.

_____ **12.** An American, Richard Morris Hunt, designed the pedestal.

_____ **13.** The site chosen for the statue was Bedloe's Island in New York Harbor.

_____ **14.** The statue and its pedestal together would reach 305 feet.

_____ **15.** It is made of copper, but the statue now appears green due to weathering.

_____ **16.** The statue was unveiled in 1886 and became the tallest human-made structure at that time.

_____ **17.** In the 1980s the statue was restored for the 1986 centennial celebration.

_____ **18.** A plaque inside the statue displays a poem by the poet Emma Lazarus.

_____ **19.** The poem welcomes immigrants to the United States, and it continues to inspire immigrants today.

_____ **20.** The Statue of Liberty has come to signify the wealth of opportunities available in the United States.

Lesson 25
Complex and Compound-Complex Sentences

A complex sentence contains one main clause and one or more subordinate clauses.

When she heard the applause, Beth felt proud.

A compound-complex sentence has more than one main clause and one or more subordinate clauses.

Although we had difficulty deciding, we finally chose a destination, and Dad bought the airline tickets.

▶ **Exercise 1 Circle the number in front of each complex sentence.**

(a.) We went to the eastern United States for our vacation although we'd been there before.

1. Frederick Douglass, who fought to end slavery, was a leader in the abolitionist movement.

2. Born Frederick Bailey in 1817, he grew up as a slave on a Maryland plantation.

3. Unlike most slaves, Douglass learned to read and write.

4. He escaped to the North in 1838, where he changed his name to avoid being caught.

5. After he spoke at a meeting of the American Anti-Slavery Society in 1841, Douglass became a spokesman for the society.

6. In his speeches, Douglass recalled life as a slave, and he called for an immediate end to slavery.

7. His autobiography, *Narrative of the Life of Frederick Douglass,* was published in 1841.

8. His book was popular in the North and in Europe.

9. Douglass became known as a leader in the crusade against slavery.

10. Douglass's notoriety jeopardized his freedom.

11. He spent two years in the British Isles, where he tried to win support.

12. In 1841 Douglass became the editor of the *North Star,* an antislavery newspaper.

13. He married Anna Murray in 1838, and the two had five children together.

14. When the Underground Railroad began, Douglass helped slaves escape to the North.

15. During the Civil War, Douglass wanted it known that the war was a move to abolish slavery.

16. He served as an advisor to President Lincoln, who saw Douglass as a representative for African Americans.

17. In 1862, Lincoln issued the Emancipation Proclamation, which freed slaves in places not held by Union troops.

18. Although slavery was abolished with the Thirteenth Amendment, Douglass pursued the right of blacks to vote.

19. He became a U.S. Marshal in 1877 and was later appointed consul general to Haiti.

20. Douglass continued to fight for reform until his death in 1895, when he collapsed following a woman suffrage meeting.

▶ **Exercise 2** **Draw one line under each main clause and two lines under each subordinate clause. Then write *c* if the sentence is complex or *cc* if the sentence is compound-complex.**

_____c_____ As we neared the hot-air balloon festival, the sky looked like a fairyland.

_____ **1.** Until they were called home, the children played happily.

_____ **2.** When we went to the opera, we saw Luciano Pavarotti, but we didn't get to see Placido Domingo.

_____ **3.** Although I didn't brew it long, the coffee tastes bitter, and I will not drink it.

_____ **4.** As the morning bell rang, the students rushed quickly into class.

_____ **5.** I have always volunteered at the hospital because I enjoy helping others.

_____ **6.** After the election is over, I will call you with results, and hopefully, our candidate will have won.

_____ **7.** Dr. May was the only doctor who was available in the middle of the night.

_____ **8.** Kelsey will finish her paper by noon, which is the deadline for the project.

_____ **9.** My journalism teacher, whose opinion I respect, told me my article was good.

_____ **10.** Since no one had a question for the speaker, the lecture ended early, and we went out for hamburgers.

_____ **11.** When my sister went to college, my parents got her a used car.

_____ **12.** After the doctor examined her, Darcy still felt ill, but she felt better in the morning.

_____ **13.** The dog finally caught the ball as it drifted into the neighbor's yard.

_____ **14.** As long as you keep your eyes open, you will see the exit ramp.

_____ **15.** Although he did not understand the reasons, Josh accepted the divorce.

_____ **16.** Since he has learned English, Miguel has been more outgoing.

_____ **17.** Paul's speech will emphasize the budget because we must reduce the deficit, and his book will say the same.

_____ **18.** The park where we used to play is now the site of a shopping mall.

Grammar

Lesson 26
Adjective Clauses

Grammar

An **adjective clause** is a subordinate clause that modifies a noun or pronoun. Remember that a subordinate clause contains a subject and verb but cannot stand alone. An adjective clause usually begins with a relative pronoun, such as *who, whom, whose, that,* and *which,* or a subordinating conjunction, such as *where* or *when.*

The book **that I lent him** is now overdue. (The adjective clause modifies the noun *book.*)

Sometimes the relative pronoun or subordinating conjunction is left out.

The book **I lent him** is now overdue.

An adjective clause can be essential or nonessential to the meaning of a sentence. An essential adjective clause is an adjective clause that cannot be omitted from a sentence without changing its meaning. A nonessential adjective clause can be omitted from a sentence, and the meaning of the sentence will remain the same.

Essential: The player **who batted last** scored the winning run.
Nonessential: Jerome, **who batted last**, is the best player on the team.

▶ **Exercise 1** **Underline the adjective clause, and circle the noun or pronoun it modifies.**

The (lamb) that Dena showed at the fair placed second in its division.

1. The basketball player whom I admired most retired last year.

2. The company that I worked for last summer went out of business.

3. The Battle of Gettysburg, which lasted three days, ended in victory for the Union soldiers.

4. The chair that we bought at the garage sale looks great in the living room.

5. The telegraph, which was the forerunner of the telephone, transmits signals over a wire.

6. The swimmers who won the meet were treated to dinner.

7. Do you remember the time when we marched in the parade?

8. The spaghetti that Duane made for dinner tasted great.

9. The pier where we docked the boat is the one on the left.

10. The author who wrote the book was signing autographs at the bookstore.

11. Rich was the chef whose secret recipes everyone wanted.

12. The contributor who made the large donation was never identified.

13. The suburb that we live in is undergoing many changes.

14. My parents were married in the park where they met.

15. The coin, which was shiny and new, was given to me by my grandfather.

16. The surgery that was supposed to cure her only made her feel worse.

17. Music and dancing are hobbies that we both love.

18. The people who are unable to attend will be invited again.

19. Ian found a book that someone had left in the gym.

20. Frank Lloyd Wright is recognized as the man who changed modern architecture.

21. The stairs that led to the attic were creaky.

22. Jessica found a bird that had fallen out of its nest.

23. The skyscrapers that rose above the city were shrouded in fog.

24. Juan is the boy who plays all intramural sports.

25. The trail they followed was marked with handkerchiefs.

26. His speech, which made perfect sense to me, was misinterpreted by some.

27. Cyclists who wear helmets have a better chance of surviving accidents.

28. The clothes that hung on the line were just washed.

29. The student who played Tiny Tim is in my geometry class.

30. I remember the year when I got my first bike.

31. The experiment, which worked perfectly, proved that the substance was soluble.

32. Luke remembered the day when he nearly fell through the ice.

33. The forecast, which called for rain, was incorrect.

34. At dark we reached the area where we had planned to set up camp.

35. The place where I belong is with my family.

36. Those who chose the wrong trail walked in circles for hours.

37. People who hoped to see the comedian up close were disappointed.

38. The bus that picks us up in the morning is not the one that drops us off after school.

39. Plays he has directed have won many awards.

40. Anyone who wants to join the army must be disciplined.

41. The books that had been missing were found in the basement.

42. That elephant, which is indigenous to Africa, cannot survive in the cold.

43. Anyone who tried to change Kyle's mind failed miserably.

44. The picnic lunch that we packed this morning should feed the whole group.

45. Students who want to go on the field trip must bring a permission slip.

▶ **Exercise 2** **Underline the adjective clause in each sentence. Write *N* next to the nonessential clauses and *E* next to the essential clauses.**

___E___   Players <u>who are always on time for practice</u> set a good example for their teammates.

_____ **1.** My rollerskates, which I paid fifty dollars for, are now too small for me.

_____ **2.** The city that we visited on vacation was my father's home town.

_____ **3.** The kicker who missed the field goal was disappointed for days.

_____ **4.** The call, which was unexpected, came on a Saturday night.

_____ **5.** The program that we were watching was interrupted.

_____ **6.** The house that we lived in for nine years has been sold.

_____ **7.** The boy whose bike had been stolen cried loudly.

_____ **8.** Food that is not stored properly will spoil.

_____ **9.** The camels roamed the desert, where water was scarce.

_____ **10.** Stephanie studied every night, which helped her become a better student.

_____ **11.** Materials that are not recyclable go in the other bin.

_____ **12.** The piano, which had been tuned recently, sounded wonderful.

_____ **13.** The data that we gathered was of no use to us.

_____ **14.** The oil, which was leaking everywhere, caused quite a mess.

_____ **15.** My friend, who goes to a different school, came to visit me.

_____ **16.** Helen grew up during the fifties, when times were much different.

_____ **17.** One thing that my father and I shared was a love of fishing.

_____ **18.** The quarry, which was not safe to swim in, was being filled with dirt.

_____ **19.** Those flowers, which have a strong scent, make me sneeze.

_____ **20.** Dogwood trees, which are very beautiful, can be white or pink.

▶ **Exercise 3** **Insert an adjective clause to modify the noun or pronoun in italics.**

The *lake,* _____which looked so glassy yesterday,_____ had whitecaps today due to the high winds.

1. The *video game* _____ is difficult for beginners.

2. There is the *table* _____ .

Grammar

3. Eli found a *puppy* _____.

4. The *campground* _____ was nearly full.

5. *Anyone* _____ can be on the team.

6. My *cousin* _____ comes to visit often.

7. The *driver* _____ was not responsible for the accident.

8. This is the *firefighter* _____.

9. In the *desert,* _____, plant and animal life are scarce.

10. I forgot about the *appointment* _____.

11. The *actor* _____ gave an acceptance speech.

12. The car wash was held in the *morning,* _____.

13. The bowling *league* _____ celebrated for two hours.

14. At the start of the *meeting* _____, breakfast was served.

15. Joy read a *magazine* _____.

16. José spent the *money* _____ on a gift for his sister's birthday.

17. The mountain *trail* _____ was steep and rocky.

18. Vanessa goes to the *gym* on Main Street, _____.

19. Our first *assignment,* _____, was due on Tuesday.

20. The sea *air* _____ gave us a chill.

▶ **Writing Link Write a paragraph describing your neighborhood that includes at least three or more adjective clauses.**

_____

_____

_____

_____

_____

_____

_____

_____

_____

_____

Lesson 27
Adverb Clauses

An **adverb clause** is a subordinate clause that modifies a verb, an adjective, or an adverb. It is used to tell *when, where, why, how, to what extent,* or *under what conditions.* An adverb clause is usually introduced by a subordinating conjunction.

I cry **whenever I see a sad movie.** (The adverb clause modifies the verb *cry.* It tells *when.)*

An adverb clause that seems to have missing words is called **elliptical**. The words that are left out are understood in the clause.

Steve runs faster **than I** [run].

▶ **Exercise 1 Underline the adverb clause in each sentence.**

When they arrived at the space camp, the aspiring astronauts grew nervous.

1. After I finished doing the dishes, I helped my dad mow the lawn.

2. The little girl was upset because her puppy was lost.

3. That old house looked spookier than any other house in the neighborhood.

4. Jeremy left for the football game before I could offer him a ride.

5. Jennifer will go on the retreat unless it rains.

6. Dino ran the 100-yard dash much faster than I did.

7. Because the sweaters were on sale, Stuart bought three.

8. Eve was more interested in geography than her brother was.

9. Will you wait in the car until it's time to leave for school?

10. Alex waxed the car until it looked brand new.

11. We met where his street intersects mine.

12. I heard a strange noise when I turned on the computer.

13. While it was snowing outside, Simon was daydreaming about sunny beaches.

14. The band began a food drive so that we could help the hungry.

15. Because she couldn't find an opener, Sandy didn't open the can.

16. Whenever I go to that restaurant, I run into a friend.

17. I dropped my wallet as I was crossing the street.

Grammar

18. You will see a gas station wherever you look in that city.

19. Although I had never seen my aunt before, I recognized her instantly.

20. Grandma and Grandpa have lived in the same house since they were married.

21. The charity event will be a success as long as it doesn't rain.

22. Whenever we ice-skate, we put on our mittens.

23. He will go away unless you apologize.

24. Wherever we went, we put up flyers announcing the play.

25. If we understood the rules, we would be able to play the game.

26. We walked slowly away from the barking dog because it frightened us.

27. Because he is a fine athlete, Terry will compete for a scholarship.

28. Tim has been driving everywhere since he got his driver's license.

29. Rosa grew taller than her older sister.

30. While we were on the plane to Hawaii, I had a wonderful dream.

31. We rode the bus because the car was being serviced.

32. After Sabine went back to France, we promised to write letters every week.

33. Sean is a better cook than I.

34. You will do well on the essay questions as long as you answer each question completely.

35. Grandpa bought the telescope because my brother loves to look at the stars.

36. I like to exercise as soon as I get up each morning.

37. Those chemicals are not dangerous unless they are combined.

38. After they left the theater, John and Kim went out to dinner.

39. Whenever I get a cold, I feel miserable.

40. We will stick to the schedule as long as there are no objections.

41. My muscles ached after I did the exercises.

42. Though he was in no immediate danger, we were still concerned.

43. The audience was restless until the performance began.

44. We had a substitute teacher because our regular teacher was ill.

45. Sherry has a heavier southern accent than I have.

► **Exercise 2** **Underline the adverb clause in each sentence. Circle the verb, adverb, or adjective it modifies.**

<u>While they were in the shelter of the cliff</u>, Mali and Aaron (felt) safe from the storm.

1. Whenever I move my rook, she takes my bishop.

2. Because he was under oath, the witness answered honestly.

3. We stayed until the end of the program.

4. Although I am busy, I will help you paint the room.

5. Ryan felt awful until he took the medicine.

6. Bridget walked away as if she were angry.

7. While the first coat of paint dried, we rested.

8. Helena sings better than Lisa.

9. Raymond was feeling worse than I was feeling.

10. The telephone rings whenever I take a shower.

11. While I'm at the store, I can get you something.

12. The discussion made me angrier than it made him.

13. Because I need extra money, I baby-sit every weekend.

14. Though it took a long time, we waited patiently.

15. The ride is safe as long as you wear your safety belt.

16. When the time came to volunteer, Maryann raised her hand first.

17. Kevin was frustrated because he couldn't solve the problem.

18. Rebecca can climb higher than I can climb.

19. Because she believes in protecting the environment, Julie recycles.

20. Whenever she sang, audiences cheered.

► **Exercise 3** **Underline each adverb clause and adjective clause. Write *adv.* if the underlined clause is an adverb clause or *adj.* if it is an adjective clause.**

**adj.** The first person <u>whose name is called</u> will be the team leader.

_____ 1. I call on Malcolm whenever I need help with algebra.

_____ 2. The horse will respond as long as you give the signals correctly.

_____ 3. Ernesto had many fine qualities that made him very popular.

_____ 4. The twins agreed to stay home as long as we agreed to bring them something.

Grammar

_____ 5. Anyone who calls the office will hear the recording of Jane's message.

_____ 6. Jamie sneaked up on me while I was eating my lunch.

_____ 7. Since there was no time to argue, we quickly decided to vote on it.

_____ 8. The book that I cherish the most is the one on this shelf.

_____ 9. Although I was not injured, the accident gave me quite a scare.

_____ 10. The runners who finished the race were out of breath.

_____ 11. I look for these dolls wherever I go.

_____ 12. I found a dollar as I was walking to Joel's house.

_____ 13. The scarecrow that stood out in the rain was soaking wet.

_____ 14. We looked for fireflies at night whenever we had time.

_____ 15. Ruth gave her jacket to someone who needed it more.

_____ 16. The turkey, which was in the oven, smelled delicious.

_____ 17. The telephone that I got for my birthday was a pleasant surprise.

_____ 18. Derek panicked after he saw his new haircut.

_____ 19. Ben Franklin, whose picture appears on the one-hundred-dollar bill, was a famous

statesman and scientist.

_____ 20. Doug was proud after he completed his term paper.

▶ **Writing Link** **Write a paragraph about a family pet. Use at least three adverb clauses.**

_____

_____

_____

_____

_____

_____

_____

_____

_____

_____

Lesson 28
Noun Clauses

A **noun clause** is a subordinate clause that is used as a noun. A noun clause may be used as a subject, a direct object, an indirect object, an object of a preposition, an appositive, or a predicate nominative.

A noun clause usually begins with one of these words: *how, that, what, whatever, when, where, which, whichever, who, whom, whoever, whose, why.*

                            direct object
Cindy did not know where the beakers were kept.

             subject
What makes them different is their ability to change colors to blend with their environment.

▶ **Exercise 1** **Circle each sentence that contains a noun clause.**

(Whenever we choose to leave for the game is fine with them.)

1. The board proposed that all residents be required to recycle.

2. Whatever you choose will make a fine gift.

3. Mike defended his position on the issue.

4. The community college offers a course in fencing.

5. The scientist predicted how the chemicals might react.

6. Ted should have been at the swim meet an hour ago.

7. The rest of the group arrived later.

8. You may take whichever puppy you want.

9. The raccoons eat whatever they can find.

10. The spilled soda did not stain the carpet.

11. Many people thought that the defendant was not guilty.

12. Onlookers were disappointed when the shuttle lift-off was delayed.

13. Marla was encouraged to enter her poems in a contest.

14. Many people believe that you can do anything if you try.

15. Melissa told the teacher that her test was marked incorrectly.

16. Whatever we give will be appreciated by the charity.

17. Ethan started his own business at the age of thirteen.

18. Your opinion of the show was what I thought, also.

19. The little boy mimicked whatever Kirk did.

20. I did not hear what Brenda said.

▶ **Exercise 2** **Underline the noun clause or clauses in each sentence.**

I do not care which route we take to the cabin.

1. Sam did not know where the art exhibit was.

2. I do not know why Tonya chose to go with them instead of us.

3. I dreamed that I was the president of the United States.

4. What makes them so special is their ability to see the good in everyone.

5. The refugees were grateful for whatever they received.

6. Kay is who will be the baby-sitter.

7. Whoever was in charge of that experiment made it easy to understand.

8. That the boys had nothing in common became apparent.

9. Brent's patience and understanding were what we appreciated most.

10. Chantal was not interested in what the others wanted to do.

11. Whoever can play the piano will be the first on the list.

12. Kyle always felt that he'd like to live in Australia.

13. Ron told us that there were no seats left in the auditorium.

14. Why Jay left the party early was a mystery to everyone.

15. How anyone could dislike homemade bread amazes me!

16. How well the task is done is an important issue.

17. The principal told me that the band show was a great success.

18. That Holly had run out of gas was true.

19. What we didn't know was that the surprise was waiting for us outside.

20. That Florence was the best player was accepted by everyone.

21. Cheryl hears what she wants to hear.

22. I cannot understand how anyone can enjoy going to the dentist.

23. We gave directions to whoever asked us.

24. What Carl does not realize is that he has a great career ahead of him.

25. My friends argued about how we should build the science project.

26. Where the exhibit will be held has yet to be determined.

27. Whoever made that comment should be recognized.

28. That we need more police on patrol was the point of his speech.

29. You cannot know that the test will be easy.

30. What the athletes wanted was to do their best.

31. Your review of the novel was what I believed, too.

32. Our wish is that the puppy will find a good home.

33. No one could predict how long the rally would go on.

34. That the candidate was qualified was not an easy thing to prove.

35. Pass your paper to whoever is on your left.

36. Patrick was happy about what happened at the tennis match.

37. Joni always answered with whatever she thought.

38. The art students were asked what the painting represents.

39. Why we have so little time is bewildering to me.

40. Because I'm starved, whatever you cook will be fine with me.

41. I will call whomever you wish.

42. Nina could not understand why the dress was so expensive.

43. Many people think that dogs make the best pets.

44. What the judges decided was not acceptable to Marcus.

45. Did you know that the exploration of caves is called *spelunking*?

▶ **Exercise 3** **Underline the noun clause in each sentence. Then label it** *d.o.* **for direct object,** *subj.* **for subject,** *p.n.* **for predicate nominative, or** *o.p.* **for object of a preposition.**

                subj.
    Where they found the missing necklace remains a secret.

1. That the team did not want to practice was no great surprise.

2. I do not know where she works after school.

3. Your opinion of the class is what I think, too.

4. Whoever sleeps will be the victim of our practical jokes.

5. We will make up a skit with whatever props we are given.

Grammar

6. That is why I could not go to the movie.

7. Will the teacher explain what DNA is?

8. We paid special attention to how she wove the baskets.

9. The directions did not indicate where one should go in case of fire.

10. My problem is that the book was due last week.

11. Whoever has visited Chicago has seen many skyscrapers.

12. You may have heard that we got a new principal.

13. Ben decided to dance with whoever asked him.

14. I did not know how long the debate would go on.

15. That the bitter cold will be here soon is unfortunate, but true.

16. Ashley does whatever she wants to do.

17. Hiroko asked why I did not go to camp.

18. What appeared to be true was ruled out after further investigation.

19. The mittens were left by whichever person sat there last.

20. What makes me laugh is his crazy sense of humor.

▶ **Writing Link Write a paragraph about a book you have read recently. Use at least three noun clauses in your paragraph.**

_____

_____

_____

_____

_____

_____

_____

_____

_____

Lesson 29
Kinds of Sentences: Declarative and Imperative

A **declarative sentence** makes a statement and usually ends with a period.

Diet soda is my favorite drink.

An **imperative sentence** gives a command or makes a request. The subject "you" is understood.

(You) Report any safety violations to the supervisor.

▶ **Exercise 1** Label each sentence *dec.* for declarative sentence or *imp.* for imperative sentence.

imp.   Always wear eye protection in the laboratory.

_____ 1. The backyard was flooded after the strong rains.

_____ 2. Come to my house after band practice.

_____ 3. Slowly pour the solution into the beaker.

_____ 4. The spaghetti was cold by the time we sat down to eat.

_____ 5. My glasses were bent after my little sister sat on them.

_____ 6. The drugstore was closed by the time I arrived there.

_____ 7. Go to the nearest ticket booth, and get two tickets for the concert.

_____ 8. My throat was sore after I had my tonsils taken out.

_____ 9. Send a letter to your representative if you have a complaint.

_____ 10. Please wash my white shirt by Monday.

_____ 11. The sand was so hot we couldn't walk on it.

_____ 12. We've lived in the same house since I was born.

_____ 13. An isosceles triangle has two equal sides.

_____ 14. Have faith in my abilities.

_____ 15. Drink your hot chocolate before it gets cold.

_____ 16. The tent is too small for the whole family to use.

_____ 17. When Tuesday comes, take out the trash.

_____ 18. Jack is taller than his father.

_____ 19. Antonio was the best gymnast at the competition.

_____ **20.** Remind me to return my library books.

_____ **21.** The family that moved in next door is very nice.

_____ **22.** Stay away from that wild horse.

_____ **23.** Call the fire department if you suspect fire.

_____ **24.** Take Mel to see the penguins.

_____ **25.** Science fiction has never interested me.

_____ **26.** Eduardo always reads the comics first.

_____ **27.** Gather your belongings and come with me.

_____ **28.** Violin music makes me sleepy.

_____ **29.** Lock the door on your way out.

_____ **30.** My science textbook had been lost all year.

_____ **31.** Linda loves to watch old westerns on television.

_____ **32.** Please wear your seat belt in my car.

_____ **33.** Stay in the hospital until you feel well.

_____ **34.** We saw *The Nutcracker* at the theater downtown.

_____ **35.** Hold on to my hand until I can skate by myself.

_____ **36.** We played board games until midnight.

_____ **37.** Donna grew up on a farm.

_____ **38.** Watch your step on the ice.

_____ **39.** After he got a tutor, Jesse's work showed improvement.

_____ **40.** Yolanda showed me the newest dance steps.

_____ **41.** Don't touch the freshly painted walls.

_____ **42.** Smile so that I can take your picture.

_____ **43.** Read all about it in the newspaper today.

_____ **44.** The photos made me remember my childhood.

_____ **45.** Inform the guidance counselor whenever you need extra help.

Lesson 30

Kinds of Sentences: Interrogative and Exclamatory

An **interrogative sentence** asks a question and ends with a question mark.

Are your allergies bothering you?

An **exclamatory sentence** shows strong or sudden feeling. It ends with an exclamation point.

We won the game!

▶ **Exercise 1** **Insert a question mark if the sentence is interrogative, or an exclamation point if the sentence is exclamatory.**

Don't drop that fragile vase!

1. How did you find out about the surprise party

2. Watch out for the falling rocks

3. Is this the place where Lee surrendered

4. Were you frightened by the loud noises

5. When will the train be leaving

6. Where are the tryouts for the play held

7. Don't spill your drink

8. I can't believe you said that

9. The bell rang ten minutes ago

10. What time does the movie start

11. Do you like sugar in your tea

12. Run as fast as you can

13. Has Seema asked you for help with history

14. I caught you taking the last cookie

15. Does the meeting start at seven

16. Would you pick up some eggs at the store

17. Do you know where Dylan is

18. Is that your radio

19. Don't be so eager

Grammar

20. Please help me find Mother's favorite earring

21. Can you find the Big Dipper in the night sky

22. You scared me to death

23. Are you allowed to stay out late

24. Has Marcia been asked to the dance

25. Is there enough time to play soccer before we go shopping

26. Which station do you listen to the most

27. Don't stand so close to the campfire

28. Erik just took the lead

29. Why have you been so quiet

30. Is this oboe yours

31. That's no excuse

32. How did you hear the news

33. What was decided during the peace talks

34. Never give up

35. I won first-chair violin

36. Which tie looks better with this suit

37. Will we meet at the same time tomorrow

38. Was our team defeated last night

39. What will happen if I change my mind

40. I can't believe he missed that shot

41. Where do we sign up for intramural basketball

42. How many cookies did Darryl eat

43. Do you know how to use the copier

44. Hurry, or we'll be late

45. Who painted the picture hanging in the lobby

Lesson 31
Sentence Fragments

A **sentence fragment** is an incomplete sentence. It may lack a subject, a verb, or both. Alternatively, it may be a subordinate clause that cannot stand alone. Correct it by adding the missing phrase or words.

Although he bought the tie for his brother. (Fragment)
Although he bought the tie for his brother, he kept it for himself. (Sentence)

▶ **Exercise 1 Write *frag.* next to each sentence fragment. Write *s* next to each complete sentence.**

<u>frag.</u>   In the event of a disaster.

_____ **1.** Georgia O'Keeffe became one of the best-loved American artists.

_____ **2.** Because she had an innovative style.

_____ **3.** Works from charcoals to watercolors to pastels.

_____ **4.** O'Keeffe, feeling that her creations were personal, kept to herself.

_____ **5.** By distancing herself from historians, biographers, and critics.

_____ **6.** She developed a very individual style.

_____ **7.** Which became apparent in 1915.

_____ **8.** O'Keeffe studied at the Art Institute of Chicago and the Arts Students League in New York.

_____ **9.** Her works soon came to the attention of Alfred Stieglitz, a photographer and art exhibitor.

_____ **10.** In 1917, O'Keeffe had her first art show at the New York gallery owned by Stieglitz.

_____ **11.** Whom she later married.

_____ **12.** Paintings of flowers, some of her most famous works.

_____ **13.** Appeared in the mid-1920s.

_____ **14.** She created many paintings that were based on the American Southwest.

_____ **15.** Where she first visited in 1929.

_____ **16.** Establishing her home in New Mexico in 1949.

_____ **17.** *The Pelvis Series* includes some of her best work.

_____ **18.** A series of paintings of animal bones against stark backgrounds.

Grammar

_____ **19.** O'Keeffe's art helped to bridge the gap between American and European art of the early twentieth century.

_____ **20.** Until her death in 1986.

▶ **Exercise 2 Tell whether you would add a subject *(s)*, verb *(v)*, or a main clause *(m)* to form a complete sentence.**

___v___ A blue bus carrying fifteen adults and four children.

_____ **1.** As if he were in a daze.

_____ **2.** Each year thousands of crops lost to flooding.

_____ **3.** How to spell the words for the test.

_____ **4.** Advised against eating fatty foods.

_____ **5.** A heart doctor known as a cardiologist.

_____ **6.** Charges no admission for students.

_____ **7.** Since we forgot our skis.

_____ **8.** The Smiths installing a security system in their home.

_____ **9.** Which the school paper published.

_____ **10.** Animals from the city zoo arriving this afternoon.

_____ **11.** Warned us not to swim right after eating.

_____ **12.** Are living in mobile homes until their houses are rebuilt.

_____ **13.** A child singing in the chorus.

_____ **14.** Gives the user plenty of information.

_____ **15.** Because I cannot be at the meeting.

_____ **16.** A chocolate cookie melting in the sun.

_____ **17.** Every year plants trees near the school.

_____ **18.** Although I bought the gift for Trisha.

_____ **19.** Requires permission from a parent or guardian.

_____ **20.** Hiking on lichen-covered rocky slopes.

_____ **21.** Stir the hard-packed prairie soil.

_____ **22.** A squirrel monkey pouncing on insects.

_____ **23.** Include the prevention of water-runoff pollution.

_____ **24.** One of the most livable cities in the country.

Lesson 32
Run-on Sentences

A **run-on sentence** contains two or more complete sentences written as one.

Incorrect: There was a mistake on our bill, the server took care of it. (two main clauses separated by a comma instead of a period)

Correct: There was a mistake on our bill. The server took care of it. (Break up with a period or semicolon.)

Incorrect: I ran into Margaret she is leaving for Florida tomorrow. (two main clauses with no punctuation between them)

Correct: I ran into Margaret; she is leaving for Florida tomorrow. (Break up with a period or semicolon.)

▶ **Exercise 1** Write *run-on* next to each run-on sentence.

_____run-on_____ Prizes encourage excellence one particular prize is the Pulitzer Prize.

_____ **1.** The Pulitzer Prize is awarded each year, it awards excellence in journalism, letters, and music.

_____ **2.** The awards were established by the powerful publisher Joseph Pulitzer.

_____ **3.** Pulitzer owned the *St. Louis Post-Dispatch* he purchased the *New York World* in 1883.

_____ **4.** Pulitzer helped to shape the modern newspaper.

_____ **5.** He added many features to his newspapers, including sports, comics, fashions, and illustrations.

_____ **6.** Pulitzer's papers also gained a reputation for sensational reporting.

_____ **7.** Pulitzer left money to Columbia University the awards were established in 1917.

_____ **8.** In addition to establishing the awards, his money funded a school of journalism for Columbia.

_____ **9.** Pulitzer planned four awards for journalism and four for letters more categories were added later.

_____ **10.** The letters category includes drama, poetry, history, biography or autobiography, fiction, and general nonfiction.

_____ **11.** The Pulitzer Prizes for journalism are given for work that appears in U.S. newspapers.

_____ **12.** Each prize is $1,000, except the prize for public service, which is a gold medal.

Grammar

Grammar

_____ 13. Anyone may make a nomination, the nomination must include the work.

_____ 14. Following a preliminary judging, the candidates are judged by an advisory board.

_____ 15. The advisory board can nominate other candidates.

_____ 16. Works with American themes seem to be preferred.

_____ 17. The winning names are given to Columbia University trustees.

_____ 18. Pulitzer's career was ended by his failing health he had paved the way for future journalists.

_____ 19. Joseph Pulitzer Jr., his grandson, serves on the advisory board.

_____ 20. The Pulitzer Prize is a highly regarded honor, it signifies great achievement.

▶ **Exercise 2 Write *run-on* next to each run-on sentence.**

___run-on___   Joan went to the bank Chris waited at home.

_____ 1. Pearl Buck won a Pulitzer Prize in 1932 she was a novelist.

_____ 2. Pearl spent much of her childhood in China because her parents were missionaries.

_____ 3. After attending Randolph-Macon Woman's College, she returned to China and became a teacher.

_____ 4. Pearl Buck wrote many stories about Chinese life, she did not achieve success until 1931 when *The Good Earth* was published.

_____ 5. This work was recognized with a Pulitzer Prize, she continued to write novels.

_____ 6. *The House of Earth* is a trilogy composed of *The Good Earth, Sons,* and *A House Divided.*

_____ 7. In 1935, Pearl Buck moved back to the United States she started writing biographies at this time, as well.

_____ 8. The following year, she published biographies of her mother and father.

_____ 9. She worked on many projects, she wrote short stories, an autobiography, and more novels.

_____ 10. Pearl Buck also wrote novels under the pen name of John Sedges.

☑ Unit 4 **Review**

▶ **Exercise 1** **Label the sentences below with** *imp.* **for imperative,** *int.* **for interrogative,** *d* **for declarative, or** *e* **for exclamatory.**

___d___   Before leaving the house, he had a glass of orange juice.

_____   **1.** Be considerate of the feelings of others.

_____   **2.** What class do you have first period?

_____   **3.** Does that old air pump still work?

_____   **4.** We called the police when we heard the noise.

_____   **5.** I learned that move in my karate class.

_____   **6.** That's the silliest thing I've ever heard!

_____   **7.** The newspaper arrived late on Sunday.

_____   **8.** Don't slam the door!

_____   **9.** Use your binoculars to see the birds more clearly.

_____ **10.** Which of the twins volunteers at the nursing home?

_____ **11.** Darcy's family went to New Orleans during Mardi Gras.

_____ **12.** What do you think are society's toughest problems?

_____ **13.** Bring me a rake from the garage.

_____ **14.** Where is the pizza with anchovies?

_____ **15.** Watch out for that car!

_____ **16.** Science is my favorite subject.

_____ **17.** Are you getting your hair cut today?

_____ **18.** Give me the hammer beside you.

_____ **19.** The magician's tricks were incredible!

_____ **20.** Seeing our relatives over the holidays will occupy most of our time.

_____ **21.** Permit the unfortunate boy to have my seat.

_____ **22.** What will happen to my companions?

_____ **23.** The crowd in Madison Square Garden responded enthusiastically.

_____ **24.** I hope you are having fun!

Cumulative Review: Units 1–4

▶ **Exercise 1** Draw one line under each simple subject and two lines under each simple predicate. In the blank, identify the kind of sentence by writing *dec.* (declarative), *imp.* (imperative), *int.* (interrogative), or *exc.* (exclamatory).

exc.   How cold this <u>winter</u> <u><u>has been</u></u>!

_____ **1.** The store sent the customer the wrong package.

_____ **2.** Show me your hall pass.

_____ **3.** The captain and the crew of the starship *Enterprise* were very experienced.

_____ **4.** How much did you pay for that dress?

_____ **5.** There is smoke coming from under that door!

_____ **6.** Susan went to the library to gather information for her report.

_____ **7.** Please don't cut in front of the line.

_____ **8.** Does anyone know the location of his office?

_____ **9.** Our senator campaigned to become president.

_____ **10.** Their new house withstood the hurricane better than the last one.

▶ **Exercise 2** Underline the subordinate clause in each sentence. Write *adj.* (adjective), *adv.* (adverb), or *n* (noun) in the blank to tell what kind of clause it is.

adj.   Students <u>who sing in the choir</u> are dismissed early.

_____ **1.** We arrived at the theater after the movie had begun.

_____ **2.** My problem is how I can finish this lengthy book in one week.

_____ **3.** The stylish woman who spoke at the banquet is the founder of the local department store.

_____ **4.** There will be a quiz after we watch the film on the battles of the Civil War.

_____ **5.** Sarah was worried about whether she had made the basketball team.

_____ **6.** The realtor who sold us this house designed it himself.

_____ **7.** We were fortunate to arrive home before the snowstorm hit.

_____ **8.** Shall I wait for you at your locker while you go to the office?

_____ **9.** No one could understand what the directions were explaining.

_____ **10.** The classical music that Mrs. Griffin likes the best is by Beethoven.

Unit 5: Diagraming Sentences

Lesson 33

Diagraming Simple Sentences

Grammar

Write the simple subject and the verb on a horizontal line and then draw a vertical line between them. Draw a shorter vertical line between the verb and the direct object. If there is a predicate nominative or a predicate adjective instead of a direct object, slant the shorter line toward the subject. Place an indirect object on a horizontal line under the verb, and draw a slanted line from the horizontal line to the verb. The following examples show how to diagram simple sentences.

The new student worked very hard.   Rosa and Maria gave their brother a haircut.

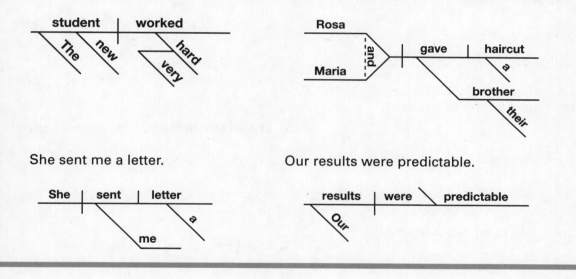

She sent me a letter.   Our results were predictable.

▶**Exercise 1** **Diagram the following simple sentences.**

1. Bruno finished his homework.

3. The tennis coach plays the mandolin.

2. This recipe requires sugar and oil.

4. Did Inez call anyone?

Grammar

5. My best friend and her cousin made me cookies.

6. I used my laptop computer yesterday.

7. The team played very well today.

8. Is Ruth's aunt a lawyer or a dentist?

9. The cheetah is an endangered species.

10. Write the answer clearly.

11. Can you tune your guitar?

12. Isaac and Yuri sing and play the piano.

13. Mrs. Lopez washed and waxed her truck.

14. The students completed a community project.

15. My pets include a fish, a cat, and a gerbil.

16. May I be excused?

17. Give me the licorice!

18. David grades the history quizzes.

Lesson 34
Diagraming Simple Sentences with Phrases

The following examples demonstrate how to diagram sentences with phrases.

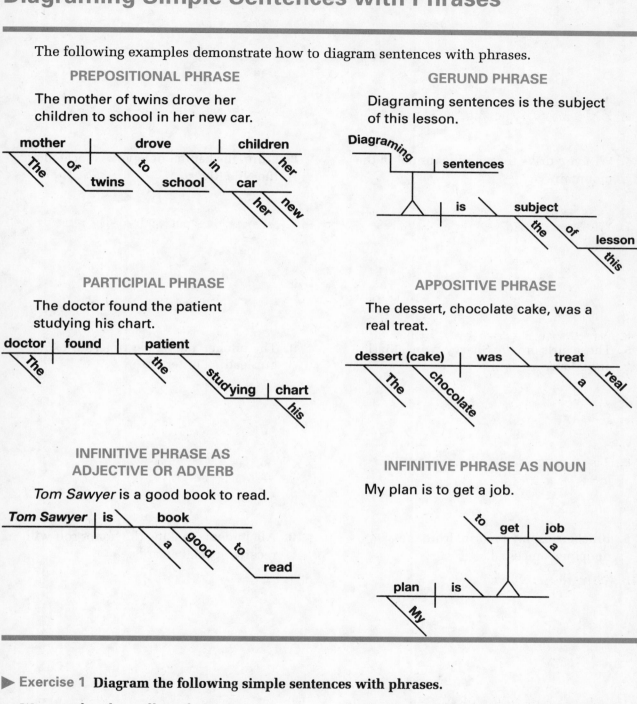

PREPOSITIONAL PHRASE

The mother of twins drove her children to school in her new car.

GERUND PHRASE

Diagraming sentences is the subject of this lesson.

PARTICIPIAL PHRASE

The doctor found the patient studying his chart.

APPOSITIVE PHRASE

The dessert, chocolate cake, was a real treat.

INFINITIVE PHRASE AS ADJECTIVE OR ADVERB

Tom Sawyer is a good book to read.

INFINITIVE PHRASE AS NOUN

My plan is to get a job.

▶ **Exercise 1** **Diagram the following simple sentences with phrases.**

1. We stayed at the mall until evening.

2. Somebody sent this book to my mother by mistake.

3. The captain of the team spoke to us during practice.

4. Will you drive through the tunnel in the mountain?

5. Those girls are the Sharvy twins, Marla and Maureen.

6. Blueberries, my favorite fruit, are delicious on cereal.

7. The man in the blue sweater is Mr. Boudoulas, my English teacher.

8. Cairo, the capital of Egypt, is located on the Nile River.

9. The pitcher, taking her time, struck out our leading hitter.

10. All students making the honor roll will receive special awards.

Lesson 35
Diagraming Sentences with Clauses

The following examples demonstrate how to diagram sentences with clauses.

COMPOUND SENTENCES

He removed the lid, and the small dog barked playfully.

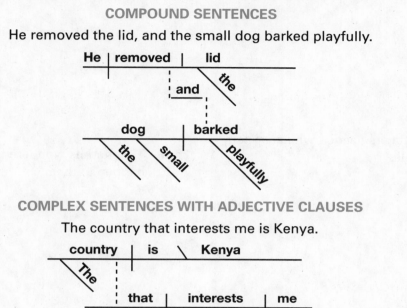

COMPLEX SENTENCES WITH ADJECTIVE CLAUSES

The country that interests me is Kenya.

COMPLEX SENTENCES WITH ADVERB CLAUSES

Because the foreign exchange student had never been skiing, he went in my place.

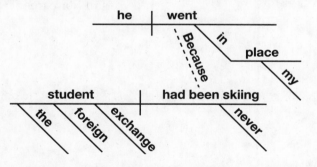

COMPLEX SENTENCES WITH NOUN CLAUSES

Elston believed that Echo was his friend.

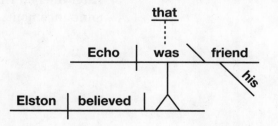

▶ Exercise 1 **Diagram the following sentences with clauses.**

1. After the hurricane ceased, workers began a massive clean-up operation.

2. The class officers needed whatever help was available.

3. The press secretary spoke initially, and then the president held a news conference.

4. The nurse prepped the patient, and the doctor performed the surgery.

5. The grass needs mowing, and the rose bush needs pruning.

6. The victims wondered how this could happen to them.

7. The author wrote short stories when she began her career.

8. After the bell rings, the principal makes announcements.

Grammar

9. Claudine knows that Rupert will help.

13. Alligators seem slow, although they can move quickly.

10. The ski club decided where the contest would be held.

14. Can you see how the treasure was lost?

11. As far as I am concerned, you may go on the camping trip.

15. What you choose for a career will affect your entire life.

12. The custodian knew where the missing keys were.

16. Jay is spending a week in New York so he will have time to attend a concert.

Grammar

Grammar

17. You will complete the art project whenever you have the time.

18. My dad, whom you know, bought a new set of golf clubs.

19. One of the players on whom we rely was injured at the last game.

20. The treasurer warned that funds are low.

21. The tomb that held the mummy was ornately decorated.

22. The team that won the tournament was the Tigers.

23. Prizes will be awarded to whoever arrives first.

24. We wrote a poem about how we felt.

☑ Unit 5 **Review**

▶ **Exercise 1 Diagram the following sentences.**

1. The novelist wrote movie scripts until she left Hollywood.

2. The class officers said that we could march in the parade.

3. Jessie attended the workshop to learn to paint with watercolors.

4. Maureen's goal is to play drums in Lon's band.

5. The soccer field was rocky and hard.

6. The general, a veteran of two wars, accepted the medal and addressed the crowd.

7. Gasping for air, Ella reached the top of the mountain.

8. Jim is friendly, but he must try to meet more people.

Cumulative Review: Units 1–5

▶ **Exercise 1** Draw one line under all nouns and two lines under all verbs. Write *adj.* above any adjective, *adv.* above any adverbs, and *d.o.* above any direct object. You may ignore any articles.

               adj.   d.o.
Running provides good exercise.

1. The prosecutor spoke convincingly to the jury.

2. Several rose bushes are still blooming in the garden.

3. The department store sold its holiday decorations at half price.

4. The hungry herd of bison grazed lazily on the open range.

5. Mr. Jackson gave his class bad news concerning the field trip.

6. Which river is longer, the Nile or the Amazon?

7. Ms. Wong answered my sincere question in a somewhat mocking tone.

8. A large truckload of dairy products has spilled onto the road.

9. I will give you my secret recipe for very moist brownies.

10. Many Chinese dynasties caused great changes.

11. The car in front of us stopped quite suddenly.

12. Jake called the radio station twice.

13. The Incas ruled one of the largest and richest empires in the world.

14. The secret will be safe with me.

15. Sharon bought a tiny trinket at the bazaar.

16. We proudly displayed the American flag.

17. The ambulance has already radioed the emergency room with vital information.

18. The interview went more smoothly today.

19. You swim very well for a novice.

20. Amanda teaches her parrots slang words.

▶ **Exercise 2** Draw one line under each main clause. Draw two lines under each subordinate clause. Identify each sentence by writing *simple, compound, complex,* or *compound-complex* in the blank.

_____compound_____   <u>Ruben visited New Jersey,</u> and <u>he stayed near Atlantic City.</u>

_____   **1.** During their sailing adventure last week, the crew survived a sudden storm.

_____   **2.** The Olympic team felt empowered by the cheers of their fellow countrymen.

_____   **3.** The artist created miniature figurines, and his friend sold them in his shop.

_____   **4.** When he fell behind on the trail, Stephen wondered if he would lose sight of his group, but soon he caught up with them again.

_____   **5.** Solada, while mixing up the cookies, began to wonder what she had done wrong because the dough looked strange.

_____   **6.** At the hospital, the staff disposed of certain materials in a special manner to meet federal requirements.

_____   **7.** The director of the play gave the actors advice.

_____   **8.** Kyle is very musical, and he wants to do well at the competition.

_____   **9.** While he was climbing the ladder, the firefighter slipped and nearly dropped the small animal he was carrying.

_____   **10.** Families need to take vacations together, but usually their conflicting schedules make this difficult.

_____   **11.** After he finished writing one book, Kevin began another, and his career was on its way.

_____   **12.** Although the highway was now officially open, the Moehlers felt it was still not safe to travel, so they cancelled their trip.

_____   **13.** The concerned and caring youth group gave food items to anyone who needed them.

_____   **14.** Although I have many good memories, skating on the pond behind our home is my favorite one.

Grammar

Name _____ Class _____ Date _____

▶ Exercise 3 **Diagram the following sentences.**

1. The daring cowboy rode the spirited mustang.

2. June enjoys Chicago-style pizza.

3. Have you read the article explaining the monarch butterfly's migration to Mexico?

4. Renée enjoys playing the piano.

5. Recycling will help the environment.

6. You need a telescope to see the rings of Saturn.

7. To train a dog well requires much patience.

8. A police officer's job is to protect the public.

9. Sheila and Dave paid attention to what the acrobat did next.

10. They argued about who would watch the game.

Grammar

Unit 6: Verb Tenses and Voice

Lesson 36

Regular Verbs: Principal Parts

Verbs have four main parts: a base form, a present participle, a simple past, and a past participle. A regular verb forms its past and past participle by adding -ed or -d to the base form. All verbs form the present participle by adding -ing to the base form. Both the present participle and the past participle require a helping verb.

Base Form: The sisters **talk** to each other every day.
Present Participle: The sisters **are talking** about their summer vacations.
Past Form: The sisters **talked** earlier this morning.
Past Participle: The sisters **have talked** often about their children.

Grammar

▶ **Exercise 1** **Complete each sentence by writing the form of the verb indicated in parentheses.**

Grandma has _____discussed_____ her childhood. (past participle/discuss)

1. Clancy is _____ for his hockey stick. (present participle/search)

2. Yesterday he _____ high and low but with no luck. (past/hunt)

3. Clancy and his twin sister, June, have often _____ what happened to their belongings. (past participle/wonder)

4. Last week Clancy _____ his softball and glove on the kitchen table before he went to his room to study. (past/place)

5. When he came back, Clancy _____ his ball and glove under the stove. (past/discover)

6. Recently, June _____ a muddy trail outside, where she found the dirty boots she had left in the hallway. (past/follow)

7. Clancy and June are _____ if they should hire a private detective to find the culprit. (present participle/wonder)

8. Clancy and June have _____ to leave one of their belongings in a certain place and then watch to see what happens. (past participle/decide)

9. They _____ a baseball glove in the kitchen. (base form/leave)

10. However, their dogs _____ to go for a walk. (base form/want)

11. Fido and Spike, who _____ to see them, jump up eagerly when they open the door. (base form/love)

12. On their walk, Clancy and June see that the dogs have _____ a spot under the fence. (past participle/burrow)

13. Curious, they hurry over to the hole the dogs have _____. (past participle/excavate)

14. Looking into the hole, they _____ with laughter. (base form/howl)

15. There in the hole are _____ three of their missing items—a scarf, a pair of gloves, and a knee pad. (present participle/rest)

16. "We have _____ the mystery," Clancy laughs. (past participle/solve)

17. "When you see us with a ball or a glove, you know we are _____ you," adds June. (present participle/abandon)

18. "You _____ that if we don't have our belongings, we can't leave you," says Clancy. (base form/reason)

19. "Well," says June, "I think I _____ what to do." (base form/know)

20. "From now on you can go with us and _____ from the sidelines," the twins agree. (base form/watch)

▶ **Exercise 2** **Write the three principal parts of each verb—present participle, past, and past participle.**

cough   _coughing, coughed, coughed_____

1. admit _____

2. study _____

3. hike _____

4. return _____

5. complete _____

6. refuse _____

7. plot _____

8. pitch _____

9. dance _____

10. elect _____

11. recycle _____

12. conserve _____

13. disappear _____

14. tape _____

15. practice _____

Lesson 37
Irregular Verbs: Principal Parts

Grammar

Irregular verbs form their past and past participle in ways different from the *-ed* and *-d* additions used for regular verbs. See the examples below for the verb *to be*.

Present Participle: I **am being** very patient with you.
Past Form: I **was** sixteen yesterday. You **were** at my party.
Past Participle: I **have been** happy today.

The principal parts of some common irregular verbs are shown below.

Base Form	Present Participle	Past Form	Past Participle
break	(am, is, or are) breaking	broke	(has, have, or had) broken
come	coming	came	come
do	doing	did	done
drive	driving	drove	driven
give	giving	gave	given
go	going	went	gone
have	having	had	had
know	knowing	knew	known
say	saying	said	said
see	seeing	saw	seen
sing	singing	sang	sung
speak	speaking	spoke	spoken
tell	telling	told	told
think	thinking	thought	thought
write	writing	wrote	written

Notice that these verbs, though irregular, still form their present participle form by adding *-ing*.

▶ **Exercise 1**   **Underline the word in parentheses that correctly completes each sentence. In the space provided, identify the form of the verb used as** *base form, present participle, past form,* **or** *past participle.*

___base form___   My fish (<u>swim</u>, swimming) all day long.

_____   **1.** Howard (spoke, speaking) for one hour.

_____   **2.** How many miles have you (drive, driven) today?

_____   **3.** The chorus (sung, sang) the school song.

_____   **4.** I (know, known) how much Carla likes horses.

_____   **5.** I (think, thought) of the answer after the test.

_____   **6.** We are (giving, given) some money to the hunger center.

Grammar

_____ **7.** Marsha has not (wrote, written) to me lately.

_____ **8.** The team has (gone, went) to the scrimmage early.

_____ **9.** I hope the birthday gift has (came, come) in time.

_____ **10.** She has (did, done) that assignment already.

_____ **11.** My pets often (break, broke) things while I am away.

_____ **12.** They (say, saying) we can borrow their video.

_____ **13.** Are you (tell, telling) me you have the flu?

_____ **14.** We (seen, saw) the lovely sunset yesterday.

_____ **15.** The neighbors are (having, have) a party tonight.

_____ **16.** What are you (doing, done) for Thanksgiving?

_____ **17.** The explorer has (spoke, spoken) to the group before.

_____ **18.** She has (gave, given) the problem much thought.

_____ **19.** Cara just (wrote, write) in her journal.

_____ **20.** I have (knew, known) Mr. Janus for years.

_____ **21.** That music is (driven, driving) me crazy!

_____ **22.** The club members (see, seen) a movie once a week.

_____ **23.** We have (thought, think) of a name for the baby.

_____ **24.** Deliveries (come, coming) early in our neighborhood.

_____ **25.** I'm (tell, telling) you I don't know!

_____ **26.** The climber (gone, went) to the top of the cliff.

_____ **27.** I have (break, broken) two glasses today.

_____ **28.** They have (say, said) they are sorry.

_____ **29.** I (gave, given) you a snack already!

_____ **30.** She has (driving, driven) that route many times.

_____ **31.** Who is (sang, singing) in the shower?

_____ **32.** I (told, tell) you I would think about it.

_____ **33.** We have (had, have) enough of this noise!

_____ **34.** Stan has (did, done) his good deed for today.

_____ **35.** I (known, knew) I had seen you before.

_____ **36.** With his new glasses, he is (seen, seeing) more clearly.

Lesson 38
Tense of Verbs: Present, Past, and Future

Verb tenses show time. They tell when events happen, happened, or will happen.

The present tense and the base form of a verb are the same, except for the third person singular (he, she, or it), which adds *-s* or *-es*. The verb *be* is also an exception to this rule.

The present tense may express an action that is repeated or ongoing. It can also express an action that is happening right now or a situation that is always true.

Malachi **plays** the trumpet well. (repeated action, always true)
I **feel** a cold draft. (right now)

The past tense expresses an action that has already occurred. In regular verbs, the past tense is formed by adding *-ed* or *-d* to the base form. In irregular verbs, the past tense takes a variety of forms. The verb *be* uses two past tense forms—*was* and *were.*

We **trounced** our archrivals last night. (regular)
Jackie **leapt** for the branch and missed. (irregular)

The future tense expresses an action that will take place in the future. The future tense is formed by adding *will* to the base form.

I **will reserve** tickets on the morning flight.
The students **will debate** the issues tomorrow.

▶ Exercise 1 **Complete each sentence by writing the form of the verb in parentheses.**

The football team _____ scored _____ a touchdown. (past tense/score)

1. Cosmo _____ for Europe Tuesday. (future tense/leave)

2. The travel agent _____ a fantastic trip for him. (past tense/plan)

3. Michelle _____ to hear all the details. (present tense/want)

4. Cosmo _____ to tell us at lunchtime. (present tense/promise)

5. All our friends _____ under the elm tree. (future tense/eat)

6. We _____ at noon. (future tense/meet)

7. Because he had so many things to do, Cosmo _____ late. (past tense/arrive)

8. Michelle and our friends _____ patient. (past tense/be)

9. However, I _____ around the tree. (past tense/pace)

10. Cosmo _____ us jovially and sat down to eat his lunch. (past tense/greet)

11. "We _____ to finish eating before you begin," I said. (future tense/try)

12. "I _____ you about my trip in a minute," Cosmo replied. (future tense/tell)

Grammar

13. George _____ toward the basketball court. (present tense/wander)

14. He _____ if anyone is interested in a game. (present tense/ask)

15. Cosmo _____ that he is ready to describe his trip. (present tense/announce)

16. George _____ back just in time to hear about the journey. (past tense/come)

17. Cosmo's first stop _____ Rome. (future tense/be)

18. He _____ to visit relatives who live nearby. (present tense/plan)

19. He also _____ to find the perfect plate of pasta. (present tense/hope)

20. "What about the famous places?" Michelle _____. (past tense/demand)

21. Smiling, Cosmo _____ that he planned to see many of the well-known sights. (past tense/explain)

22. The Vittoriano _____ a monument to Victor Emmanuel II, the first king of united Italy. (present tense/be)

23. Romans _____ the Piazza del Popolo to serve as a ceremonial entrance to the city. (past tense/construct)

24. Michelle, who is interested in architecture, _____ us that the Spanish Steps were built from a French design. (present tense/inform)

25. I _____ to wonder what other cities Cosmo would visit. (past tense/begin)

26. He _____ he would also be going to Venice. (past tense/say)

27. This Italian city _____ famous for its many canals. (past tense/become)

28. In Venice, people often _____ in a *gondola,* a special kind of boat. (present tense/travel)

29. Cosmo is certain he _____ in one. (future tense/ride)

30. He _____ in Venice for the *Biennale,* an art festival. (future tense/stay)

31. Then he _____ to Paris. (future tense/journey)

32. I _____ about the capital of France in history class. (past tense/learn)

33. The Seine River _____ through the city. (present tense/flow)

34. Built for the International Exposition of 1889, the Eiffel Tower _____ unattractive to some people. (past tense/look)

35. However, it _____ to be the most recognizable symbol of Paris. (present tense/continue)

36. Cosmo _____ quick to encourage me to take a similar trip. (past tense/be)

37. I _____ ruefully and shook my head. (past tense/smile)

38. I _____ until I have saved more money. (future tense/wait)

Lesson 39
Perfect Tenses: Present, Past, and Future

The present perfect tense is used to express an action that took place at some indefinite time in the past. The present perfect tense is formed with the past tense of the verb and the helping verb *has* or *have.* The present perfect tense can also be used to express an action that began in the past and continues now.

She **has read** that book.
I **have tried** several times to reach my grandmother.

The past perfect tense is used to show that one action in the past began and ended before another action in the past started. The past perfect tense is formed with the past participle of the verb and the helping verb *had.*

They **had seen** the movie before I **rented** it. (past perfect tense, past tense)

The future perfect tense is used to show that one action or condition in the future will begin and end before another event in the future starts. The future perfect tense is formed with the past participle of the verb and the construction *will have.*

By the time the school year ends, I **will have completed** ten book reports.

▶ **Exercise 1** **Draw two lines under each simple predicate in the main clause. Write the verb tense: *present perfect*, *past perfect*, or *future perfect*.**

__past perfect__   He <u>had watched</u> football all day long.

_____   1. By Saturday, we will have finished our recycling project.

_____   2. My dog had stolen the cat's food.

_____   3. The gymnast has never lost her confidence.

_____   4. The farm workers had generally gone before dawn.

_____   5. By Tuesday Tisha will have landed her plane for the first time.

_____   6. Raul has exhausted himself with his project.

_____   7. I had turned at the wrong corner.

_____   8. Before next week, Ms. Rashad will have corrected over one hundred themes.

_____   9. Mother has already found her lost ring.

_____ 10. By mid-afternoon the tide will have gone out.

_____ 11. She has always wanted a book on whales.

_____ 12. The explorers had hoped to reach the peak by nightfall.

Grammar

_____ **13.** My grandmother has taught me both knitting and quilting.

_____ **14.** They will have finished dinner before the performance.

_____ **15.** The flower pot had narrowly missed the bystanders.

_____ **16.** We have warned you about this before.

_____ **17.** The VCR has failed to record three times this week.

_____ **18.** The band will have played its program before the second half starts.

_____ **19.** I had snubbed her before she apologized.

_____ **20.** Before the speech ended, I had decided whom to vote for.

_____ **21.** By the time the sun rises, the icicles will have melted.

_____ **22.** Sue will have completed her morning exercises before her brothers get up.

_____ **23.** The dog has chewed her bone down to the nub.

_____ **24.** Trapeze artists have always fascinated me.

_____ **25.** The spy had switched off the light before the agents even reached the doorway.

_____ **26.** Kaoru has visited her brother in the hospital every day.

_____ **27.** By nightfall, I will have gotten very sick of the train.

_____ **28.** We have rehearsed this scene until it is perfect.

_____ **29.** The dogs had gone for hours without a walk when I came home.

_____ **30.** The movie had played for a half hour by the time we got there.

_____ **31.** Our team has won ten of its last eleven games.

_____ **32.** If we wait awhile, most of the crowd will have left.

_____ **33.** Rocco will have gotten his degree by the end of the term.

_____ **34.** Doug has struggled for months to learn Spanish.

_____ **35.** That volcano has already erupted twice this year.

_____ **36.** Kyra had rearranged the furniture since the last time I visited.

_____ **37.** I have repeatedly told you not to stand on that rickety ladder!

_____ **38.** You have never missed a rock concert!

_____ **39.** We will have fallen asleep before our parents arrive.

_____ **40.** The freighter had sunk before the rescue ship could reach it.

Lesson 40
Tenses of Verbs

Grammar

The **present tense** expresses an action that is repeated, always true, or happening right now.

I **watch** for the early bus at Third Street. He **watches** for the early bus at Third Street.
I **am** happy. You **are** happy. He, she, or it **is** happy. They **are** happy.

The **past tense** expresses an action that has already occurred.

I **watched** for the bus and **caught** it at First Avenue. (regular and irregular verbs)
I **was** late, but the rest of the students **were** on time. (the verb *be*)

The **future tense** expresses an action that will take place in the future.

Shannon **will connect** the wires.

The **present perfect tense** expresses an action that took place sometime in the past.

I **have searched** everywhere for my telescope.

The **past perfect tense** shows that one action in the past began and ended before another action started.

I **had** already **completed** the puzzle when you came.

The **future perfect tense** shows that an action in the future will begin and end before another action starts.

I **will have swum** forty laps by the end of the hour.

▶ **Exercise 1** Draw two lines under the simple predicate in each sentence. Then write the tense of the verb in the space provided.

___past tense___   Many citizens signed the petition.

_____ **1.** Historians have called the time from 1870 to 1890 the Gilded Age.

_____ **2.** This name comes from a novel by Charles Dudley Warner and Mark Twain.

_____ **3.** The novel described life in the United States at that time.

_____ **4.** Before writing the book, the authors had decided on a theme.

_____ **5.** They wanted to expose the corruption beneath the pretty, polished surface of

their world.

_____ **6.** However, the Gilded Age has produced positive results as well.

_____ **7.** We will have seen these accomplishments by the end of the year.

_____ **8.** Victoria Woodhull was the first woman to attempt to run for president.

Grammar

_____ 9. She had asked to be on the ballot in the election of 1872.

_____ 10. However, she had not reached the age of thirty-five by the time of the election.

_____ 11. In 1884, the newly formed National Equal Rights party nominated Belva Lockwood, a New York lawyer, for president.

_____ 12. Some prominent women will be against her candidacy.

_____ 13. Belva Lockwood received over four thousand votes.

_____ 14. None of these votes will have come from women.

_____ 15. Women had not received the right to vote yet.

_____ 16. Women had achieved many distinctions and honors.

_____ 17. Many, such as Mary Bonney and Amelia Quinton, work to improve the lives of Native Americans.

_____ 18. Colleges have opened their doors to women.

_____ 19. Writing is one way for women to earn money in the Gilded Age.

_____ ‚20. I will have finished reading *Little Women* by Friday.

▶ Exercise 2 **Complete each sentence by writing the form of the verb listed in parentheses.**

The submarine _____ submerges _____ in the ocean. (present tense/submerge)

1. John Philip Sousa _____ a famous musician of the Gilded Age. (past tense/be)

2. He _____ music since the age of six. (past perfect tense/study)

3. He _____ an interest in band music. (present tense/develop)

4. Believe it or not, he _____ how to play every instrument used in military bands by the time he becomes leader of the United States Marine Corps band. (future perfect tense/learn)

5. After twelve years, he _____ the Marine Corps band to create a band of his own. (present tense/leave)

6. He _____ a composer as well as a band leader. (past tense/become)

7. Sousa _____ many famous marches, including "Washington Post March" and "Stars and Stripes Forever." (present perfect tense/compose)

8. His marches _____ crowds for more than a century. (present perfect tense/excite)

9. When his music was still new, Sousa's band _____ around the world. (past tense/travel)

10. Admirers of his work _____ him the March King. (future tense/name)

Lesson 41
Verbs: Progressive and Emphatic Forms

The progressive form of a verb tense expresses an action that is continuing at the time referred to in the sentence. The progressive form uses the present participle of the verb with the suitable tense of the verb *be.*

Present Progressive	They **are laughing.**
Past Progressive	They **were laughing.**
Future Progressive	They **will be laughing.**
Present Perfect Progressive	They **have been laughing.**
Past Perfect Progressive	They **had been laughing.**
Future Perfect Progressive	They **will have been laughing.**

▶ **Exercise 1** **Write the required form of each verb listed. Use the subject that heads each group as the subject of the verb.**

I; past progressive/eat ___I was eating._____

I

1. future progressive/sail _____

2. past perfect progressive/ask _____

3. present progressive/arrive _____

4. past progressive/wait _____

5. present perfect progressive/move _____

YOU

6. future perfect progressive/swim _____

7. present progressive/testify _____

8. past perfect progressive/hope _____

9. past progressive/play _____

10. future progressive/go _____

THEY

11. present perfect progressive/wonder _____

12. past progressive/follow _____

13. past perfect progressive/challenge _____

14. future perfect progressive/write _____

15. present progressive/buy _____

SHE

16. future progressive/rest _____

17. past perfect progressive/catch _____

18. present progressive/hide _____

19. future perfect progressive/knit _____

20. present perfect progressive/collect _____

The **emphatic form** adds emphasis to the verb. The emphatic form uses the base form of the verb with the addition of *do, does,* or *did.*

Present Emphatic	I **do mow** the lawn every week.
	Carla **does mow** hers twice each week.
Past Emphatic	Ralph **did mow** it while we were gone.

▶ **Exercise 2** **Complete each sentence by writing the emphatic verb form described in parentheses.**

Regardless of the weather, I _____ did visit _____ the amusement park. (past emphatic/visit)

1. Despite what you say, I _____ the car yesterday. (past emphatic/wash)

2. Although she hates them, Rachel _____ her exercises each morning. (present emphatic/complete)

3. Even though you think you're alone, I _____ your feelings. (present emphatic/understand)

4. Before I forget, Aunt Cora _____ after you left. (past emphatic/call)

5. Apparently the machine _____ on batteries. (present emphatic/work)

6. Laugh if you want to, but I _____ how to do a somersault. (present emphatic/know)

7. When you pass the park, _____ at the new monument. (present emphatic/look)

8. The electrician says he _____ the outside wiring. (past emphatic/fix)

9. They hope the game _____ on time. (present emphatic/end)

10. I _____ the garbage! (past emphatic/empty)

Lesson 42
Verbs: Compatibility of Tenses

Sometimes one event occurs before or after another event in a sentence. In these cases, it is appropriate to shift tenses.

Incorrect: By the time the police **arrived,** the thief **escaped.**

This is incorrect because the verbs are both past tense forms and suggest that the two events took place at the same time.

Correct: By the time the police **arrived,** the thief **had escaped.**

Here the tense shifts from the past (arrived) to past perfect (had escaped) to show that the thief escaped before the police arrived.

When two or more events take place at the same time in a sentence, the verb tenses must remain the same.

Incorrect: When Paul **registered** for the summer class, he **is filling** out seven forms.

This is incorrect because the tense changes from past to present, even though the events in the sentence both took place in the past.

Correct: When Paul **registered** for the summer class, he **filled** out seven forms.

▶ **Exercise 1** **Complete each sentence with the appropriate tense of the verb in parentheses.**

We went backstage to see the actor, but he _____ had gone _____ home. (go)

1. Taylor's family will plan their vacation before she _____ for school. (leave)

2. If she waits until ten o'clock, she _____ out when they are leaving. (find)

3. I had expected her to be late, but she _____ early. (arrive)

4. Taylor says they are going to Hawaii, which _____ their original destination. (be)

5. By the time she left, Taylor _____ several books about Hawaii. (purchase)

6. Last week she read about a luau, which _____ a Hawaiian banquet. (be)

7. If you look up the word *luau,* you _____ that it was originally the name for the leaves of the taro plant. (discover)

8. *Luau* had referred to dishes made with these leaves before the word _____ the name of the feast itself. (become)

9. Taylor has waited several years, so she _____ attending a luau. (enjoy)

10. If she remembers to bring her camera, she _____ photographs. (take)

11. She had hoped for nice weather, but a storm _____ . (appear)

Grammar

12. She will visit her friend Niki, whose family _____ the luau. (prepare)

13. If she watches carefully, she _____ how to cook the meal. (learn)

14. The host _____ a pig before the guests arrived. (roast)

15. *Lau lau* is a dish that _____ of luau leaves and pork wrapped in a ti leaf. (consist)

16. By the time she reached the luau, the others _____ the table. (decorate)

17. Niki's family had expected to serve twelve dishes, but their friends _____ three more. (bring)

18. Ti leaves cover the table at which the guests _____ later. (eat)

19. Before Taylor finished her poi, her host _____ the pig. (serve)

20. The meal will not be over before the dancing _____. (begin)

▶ **Exercise 2** **Draw two lines under the two verbs or verb phrases. In the blank, rewrite the second verb or verb phrase to match the tense of the first.**

Elena built a bookcase in industrial arts class, and then she paints it. __painted_____

1. The first Hawaiians were of Polynesian origin and come from the Marquesas Islands. _____

2. A group of immigrants left Tahiti and traveling to the Hawaiian Islands. _____

3. In 1778, Captain James Cook discovers the islands and will name them the Sandwich Islands.

_____

4. Kamehameha I will become monarch because he seemed to be the strongest leader. _____

5. The islands will begin to change and continuing to develop. _____

6. Other nations recognized the kingdom's independence when the country adopts a constitution.

_____

7. While Great Britain and France were fighting each other for control of the islands,

Kamehameha III seeks protection from the United States. _____

8. President Cleveland is against annexation, but the United States had received permission to

build a naval base at Pearl Harbor. _____

9. In 1959, Hawaii joins the Union, so flagmakers added a fiftieth star to the U.S. flag. _____

10. Many people consider Hawaii the most beautiful state, though each state will have its own

unique beauty. _____

Lesson 43
Voice of Verbs: Active and Passive

Action verbs can be used in two ways—in the active voice and in the passive voice. A sentence has a verb in the **active voice** when the subject performs the action. A sentence has a verb in the **passive voice** when the action is performed on the subject.

The catcher **caught** the ball. (active voice)
The ball **was caught** by the catcher. (passive voice)

The passive voice is formed by using the past participle of the verb with a form of the helping verb *be*.

The ball **is caught** by the catcher.   (present tense)
The ball **was caught** by the catcher.   (past tense)
The ball **will be caught** by the catcher.   (future tense)

The passive voice can give variety to your writing. In general, however, the active voice is more interesting, more direct, and makes for livelier writing.

▶ **Exercise 1** **Draw two lines under the verb or verb phrase. Write *A* (active voice) or *P* (passive voice) over the verb to tell which voice it is.**

               P
Study hall <u><u>was changed</u></u> to second period.

1. The puppy chewed the bone.

2. Carla is known by everybody.

3. Ron fed the birds.

4. The kitten was found by Bev.

5. The baby will be fed by Dad.

6. Curt showed the photographs.

7. The dog guards the house.

8. The team won the trophy.

9. The car was washed by Sarah.

10. Mom will lock the door.

11. George took the medicine.

12. The data were relayed by satellite.

13. Curly read the minutes.

14. A meeting will be held by the committee.

15. The vote was taken by our chairperson.

16. The rescue planes dropped food.

17. The flood destroyed three towns.

18. The mail was delivered by Jake.

19. Our house will be painted by Marge.

20. Dad bought groceries.

▶ **Exercise 2** Write *A* over the verb if the verb is in the active voice and *P* if it is in the passive voice. Then rewrite each active voice sentence in the passive voice and each passive voice sentence in the active voice.

      A

Raul planted tomatoes.   Tomatoes were planted by Raul. _____

1. Money was needed by the band. _____

2. The group's budget had been depleted by inflation. _____

3. The band members planned a fund-raiser. _____

4. The band members discussed several ideas. _____

5. The trombone players suggested an instrument sale. _____

_____

6. A car wash was proposed by the clarinet players. _____

7. Several of the drummers recommended a raffle. _____

_____

8. That idea was liked by everyone. _____

9. A new trumpet was donated by a local instrument seller, Mr. Majeske. _____

_____

10. The band members sold raffle tickets after school. _____

_____

Grammar

☑ Unit 6 **Review**

▶ Exercise **Draw two lines under each verb or verb phrase. Then write the tense of each verb in the blank before the sentence. Some sentences have more than one verb.**

_____past_____ We rode the roller coaster.

_____ 1. Sheila will finish her homework before dinner.

_____ 2. Our cooking class has watched three videos to learn how to
                                prepare this dish.

_____ 3. If you crouch very quietly, you will see the raccoon.

_____ 4. The alligator had disappeared by the time we reached the edge
                                of the swamp.

_____ 5. The teacher is talking about Thomas Edison.

_____ 6. Yesterday I toured the natural history museum.

_____ 7. We have been laughing at Sara's joke for five minutes.

_____ 8. The new train will have traveled two hundred miles by noon.

_____ 9. The playwright was hoping for a positive review.

_____ 10. Their team will be jogging around the Lincoln Memorial.

_____ 11. Colleen did hear the speech by the Russian scientist.

_____ 12. In December, she will have been knitting that scarf for six
                                months.

_____ 13. My dog, Juno, does like to jump over the fence.

_____ 14. The Tates had been expecting fifty guests, but sixty people
                                came to the banquet.

_____ 15. Uncle Yuri sends his regards to the entire family.

_____ 16. We had waited nearly an hour for the bus to arrive.

_____ 17. The florist will arrange a lovely centerpiece for Cousin Darla's
                                wedding.

_____ 18. Claude sailed his boat across Lake Erie.

_____ 19. We are watching a movie about space exploration.

_____ 20. Rochelle has been studying medicine for three years.

Grammar

Cumulative Review: Units 1–6

▶ **Exercise 1** Underline each simple subject once and each simple predicate twice. Label each preposition *prep*, each direct object *d.o.*, and each indirect object *i.o.*

                             d.o. prep.
       Peter took his cousin to the mall.

1. Tracy suddenly left the room during the lecture.

2. Ed will ski the advanced run tomorrow.

3. I gave Sandy the box with the blue label.

4. The heavy rain replenished the crop.

5. The observers were excited by the meteor shower.

6. The forward will shoot from midcourt.

7. My friend Ione is writing a collection of poems.

8. The actor applies his makeup every night before the show.

9. A lone tugboat struggled through the choppy water.

10. Ms. Watkins asked Jenny an algebra question.

11. That athlete inspires many young people to stay in school.

12. We will telephone everyone about the party.

13. Neil is always the first one out the door.

14. Wilson collects insects for his science class.

15. The current mayor will challenge her opponent to a debate.

16. The chemistry class performs two experiments each week.

17. Her kitten hid my socks in the yard.

18. The guests brought their host a vase of flowers.

19. Ben swam a mile in his best time yet.

20. Our friends will be exhausted after the events.

21. Paul rode his bicycle home through the rain.

22. My mother wins at chess most of the time.

▶ **Exercise 2** **Label each participle** *part.*, **each gerund** *ger.*, **and each infinitive** *inf.* **Then write whether the sentence is** *simple, compound, complex,* **or** *compound-complex.*

_____simple_____   ^{ger.} Jogging is a healthy way to get ^{inf.} in shape.

_____ **1.** Golfing is one of my favorite sports.

_____ **2.** I want to be a singer, but first I must study voice.

_____ **3.** Waiting by the fountain, Sven decided to sketch the town square.

_____ **4.** Although we had tickets, we were not allowed to enter the theater.

_____ **5.** The shivering skaters who still wish to compete should gather by the

judges' table.

_____ **6.** Stretching helps Bridget to warm up, and running helps her to stay

in shape.

_____ **7.** As the train pulled out of the station, Roberto took his seat, and his

fidgeting younger brother walked up and down the aisle.

_____ **8.** Unless it begins to snow, the ski resort will not be able to open.

_____ **9.** The glittering guests ascended the stairs to the awards ceremony.

_____ **10.** While Colette studies dancing, her sister studies painting.

_____ **11.** Geoff's desire to win was great, yet he skipped practice for two days.

_____ **12.** The bell may ring, or the irritating buzzer may sound when time has

expired.

_____ **13.** We are hiking to the top of the hill to do our stargazing.

_____ **14.** If the weather is mild, camping will be an option.

_____ **15.** Helga was worried, but she did not want the frightened child

to know it.

_____ **16.** The flight that Ruth and Oliver wanted to take was canceled.

_____ **17.** A pulsating beat accompanied the melody as Mike played the new

song he had composed.

_____ **18.** You need to decide what should be done, and we need to find

willing helpers.

▶ **Exercise 3** **Draw two lines under the verb or verb phrase in each sentence. Then write the tense of the verb.**

<u>present perfect</u>   The movie <u>has received</u> rave reviews.

_____ **1.** The polls had closed by seven o'clock that evening.

_____ **2.** The water in the horses' trough froze overnight.

_____ **3.** The principal will administer the test.

_____ **4.** Suki has seen several lunar eclipses.

_____ **5.** By tomorrow the council will have chosen its new president.

_____ **6.** This scarf will replace the missing one.

_____ **7.** My cousin attends the state university.

_____ **8.** This book discusses environmental problems.

_____ **9.** By yesterday evening I had written thirteen letters of application for

a summer job.

_____ **10.** The cartoonist at the fair drew several quick pictures of our family.

_____ **11.** I have given you all the facts of the case.

_____ **12.** The dog barks several times during the night.

_____ **13.** Within an hour the rocket will have splashed down in the Pacific.

_____ **14.** Katrina scoffed at the ridiculous story.

_____ **15.** The catcher has dropped the ball again.

_____ **16.** By next Sunday I will have worked four weekends in a row.

_____ **17.** This device will filter our drinking water.

_____ **18.** They have excavated the last site.

_____ **19.** The sudden wind had torn the small boat from its berth.

_____ **20.** Mr. Harris was happy with our oral reports.

_____ **21.** Sally plans to give a party for Christy.

_____ **22.** Doris and Andrew donated their profits to charity.

Unit 7: Subject-Verb Agreement

Lesson 44
Subject-Verb Agreement

The **subject and verb** in a sentence must agree. In the present tense, add *-s* or *-es* to the base form for the third-person singular.

SINGULAR
He **skates**.
She **wins**.

PLURAL
They **skate**.
They **win**.

The verbs *be, have,* and *do* change form to agree with their subjects.

SINGULAR
I **am** climbing.
You **are** climbing.
She **is** climbing.
I **have** reached the top.
You **have** reached the top.
He **has** reached the top.
I **do** climb often.
Do you climb often?
Does she climb often?

PLURAL
We **are** climbing.
You **are** climbing.
They **are** climbing.
We **have** reached the top.
You **have** reached the top.
They **have** reached the top.
We **do** climb often.
Do you climb often?
Do they climb often?

Grammar

▶ **Exercise 1**   **Underline the form of the verb that agrees with the subject.**

My younger brother (<u>has</u>, have) a large collection of toy dinosaurs.

1. Fossils (is, are) fascinating records of the past.

2. They (tells, tell) us about plants and animals of long ago.

3. Some ancient animals, such as dinosaurs, (was, were) huge.

4. A dinosaur fossil (preserves, preserve) a tooth, a bone, or even a major part of the skeleton.

5. Fossil hunters (has found, have found) dinosaur remains around the world.

6. Dinosaurs (was fixed, were fixed) in time in a number of ways.

7. Some (was frozen, were frozen) in glaciers.

8. Such a dinosaur (is, are) like the frozen food in your freezer.

9. Other dinosaurs (was caught, were caught) in tar pits and preserved there.

10. Fossil evidence (shows, show) that many dinosaurs died in a short period of time.

11. Scientists (believes, believe) that a major disaster occurred in the past.

12. Different theories (exists, exist) about why this happened.

13. One theory (states, state) that a comet collided with Earth and stirred up so much dust that the sun's light was blocked out.

14. At any rate, we (does know, do know) that dinosaurs no longer roam the earth.

15. Scientists (studies, study) dinosaur remains to find out what life was like in ancient times.

16. Stomach contents (reveals, reveal) what animals and plants lived at the same time.

17. Recently a fossilized dinosaur egg (was found, were found).

18. The unhatched baby dinosaur (have been, has been) preserved in the egg.

19. A fossil hunt (is, are) an exciting pastime.

20. Anyone who (excavates, excavate) a dinosaur has many stories to tell.

▶ **Exercise 2** **Choose the verb in parentheses that agrees with the subject. Write your choice in the blank.**

The students _____ were _____ about to study a unit on fossils. (was, were)

1. Imagine you _____ walking in the woods one day. (is, are)

2. You _____ the dried tracks of a deer in the muddy bank along a stream. (sees, see)

3. Of course the tracks probably _____ only days before you saw them. (was made, were made)

4. The dried tracks _____ the beginnings of a fossil. (is, are)

5. If a sudden rainstorm _____ the tracks up with mud, the deer print will be preserved, at least for a time. (fills, fill)

6. Several materials _____ good fossils. (makes, make)

7. A bone _____ good fossil material because of its hardness. (is, are)

8. Animal shells also _____ good fossils. (produces, produce)

9. Despite their softness, jellyfish _____ fossil imprints. (does leave, do leave)

10. Sometimes an insect _____ in amber. (is fossilized, are fossilized)

11. Amber _____ the hard sap of very old trees. (is, are)

12. As an insect sticks in the amber, the amber _____ around it. (hardens, harden)

13. Most fossils, however, _____ in layers of rock. (has formed, have formed)

14. Animal skeletons fall to the bottom of rivers and lakes, where they _____ with mud or silt. (is covered, are covered)

15. If the animal's skeleton is hard, it _____ a better fossil. (makes, make)

Lesson 45
Subject-Verb Agreement and Intervening Prepositional Phrases

The subject of a sentence is never contained within a prepositional phrase. The verb must agree with the subject of the sentence, not the object of a preposition.

The **color** of the thunderclouds **worries** me. (The subject is *color,* a singular noun. *Of the thunderclouds* is a prepositional phrase with a plural object. However, the verb *worries* agrees with the singular subject.)

The **players** on the team **have** new uniforms. (The subject is *players,* a plural noun. *On the team* is a prepositional phrase with a singular object. However, the verb *have* agrees with the plural subject.)

▶ **Exercise 1** **Underline the verb in parentheses that correctly completes the sentence by agreeing with the subject.**

A vase of roses usually (stand, <u>stands</u>) on the piano.

1. The rain forests of the earth (occurs, occur) in places where there is much rainfall.

2. The rain forest ecosystem, to biologists, (is, are) the source of much diversity.

3. Rain forests in a tropical area (is, are) warm and humid.

4. The number of tree species (is estimated, are estimated) to be about 3,000.

5. The area around the trees (is filled, are filled) with mosses, vines, and other water-loving plants.

6. The rain forest, with complex food chains, (recycles, recycle) nutrients constantly.

7. No dead plants on the ground (is, are) left there for long.

8. Plant matter from different species (decays, decay) quickly and is reused as food.

9. Plant life, with many animal species, (keep, keeps) the rain forest teeming with noise and motion.

10. The mammals of a rain forest (includes, include) leopards, jaguars, bats, and different monkeys.

11. Hoots, chirps, and roars from every corner (echoes, echo) throughout the day.

12. An explorer of rain forests also (thrills, thrill) at the wide variety of colorful birds.

13. Scientists interested in insects (has discovered, have discovered) hundreds of new species.

14. The animals on the forest floor (numbers, number) far fewer than those that live in the trees.

15. Not every traveler to these tropical paradises (focuses, focus) on animals.

16. Some visitors on a search for new healing substances (looks, look) at medicinal plants.

17. Students of the rain forest (is alarmed, are alarmed) at its rate of destruction.

18. Businesses of every kind (destroys, destroy) many acres each day.

19. Earth with its many problems (needs, need) this valuable source of life.

20. Many groups with an interest in the rain forest (works, work) hard to preserve this treasure.

▶ **Exercise 2** **Underline the verb in parentheses that agrees with the subject.**

A rainfall of several hours (<u>soaks</u>, soak) the ground.

1. Ecosystems with little water (is called, are called) deserts.

2. The rainfall from many years often (does, do) not equal the amount that falls in one year elsewhere.

3. Still, clusters of plant life (is, are) common in some deserts.

4. Temperatures in a desert (varies, vary) by many degrees.

5. In fact, people from another region (is, are) surprised to learn that deserts can be cold.

6. Deserts at high elevation or latitude (have, has) freezing temperatures.

7. Deserts of America (reaches, reach) daytime temperatures of over one hundred degrees.

8. Temperatures at night (measures, measure) many degrees cooler.

9. Deserts, in spite of their dryness, (are, is) home to an amazing variety of animals and plants.

10. Species in a desert (has, have) different adaptations to the lack of water.

11. Sharp spines on a cactus (serves, serve) as leaves and help prevent water loss.

12. The root systems of cacti (spread, spreads) out to collect as much water as possible.

13. The roots on a mesquite tree (extends, extend) far into the earth, looking for sources of water.

14. A cactus with flowers (makes, make) an attractive houseplant.

15. Visitors to the desert (expresses, express) surprise at the wide spaces between plants.

16. A desert area with few plants (conserves, conserve) the available water better than an area with many plants.

17. Animals with little need for water (does, do) best in the desert.

18. Oils from dry seeds (provides, provide) the kangaroo rat all the liquid it needs.

19. Camels of the Sahara (stores, store) water in their fatty humps.

20. Animals with adaptability (thrives, thrive) in a land of little water.

Grammar

Lesson 46
Subject-Verb Agreement and Linking Verbs

In sentences with linking verbs, the verb agrees with the subject, not with the predicate nominative.

The **flowers** in the pot **are** a **gift**. (The verb, *are*, agrees with the subject, *flowers*, not the predicate nominative, *gift*.)

The **result** of the experiment **was** more effective medications. (The verb, *was*, agrees with the subject, *result*, not the predicate nominative, *medications*.)

▶ Exercise 1 **Underline the verb in parentheses that agrees with the subject.**

Jake's excuse for tardiness (is, are) his morning chores.

1. Outdoor activities (seems, seem) the best method for teaching the nature class.

2. The total cost (was, were) hundreds of dollars more than we expected.

3. Exercising and dieting (remains, remain) a healthful way to live.

4. The game scores (was, were) a major disappointment.

5. Jana's injured teeth (is, are) a source of much pain to her.

6. Pinks and oranges (makes, make) a beautiful sunset.

7. My greatest success this year (is, are) my grades.

8. The Porpoises (is, are) the best swimming team in town.

9. The band director's biggest disappointment (remains, remain) the clarinets.

10. The man's remarks (was, were) an embarrassment to his listeners.

11. Our most important resource (is, are) our children.

12. The Carters (is, are) a happy couple.

13. The two lovely monuments (remains, remain) a testament to human courage.

14. The two robberies (was, were) a mystery to the police.

15. The problem (is, are) too many cooks in the kitchen.

16. The cause of the accident (was, were) faulty brakes.

17. The noisy neighbors (was, were) a constant problem.

18. The cost of pollution (is, are) higher medical bills.

19. The reason for the delay (is, are) the strikes in the trucking industry.

20. The sounds of the birds (was, were) the only disturbance.

▶ Exercise 2 **Draw one line under the simple subject. Draw two lines under the verb in parentheses that agrees with the subject.**

The <u>results</u> of the election (is, <u><u>are</u></u>) finally available.

1. Bill's best feature (is, are) his beautiful brown eyes.

2. Your postcards from Hawaii (was, were) a welcome treat.

3. The library books (is, are) a donation from a patron.

4. The videos about whales (is, are) my favorite present.

5. The gas tanks on those trucks (is, are) a safety problem.

6. Angie's and Carla's haircuts (looks, look) a sight!

7. The joy of Stella's life (is, are) her nieces and nephews.

8. Last night's losses (seems, seem) a shame.

9. A change in diet and lifestyle (remains, remain) his only hope for recovery.

10. The falling leaves (becomes, become) a blanket of red and gold.

11. The result of last night's poor score (was, were) extra hours of practice for the team.

12. The delivery (was, were) several truckloads of appliances.

13. The pioneers' light source (was, were) candles.

14. Our worst problem (is, are) the bats in the attic.

15. The pep club's donation (was, were) two dozen boxes of used clothing.

16. Endangered species (is, are) a continuing environmental problem.

17. The result of Bob's knee injury (was, were) torn ligaments.

18. The individual bright colors (becomes, become) a dull blur at dusk.

19. The main issue in the campaign (is, are) taxes.

20. The genie's gift (was, were) three wishes.

▶ Writing Link **Write three or four sentences about a report you have prepared for one of your classes. Make your verb agree with your subject in each sentence.**

_____

_____

_____

_____

_____

_____

Lesson 47
Subject-Verb Agreement in Inverted Sentences

In most sentences the subject comes before the verb. However, some inverted sentences begin with a prepositional phrase followed by the verb and then the subject. The verb in such sentences must always agree with the subject, not the object of the prepositional phrase.

            V   S   V   S
Up the tree **crawls** the **bear.**   Up the tree **crawl** the **bears.**

In sentences that begin with *here* or *there,* do not confuse either word with the subject. Look for the subject following the verb.

          V   S   V   S
There **is a bear** in that tree.   Here **come** the **bears** down the tree!

Questions are inverted sentences. In such constructions, a helping verb often comes before the subject.

     V   S   V   V   S   V
Does the **bear live** in a den?   **Do** the **bears fish** for salmon?

▶ **Exercise 1 Draw a line under the subject. Choose the verb in parentheses that agrees with the subject, and write it in the blank.**

On the sidelines _____*stand*_____ many eager <u>players</u> ready for action. (stand, stands)

1. _____ you _____ for the festivities tomorrow? (Is prepared, Are prepared)

2. Here _____ the fliers about the founder's day celebration. (is, are)

3. Beside that bench _____ a stack of decorations. (is, are)

4. On the walls _____ the decorations we already put up.(hangs, hang)

5. Along the sidewalks _____ a long banner. (extend, extends)

6. Here _____ Luella, the chairperson of the committee. (comes, come)

7. In her hands _____ a list of tasks to be completed. (is, are)

8. _____ a few of those tasks _____ you? (Does interest, Do interest)

9. Under the trees _____ the people who want to help. (gather, gathers)

10. From the apartment building _____ the sounds of the band practicing. (pours, pour)

11. There _____ an article about this event in today's paper. (was, were)

12. _____ the paper _____ our plans? (Does support, Do support)

13. There on the sidewalk _____ the photographers. (waits, wait)

14. Down the street _____ a series of floats. (moves, move)

15. _____ the photographers _____ a picture of the floats? (Does shoot, Do shoot)

16. Behind the floats _____ three huge balloons. (soars, soar)

17. There _____ a photograph of our founder on each of them. (is, are)

18. _____ the crowd _____ the photographs? (Does recognize, Do recognize)

19. From the crowd _____ sounds of enjoyment. (comes, come)

20. There _____ good reasons to plan another celebration next year. (is, are)

▶ **Exercise 2** **Draw a line under the subject. Choose the verb in parentheses that agrees with the subject and write it in the blank(s).**

Near one of those curbs _____ stands _____ a bus-stop shelter. (stand, stands)

1. _____ a rock concert _____ like a good idea? (Does sound, Do sound)

2. Here _____ some suggestions for our next fund-raiser. (is, are)

3. From her agent _____ a message from rock star Linda Light. (comes, come)

4. On her every word _____ our committee. (hangs, hang)

5. Into the building _____ the workers. (hurry, hurries)

6. Into the newspapers _____ a notice of her appearance. (goes, go)

7. Up on the wall _____ many enticing posters. (appears, appear)

8. On the radio _____ an announcement about the concert. (airs, air)

9. _____ the printer _____ our tickets ready? (Does have, Do have)

10. _____ the ticket sellers _____ the correct price? (Does know, Do know)

11. Here _____ a review of Linda's concerts last week in Detroit. (is, are)

12. There _____ several songs that she did as an encore. (is, are)

13. Across the gym _____ Grayson for help with the electronic system. (yells, yell)

14. Outside the building _____ a reporter from the local paper. (parks, park)

15. Inside the office _____ the phones. (rings, ring)

16. There _____ a huge demand for tickets. (is, are)

17. Here _____ the passes we need to keep for the press. (is, are)

18. _____ the school radio station _____ to tape the concert?
(Does plan, Do plan)

19. Behind the curtain _____ the microphone. (sits, sit)

20. In all our hearts _____ anticipation. (lurks, lurk)

Lesson 48
Subject-Verb Agreement and Special Subjects

A **collective noun** names a group (see Lesson 1, pp. 47–48). In a sentence, a collective noun is **singular** when it names the group as a whole. It is **plural** when it refers to individual members of a group.

Singular: The team **takes** the bus.
           The cast **rehearses** the play.
Plural: The team **get** regular physical exams.
           The cast **sign** autographs for the audience.

Some nouns ending in -*s,* such as *mumps, measles,* and *mathematics,* take singular verbs. Other nouns ending in -*s,* such as *scissors, pants, binoculars,* and *eyeglasses,* take plural verbs. Many nouns that end in -*ics* are either singular or plural, depending on the context.

Singular: Mathematics **is** my favorite subject.
Plural: My pants **are** muddy from the river.
Singular: Politics **is** that professor's area of expertise.
Plural: That candidate's politics **were** dirty during the campaign.

A noun of amount can refer to a single unit, in which case it is singular. It can also refer to several individual units, in which case it is plural.

Singular: Ten **weeks is** the period of the first term.
Plural: Ten **weeks are** needed to complete that research.

▶ **Exercise 1** Underline the subject. Fill in the blank with the verb in parentheses that agrees with the subject in the context of the sentence.

The recycling <u>club</u> _____ asks _____ for the entire neighborhood's support. (asks, ask)

1. The band _____ school songs at halftime. (plays, play)

2. Congress _____ to adjourn early this session. (plans, plan)

3. Measles _____ no longer the dread disease it once was. (is, are)

4. The six months _____ since my best friend moved. (has dragged, have dragged)

5. The orchestra _____ in black for concerts. (dresses, dress)

6. My family _____ sick with the flu. (is, are)

7. Your binoculars _____ a big help at our star party. (was, were)

8. Seven feet _____ a long distance to jump. (is, are)

9. Three eggs _____ too many for this recipe. (is, are)

10. Athletics _____ the only thing Jack wanted to pursue. (was, were)

11. The cast _____ each bringing a dish to the theater party. (was, were)

12. Statistics _____ a link between smoking and lung cancer. (shows, show)

13. Twenty dollars _____ too much for this video. (is, are)

14. My doctor says aerobics _____ a good way to get fit. (is, are)

15. Your scissors _____ under the desk. (was, were)

16. Twenty-four hours _____ very slowly when you're waiting for a test grade. (passes, pass)

17. The committee _____ to finish its work. (tries, try)

18. Fifty stories of the building _____ finished. (is, are)

19. My eyeglasses no longer _____. (works, work)

20. Aerobics _____ exercises that strengthen the heart and lungs. (is, are)

▶ **Exercise 2** **Underline the subject. Fill in the blank with the verb in parentheses that agrees with the subject in the context of the sentence.**

Two <u>years</u> _____pass_____ before Gwen returns to her hometown. (passes, pass)

1. _____ your pliers on the workbench? (Is, Are)

2. _____ politics his specialty? (Is, Are)

3. The public _____ campaign reform. (wants, want)

4. The six o'clock news _____ local events. (covers, cover)

5. These trousers _____ not match my shirt. (does, do)

6. The committee _____ a recycling plan today. (chooses, choose)

7. Three months _____ a season. (constitute, constitutes)

8. _____ fifty cents enough for a tip? (Is, Are)

9. Athletics _____ the subject of discussion at the school board meeting. (was, were)

10. Measles _____ usually a childhood disease. (is, are)

11. The science faculty _____ meeting at the museum. (is, are)

12. The music faculty _____ all at the concert. (was, were)

13. Ten dollars _____ the amount of the refund. (was, were)

14. Our team usually _____ two out of three games. (wins, win)

15. But the team usually _____ to the Eagles. (loses, lose)

16. Often the team _____ away their caps as souvenirs. (gives, give)

Lesson 49
Subject-Verb Agreement and Compound Subjects

Some sentences have more than one subject. A compound subject that is joined by *and* or *both...and* is usually plural. However, some compound subjects have two parts that make up one unit. These take a singular verb.

Plural: Molly and Mabel **are racing**.
Plural: Both Aunt Fran and Uncle George **have arrived**.
Singular: Milk and cookies **is** a good snack.

Compound subjects joined by *or, nor, either...or,* or *neither...nor* always have a verb that agrees with the closer subject.

Singular: Either Mark or Carlo **was** the winner.
Singular: Neither the Morgans nor Mr. Hale **is** coming to the dinner.
Plural: Neither the book nor the calendars **are** on sale.

When a compound subject is preceded by *many a, every,* or *each,* the subject takes a singular verb.

Many a student and teacher **has come** to Ms. Randolph for advice.
Every Tom, Dick, and Harry **has** an opinion.
Each tree and fence post **is covered** with political signs.

▶ **Exercise 1** Draw a line under the compound subject of each sentence. Choose the verb in parentheses that agrees with the subject, then write it in the blank.

Many a bird and squirrel _____ visits _____ our backyard feeders. (visit, visits)

1. Every orchard and farm _____ by the storm. (was damaged, were damaged)

2. Spaghetti and meatballs _____ a regular meal at our home. (is, are)

3. Neither Grace nor her sisters _____ the early bus. (takes, take)

4. Either the squirrels or the opossum _____ through the storage boxes. (chews, chew)

5. The bat and the ball _____ Ed's. (is, are)

6. Every seed, nut, and suet ball _____. (was eaten, were eaten)

7. Each bird and field mouse _____ hungry. (is, are)

8. Both movies and books _____ enjoyable. (is, are)

9. Neither the soup nor the casserole _____ hot. (is, are)

10. Either Lani or Marcia _____ in the race today. (skates, skate)

11. Both my shoes and socks _____ full of burrs. (is, are)

12. Either my dad or my brothers _____ me at the bus station. (meets, meet)

Grammar

13. Neither the dogs nor the cat _____ too much sun. (likes, like)

14. Every earring, necklace, and bracelet _____ at the fund-raiser. (was sold, were sold)

15. Each geranium and lily _____ blooming. (is, are)

16. Many a horse and cow _____ in this barn. (has lived, have lived)

17. Both my arms and legs _____ after a long climb. (aches, ache)

18. The producer and director _____ over the script. (disagrees, disagree)

19. Ham and eggs _____ for breakfast at that restaurant. (is offered, are offered)

20. Either the coach or the players _____ to answer the letter. (has, have)

21. Neither the jacket nor the shoes _____. (fits, fit)

22. Lox and bagels _____ Jacob's favorite snack. (is, are)

23. Many a spy and traitor _____ by the detective. (was caught, were caught)

24. Either the washer or the drier _____. (is running, are running)

25. Both Jesse and Malachi _____ honor students. (is, are)

26. Each video and CD _____ half price. (is, are)

27. Every surfboard and sailboat _____. (is rented, are rented)

28. Many a captain and first mate _____ to avoid that wreck. (has swerved, have swerved)

29. Neither the cat nor her kittens _____. (is sleeping, are sleeping)

30. Each chair, desk, and table _____ with books. (is covered, are covered)

31. Neither the chairs nor the table _____ in the truck. (fits, fit)

32. Both Rhoda and Pallas _____ well on spelling tests. (scores, score)

33. Oil and vinegar _____ a good salad dressing. (makes, make)

34. Neither the horses nor the cow _____ restless. (is, are)

35. Neither the hurricane nor the tornadoes _____ to hit here. (is expected, are expected)

36. Many a plaintiff and defendant _____ through these doors. (has passed, have passed)

37. Each cap and gown _____. (is reserved, are reserved)

38. Both soccer and softball _____ favorites of mine. (is, are)

Lesson 50
Subject-Verb Agreement and Intervening Expressions

Certain expressions seem to create a compound subject but do not. *Accompanied by, as well as, in addition to, plus,* and *together with* are expressions that introduce phrases that tell about the subject. However, the subject remains singular and takes a singular verb.

The **President,** as well as the Cabinet, **is expected** tonight.
The **mayor,** accompanied by her staff, **eats** lunch in the cafeteria.

▶ **Exercise 1 Draw a line under the subject. Then write in the blank the form of the verb in parentheses that agrees with the subject. Use the present tense of the verb.**

Joe, as well as his brothers, _____ delivers _____ papers in the morning. (deliver)

1. Folk, in addition to rock, _____ my favorite music. (be)

2. Weight lifting, as well as wrestling, _____ strength. (take)

3. Jupiter, plus Saturn, Uranus, and Neptune, _____ a gas planet. (be)

4. The truck, as well as a car and a bus, _____ involved in the wreck. (be)

5. The players, plus the coach and manager, _____ by bus. (travel)

6. A hoe, in addition to a rake and a ladder, _____ missing from the garage. (be)

7. The singer, accompanied by her bodyguards, _____ tonight. (arrive)

8. The doctor, together with a large staff, _____ many patients. (treat)

9. A plane, in addition to a service truck, _____ on the runway. (sit)

10. Nancy, plus her parents and grandparents, _____ to Florida for the holidays. (go)

11. My bicycle, as well as my skates, _____ repair. (need)

12. The toolshed, together with the garage and the greenhouse, _____ near the stream. (sit)

13. The bank, as well as the arcade, _____ tomorrow. (open)

14. The VCR, plus the compact-disc player, _____ a good holiday gift. (make)

15. The watermelon, as well as the cantaloupe, _____ ripe. (be)

16. Dan, in addition to his friends, _____ depressed. (seem)

17. The Big Dipper, accompanied by the Little Dipper, _____ the polestar. (circle)

18. The city, as well as the suburbs, _____ today. (vote)

19. The bike, plus the skates and the skis, _____ to Oona. (belong)

20. Cereal, together with fruit and milk, _____ a good breakfast. (provide)

▶ **Exercise 2 Draw a line under the subject. Then write the form of the verb in parentheses that agrees with the subject. Use the present tense of the verb when you write it.**

Lisa's <u>paycheck</u>, in addition to her friend's income, _____*helps*_____ pay the bills. (help)

1. A helicopter, as well as a light plane, _____ for the missing hikers. (search)

2. The mail carrier, plus the grocery delivery boy, _____ the dog. (fear)

3. The bear, in addition to her cubs, _____ in that den. (live)

4. Bread, as well as cheese, _____ well with hot soup. (go)

5. Mr. Marcos, accompanied by his sons, _____ log cabins. (build)

6. The trapeze artist, in addition to her partner, _____ in each show. (perform)

7. Cory, accompanied by his nephew, _____ his own plane. (pilot)

8. The gray suit, accompanied by a vest, _____ good on Mark. (look)

9. The candidate, as well as her opponent, _____ tonight. (speak)

10. Sandy, plus Gerry and Pam, _____ several miles each weekend. (run)

11. Science, together with geography, _____ my favorite class. (be)

12. My savings, plus a little extra, _____ me enough for my mother's present. (give)

13. Grandma, plus my Aunt Clara, _____ regularly. (visit)

14. A moat, together with armed knights, _____ the castle. (surround)

15. Tod, accompanied by his parents, _____ many people on his travels. (meet)

16. Juan, as well as Mike, _____ shortstop for the baseball team. (play)

17. Mel, in addition to Madonna and Roy, _____ the flu. (have)

18. The puppy, as well as her mother, _____ everyone around the yard. (chase)

19. Mr. Randolph, accompanied by his family, _____ driving across the country. (be)

20. Hail, as well as rain, often _____ a tornado. (accompany)

▶ **Writing Link Write three or four sentences about the activities you do with your family or friends. Write at least two sentences that use one or more of the phrases you learned about in this lesson. Be sure your verbs agree with your subjects.**

_____

_____

_____

_____

_____

Lesson 51
Subject-Verb Agreement and Indefinite Pronouns as Subjects

Not all subjects are nouns. Many subjects consist of indefinite pronouns. A verb must agree in number with an indefinite pronoun used as a subject.

Singular: Everything about the party **was** perfect.
Singular: One of the windows **is** broken.
Singular: Nothing on television tonight **interests** me.
Plural: Many of our friends **study** Spanish.
Plural: A few of the trees **are** stunted.

Some pronouns can be either singular or plural, depending upon the nouns to which they refer in the sentence.

Singular: All of the punch **is** gone.
Plural: All of the players **are** exhausted.

Indefinite pronouns fall into three groups, as shown in the following chart.

INDEFINITE PRONOUNS

Always Singular	each	everyone	nobody	anything	
	either	everybody	nothing	someone	
	neither	everything	anyone	somebody	
	one	no one	anybody	something	
Always Plural	several	few	both	many	
Singular or Plural	some	all	any	most	none

▶ **Exercise 1** **Draw one line under the indefinite pronoun subject. Draw two lines under the correct form of the verb.**

<u>Several</u> of my friends (<u>swim</u>, swims) on the school team.

1. Many of the passengers (is, are) unhappy with coach service.

2. A few of the swimmers (was, were) ready to leave the pool.

3. Everything in the window (look, looks) expensive.

4. Something in the basement (has, have) eaten the vegetables.

5. One of the dogs (hunt, hunts) alone.

6. Some of the tomatoes (was, were) spoiled.

7. Everybody in the class (has, have) voted.

8. No one (answer, answers) the phone at the Caldwells.

9. Nothing (seem, seems) to please Linda.

10. All of the grass (is, are) brown from the drought.

11. Anybody who was there (know, knows) that Randy gave a good speech.

12. One of the contestants (was, were) late.

13. Nobody in our class (like, likes) the new movie.

14. Several of the squirrels (has, have) raided the sunflower sack.

15. Most of the class (do, does) push-ups each morning.

16. None of the mothers (like, likes) this arrangement.

17. Everything at the museum (was, were) fascinating.

18. Both of my aunts (is, are) from Poland.

19. Nobody in the audience (understand, understands) the play.

20. None of the players (was, were) tired.

21. Many of the old pirate ships (has been, have been) lost in that area.

22. Neither of the deer (use, uses) the salt lick.

23. Several of the class officers (was, were) ill.

24. Nothing on the menu (interest, interests) me.

25. One of the defendants (has, have) pleaded not guilty.

26. Several of the judges (has, have) ruled on their cases.

27. Everybody in the room (was, were) freezing.

28. Several of the high-school students (earn, earns) money after school.

29. Somebody in our community (has, have) won that huge prize.

30. All (is, are) well with the world.

31. Both of the twins (sing, sings) in the choir.

32. Someone (has, have) painted the old chairs.

33. Few of the people polled (approve, approves) of the new policies.

34. All of the spaghetti (was, were) gone.

35. Everyone here (has, have) finished lunch.

36. One of the babies in the nursery (is, are) crying.

37. Few of the people invited (is, are) coming.

38. Anyone at all (is, are) eligible to enter the race.

☑ Unit 7 **Review**

▶ **Exercise 1** **Underline the subject of each sentence. Then, choose the verb in parentheses that agrees with the subject and write it in the blank.**

<u>Katia</u> _____looks_____ forward to singing in the choir. (look, looks)

1. The nerves in my body _____ when I am excited. (tingle, tingles)

2. Here _____ the tomb of the unknown soldier. (lie, lies)

3. Down by the schoolyard _____ Julia, as well as Paul. (play, plays)

4. All of the campers _____ for the coming storm. (prepare, prepares)

5. Tarzan _____ from a vine. (swing, swings)

6. The coaches of the football team _____ for the big game. (plan, plans)

7. _____ the Senate, as well as the House, approve the bill? (Do, Does)

8. Peppermint candy, as well as fruitcake and eggnog, _____ traditionally served during the holidays. (is, are)

9. Across the European countryside _____ Killile and Mary. (travel, travels)

10. The Vietnamese pot-bellied pig, as well as the common dog or cat, _____ a great pet! (make, makes)

11. The books _____ a heavy load. (was, were)

12. Into the street _____ the horses! (gallop, gallops)

13. The Olympic team _____ hard with personal coaches. (train, trains)

14. Electronics, as well as mechanics, _____ a very lucrative field. (is, are)

15. Hotcakes and sausage _____ my favorite meal. (is, are)

16. My cat _____ his food when no one is watching. (eat, eats)

17. The distance from my house to the shopping mall _____ many kilometers. (span, spans)

18. The audience _____ with laughter. (roar, roars)

19. Bridget and Mary Jo _____ their new neighbors downstairs. (visit, visits)

20. A few of the lights _____ not work. (do, does)

Cumulative Review: Units 1–7

▶ **Exercise 1** Label each noun *con.* if it is concrete, *abst.* if it is abstract, *col.* if it is collective, and *prop.* if it is proper. Underline each conjunction.

> prop.   abst.   con.
> Kanya felt happiness <u>when</u> she saw her new house.

1. Fritz's pride was hurt when he fell, but there were no other injuries.

2. Neither anger nor jealousy would help the candidate win the election.

3. The gaggle of geese rested peacefully by the shore of the lake until the dog arrived.

4. If the entire family pitched in to help, they still might be able to make it to the game on time.

5. Abe will plan little surprises for his family as long as he has a part-time job.

6. Walt Whitman once wrote: "Peace is always beautiful."

7. High aspirations keep many people motivated.

8. Whenever Sally sees a rainbow, she thinks of an imaginary pot of gold.

9. The heather in the fields was beautiful with its purplish-pink leaves.

10. We read the newspaper while we were waiting for Sid.

11. As long as our group was visiting New York City, we went for a walk in Central Park.

12. Because it was a dreary day, listlessness was felt throughout the class.

13. The water-skiing team wore wet suits whenever the water or weather was too cold.

14. Many students were feeling better about school because of the peer-helper program.

15. Anxiety ran high as the competitors for the leading roles waited for the results of the auditions.

16. Janet thought a video camera would be the best way to preserve family memories.

17. Kenji ate cookies as long as there were some on the plate.

18. The committee resolved their differences so that the meetings would run successfully.

19. The students returned to their desks before the bell rang.

20. The gruff old man showed such gentleness to the stray dog.

Name _____ Class _____ Date _____

▶ Exercise 2 **Write the correct form of the verb asked for in the blank. Underline each prepositional phrase.**

Dayung ____disposed____ of the oil in the proper manner. (past tense of *dispose*)

1. The Morgans _____ hundreds of travel brochures during their travels

   throughout the years. (present perfect tense of *accumulate*)

2. The wind _____ the snow into awesome drifts. (past tense of *arrange*)

3. The highway patrol _____ all travelers about the icy road conditions.

   (future tense of *caution*)

4. The tutor _____ Kacie to do a better job on her test. (past perfect tense

   of *enable*)

5. Winning this medal _____ my every expectation! (present tense of *surpass*)

6. Mom _____ the thermometer after each use. (present perfect tense

   of *disinfect*)

7. Marty _____ anyone who has also suffered a personal loss. (present tense

   of *console*)

8. The boy _____ the injured bird in his arms all the way home. (past perfect

   tense of *cradle*)

9. The climbing expedition hopefully _____ the summit before the blizzard

   hits. (future perfect tense of *reach*)

10. The gull _____ down eagerly to the water for its food. (past tense of *swoop*)

11. For the special occasion, the couple _____ themselves with family and

    friends. (future perfect tense of *surround*)

12. The vines _____ themselves around the fence. (past perfect tense of *twist*)

13. Attending the conference _____ the staff in preparation for the year ahead.

    (future tense of *energize*)

14. After his long illness, Marcos _____ behind in his schoolwork. (present

    perfect tense of *feel*)

15. Vanesa _____ herself from negative influences. (present tense of *alienate*)

16. You _____ the lathe and other machines by the end of this semester. (future

    perfect tense of *operate*)

17. The horses _____ slowly around the arena before the competition begins.

    (future tense of *gallop*)

18. On tests, we all _____ to do our best. (present tense of *endeavor*)

19. I _____ never _____ better food in my entire life. (past perfect

    tense of *taste*)

20. Myra's hands _____ without her gloves. (future tense of *freeze*)

▶ **Exercise 3** **Draw one line under the complete subject in each sentence. Draw two lines under the correct form of the verb.**

Every hill and valley (is, are) a beautiful sight each fall.

1. Immunization (remain, remains) a requirement for school enrollment.

2. Each of the workers on the crew (paint, paints) at a different speed.

3. Every teacher in the school (evaluate, evaluates) each student's progress.

4. Neither the cake nor the cookies (has, have) been touched.

5. (Do, Does) the hunters wear safety clothing?

6. Across the shaky bridge (rattle, rattles) the antique cars.

7. Uncle Bob and Aunt Joan (thrill, thrills) to the music of the Glenn Miller Band.

8. Neither of the teams, the Falcons or the Knights, (is, are) this year's conference champion.

9. Each rowboat and canoe (is, are) being repainted for the next tourist season.

10. The attorneys in the case (make, makes) an appeal tomorrow.

11. Slick roads and fog (is, are) a major concern for travelers.

12. The newspapers on the stand (was, were) sold out by noon.

13. Every quiz, paper, and test (has, have) been a concern for Joel.

14. None of the members of the audience (applaud, applauds) loudly.

15. Over the horizon (appear, appears) the posse.

16. Ham and cheese (seem, seems) to be my favorite sandwich.

17. Every car, truck, and bus (go, goes) across this bridge to reach the island.

18. Snowmobiling in the northern woods (is, are) a wonderful winter sport.

19. One of the fishermen (has, have) lost his rod and reel in the lake.

20. "Early to bed and early to rise" (is, are) a good suggestion to live by.

Unit 8: Using Pronouns Correctly

Lesson 52
Personal Pronouns: Case

Pronouns that are used to refer to persons or things are called **personal pronouns**. Personal pronouns have three **cases**, or forms, called **nominative**, **objective**, and **possessive**. The case of a personal pronoun depends on how it is used in a sentence. The chart below lists the personal pronouns, their cases, and their uses.

Case	Singular Pronouns	Plural Pronouns	Function in Sentence
Nominative	I, you, she, he, it	we, you, they	subject or predicate nominative
Objective	me, you, her, him, it	us, you, them	direct object, indirect object, or object of preposition
Possessive	my, mine, your, yours, her, hers, his, its	our, ours, your, yours, their, theirs	replacement for possessive noun(s)

We gathered in the cafeteria for a meeting.
Dan thought the disc was **yours**.

Taylor brought **her** to the game.

▶ **Exercise 1 Underline the correct pronoun.**

Bring the packages to (they, <u>them</u>).

1. When the early settlers arrived in this country, (they, them) had little time for school.

2. Those who wanted (them, their) children to read would teach (they, them) at home.

3. There were no schools for (their, them) children to attend.

4. The most important subject for (their, them) was how to plant.

5. As the settlements grew, formal education became more important to (they, them).

6. Reading, writing, and arithmetic helped (they, them).

7. Education became a community effort, and the entire community benefited from (it, its).

8. Schoolhouses were generally built on land not suitable for farming, and the school yard rarely had any trees in (it, its).

9. Early schoolhouses were heated by smoky fires. Later (they, them) had stoves.

Grammar

10. Families sent a load of firewood when (they, their) sent (them, their) children to school.

11. Since paper was expensive, little of (it, its) was used.

12. Each family made (it, its) own ink from ink powder.

13. Handwriting was very important. (It, Its) was often considered more important than spelling.

14. Stitching samplers was a way a young girl could show (she, her) sewing skills and (she, her) knowledge of the alphabet.

15. Since the Bible was often the only book a family owned, (it, its) was usually the first reader.

16. A male teacher was expected to have a more disciplined way about (he, him).

17. A woman was expected to quit teaching after (she, her) married.

18. Schoolmasters often used discipline that today would seem very cruel to (we, us).

19. A schoolmaster would sometimes punish (him, his) students physically.

20. One of the rules for students was this: Respect (your, yours) schoolmaster. Obey (he, him) and accept (him, his) punishments.

▶ **Exercise 2** **Label each italicized pronoun** *nom.* **(nominative),** *obj.* **(objective), or** *pos.* **(possessive) case.**

> nom.　　　　pos.
> *They* shook *their* clothes to get out the sand.

1. *Our* country's history is full of exciting tales about settling the West.

2. *We* may not realize what *our* ancestors went through to settle *our* great country.

3. In the 1840s, the pioneers began *their* trek across the Great Plains and the Rocky Mountains.

4. *They* encountered many hardships on *their* treacherous journey to *their* new homes.

5. These adventurers had to plan wisely to know what to take with *them* because *their* lives depended on these decisions.

6. The Conestoga wagon, with *its* broad-rimmed wheels and *its* white canvas roof, was *their* home for the journey that would take *them* many weeks.

7. Upon reaching *their* destination, the pioneers had to choose a place to build *their* homes and plant crops.

8. This planting would provide *them* with food for *their* first winter.

9. *It* was not an easy life for the pioneers, but *they* found *they* were all willing to help each other.

10. If *you* had lived in the 1840s, would *you* have moved west?

Grammar

Lesson 53
Pronouns with and as Appositives; After *Than* and *As*

Use the nominative case for a pronoun that is the appositive of a subject or a predicate nominative. Use the objective case for a pronoun that is the appositive of a direct object, an indirect object, or an object of a preposition.

The winners, Mitzi and **she,** collected their trophies. (nominative)
Give the tickets to the ushers, Bart and **him.** (objective)

When an appositive follows a pronoun, choose the case of the pronoun that would be correct if the appositive were omitted.

We winners collected our trophies. **We** collected our trophies. (nominative)
Give the tickets to **us ushers.** Give the tickets to **us.** (objective)

In elliptical adverb clauses using *than* and *as*, choose the case of the pronoun that you would use if the missing words were fully expressed.

I am always hungrier than **he.** (Read: I am always hungrier than he is.)
The directions puzzled Phil as much as **me.** (Read: The directions puzzled Phil as much as they puzzled me.)

Grammar

▶ **Exercise 1** **Underline the correct pronoun. Identify the case by writing *nom.* (nominative) or *obj.* (objective) in the blank. Some sentences have more than one pronoun to identify.**

<u>nom., obj.</u>   The singers, Nora and (I, me), gave our friends, Sue and (they, them), front row

seats for the concert.

_____ **1.** The contestants, Conrad and (I, me), were both nervous.

_____ **2.** The judges presented the winners, Sylvia and (I, me), with engraved plaques.

_____ **3.** The newspaper article described the three fastest runners on the team, Sarah,

Jacques, and (I, me).

_____ **4.** The best goalies on the soccer team, Amy and (she, her), both wanted to play in

the championship game.

_____ **5.** The two teachers, Mr. Barnes and (she, her), explained the rules of the

classroom to (we, us) students.

_____ **6.** The three lost campers, Rich, Manuel, and (I, me), returned to camp in the

morning.

_____ **7.** The volunteers wanted to help the flood victims, Kisha and (he, him).

_____ **8.** (We, Us) voters sent a message at the election.

_____ **9.** The two class officers, (he, him) and (I, me), have to organize the food drive before Thanksgiving.

_____ **10.** Naz and Jenny are better athletes than (they, them).

_____ **11.** No one could have been more excited than (I, me).

_____ **12.** These algebra problems confuse Rashonda as much as (I, me).

_____ **13.** Eleanor chose brighter colors for her picture than (I, me).

_____ **14.** The bus picks up An-Mei as early as (I, me).

_____ **15.** When I spilled my juice, he was more startled than (I, me).

_____ **16.** I could tell Conrad was more nervous than (I, me).

_____ **17.** No one I know is a better quarterback than (he, him).

_____ **18.** The loss of electricity was less inconvenient for me than (they, them).

_____ **19.** What do you think? (We, Us) three are the winners!

_____ **20.** When Sarah, Rhoda, and I returned from outdoor survival camp, I had more mosquito bites than (they, them).

_____ **21.** It's so frustrating. I try to work as fast as (they, them), but I always finish last.

_____ **22.** Neither of last year's leads, Ricardo or (he, him), was in the play this year.

_____ **23.** English grammar seems easy for both of the editors of the school newspaper, Joe and (she, her).

_____ **24.** The two forwards, Raoul and (he, him), shared the MVP award for the basketball team last year.

_____ **25.** I am usually satisfied with much less money than (they, them).

_____ **26.** Carlos was more disappointed than (I, me) when we were both cut from the soccer team.

_____ **27.** The two teenagers, Saul and (she, her), usually have dinner ready when their grandmother gets home from work.

_____ **28.** The new computer software was easy to master for both students, Gretchen and (he, him).

_____ **29.** We are sending blankets and winter clothes to the earthquake victims we know, Katherine and (she, her).

Lesson 54
Who and *Whom* in Questions and Subordinate Clauses

Use the nominative pronoun *who* for subjects. Use the objective pronoun *whom* for the direct or indirect object of a verb or verbal or for the object of a preposition.

Who wants to try out for the play? (nominative)
Whom did you see at the mall? (objective)
Jarod, **who** lives next door, has a trampoline. (nominative)
Gwen, **whom** he had known for years, was now an actress. (objective)

▶ **Exercise 1** Write *who* or *whom* in the blank to make each sentence correct.

My sister, _____*who*_____ likes to play basketball, is trying out for the team.

1. Franklin Delano Roosevelt, _____ was elected the thirty-second president of the United States, was born in 1882.

2. He was the only child of James Roosevelt, _____ descended from a well-to-do Dutch family in New York.

3. Franklin's mother, _____ was named Sara Delano Roosevelt, was very devoted to him.

4. Franklin was a very athletic young man _____ was an expert in boating and swimming.

5. In 1905, he married Anna Eleanor Roosevelt, _____ was a distant cousin.

6. Eleanor, to _____ Sara Roosevelt objected as a wife for Franklin, was orphaned when she was ten years old.

7. At the wedding the bride was given away by another Roosevelt _____ both Eleanor and Franklin admired.

8. This Roosevelt, _____ was Eleanor's uncle, was Theodore.

9. Theodore Roosevelt, _____ became president when William McKinley was assassinated, was one of the most popular presidents in U.S. history.

10. In 1920, Franklin ran for vice president as the running mate for James M. Cox, _____ the voters rejected in favor of Warren Harding.

11. Less than a year later, the young, athletic Franklin, _____ greatly enjoyed physical activity, was stricken with poliomyelitis.

12. His mother, _____ was forever present in Franklin and Eleanor's life, wanted him to retire from politics and live as a country squire.

13. His wife, Eleanor, _____ he relied on for advice and support, urged him to remain involved in politics.

Grammar

14. In 1928, Franklin Roosevelt, _____ had been paralyzed by polio seven years earlier, was elected governor of New York.

15. When the stock market crashed in 1929, Herbert Hoover, _____ had been elected president in 1928, was blamed for the economic disaster.

16. Many voters wondered to _____ they might turn for new leadership.

17. In 1932, the voters elected Franklin Roosevelt, _____ encouraged them by saying they had nothing to fear but fear itself.

18. FDR, _____ the world will never forget, brought America into World War II to help Western Europe defend itself against Adolf Hitler.

19. FDR, with _____ the world fought for freedom in World War II, did not live to see the Allies triumph.

20. Franklin Delano Roosevelt, _____ was one of the twentieth century's most skillful political leaders, is the only person elected to the U.S. presidency four times.

21. Anna Eleanor Roosevelt, _____ was called Eleanor, was born in 1884.

22. Her father, Elliott, _____ was Theodore Roosevelt's brother, sent her to school in England.

23. Franklin Roosevelt, to _____ Eleanor was married, embarked on a political career a few years after their wedding.

24. Eleanor and Franklin had five children, of _____ little has been written.

25. Franklin, _____ was battling polio, relied on his wife to perform many tasks.

26. She, _____ joined the Women's Trade Union League, also served as financial chairperson for the women's division of the state Democratic party.

27. President Roosevelt, _____ at times was considered a controversial figure, was almost outshone in some respects by Eleanor.

28. Some people made jokes about the woman to _____ the President entrusted many important jobs.

29. Franklin, _____ often stayed at the White House, relied on Eleanor to tour the nation and report on current conditions.

30. Press conferences for women correspondents were instituted by Eleanor, _____ broke through several gender barriers.

31. Beginning in 1936, Eleanor, _____ was First Lady, wrote a daily newspaper column.

32. She wrote for people with _____ she wished to share her experiences.

33. For those to _____ she is unfamiliar, it may be difficult to understand the depth of her influence.

34. Mrs. Roosevelt, _____ was concerned about the plight of children during the Depression, took an avid interest in the President's plans to help them.

Lesson 55
Pronoun-Antecedent Agreement in Number and Gender

An **antecedent** is the word or group of words to which a pronoun refers or that a pronoun replaces. A pronoun must agree with its antecedent in number (singular or plural) and gender (masculine, feminine, or neuter). A pronoun's antecedent may be a noun, another pronoun, or a phrase or clause acting as a noun.

Paula brought **her** grandfather to speak to the class.

▶ **Exercise 1** **Complete the sentence by adding a personal pronoun that agrees with the antecedent. Underline the antecedent.**

Carla left _____*her*_____ gloves on the kitchen table.

1. The students should have _____ books by Friday.

2. Every person must bring _____ own towel to gym class.

3. Many older Americans know the exact date _____ started _____ first job.

4. Only three club members paid _____ dues by the deadline.

5. If you think the colors clash, we will change _____ .

6. When my mom and her four sisters were children, _____ all shared one big bedroom.

7. Claude and Norman practice _____ sidestrokes every day.

8. Gloria works for two hours every day after _____ leaves school.

9. Sometimes people without experience are intimidated by computers. _____ needn't be.

10. Gabriel and Chad don't want to work after school, but _____ need the money.

11. Natasha and Paul found _____ share an interest in classical automobiles.

12. George and Susan both brought _____ snakes to science class when we studied reptiles.

13. Some students don't take class elections very seriously; _____ should.

14. Each participant can be very proud of _____ accomplishments.

15. I think my grandma is the best gardener in _____ neighborhood.

16. They finally decided Jack must have the tickets in _____ room.

17. Dad says all of _____ children spend too much of _____ time watching television.

18. Ramona and her friends left _____ biology books in the library.

19. The college sends most of _____ messages to students by electronic mail.

20. Abdul and Larry showed _____ could hit a ball out of the ballpark.

▶ **Exercise 2** **Correct each personal pronoun in italics so it agrees with its antecedent in the sentence. Cross out the incorrect pronoun, and write the correct word above it. Do not change any pronouns that already agree with the antecedent in number and gender.**

their
The musicians began tuning *her* instruments.

1. Maria and Sean thought the computer was just what *they* needed to make *their* business work.

2. The artists displayed *her* paintings in the new gallery.

3. David forgot to pay *her* club dues.

4. Most students in Ms. Cynkar's class really enjoyed *their* lessons.

5. Kristen organized *its* desk for better efficiency.

6. My friends and I attended the football game; then *he* walked uptown.

7. Fred does not neglect *his* health.

8. Jacob likes the game of soccer. *It* plays often.

9. Did Kay lose the assignment sheet from *our* notebook?

10. Angela was too busy with *her* college courses.

11. The author had become accustomed to the criticism about *their* books.

12. The pioneers spent many hours preparing *its* homes for winter.

13. Martina would like to give *his* opinion on the topic.

14. Each animal makes *their* own unique sound.

15. Sandra succeeded in attaining *her* goal.

16. Did Jack lend you *their* pencil?

17. This tree has not yet shed *their* leaves.

18. Brian decided to take responsibility for *their* own chores.

19. Each student spent extra time learning the concepts *we* hadn't mastered.

20. At dawn, Miguel folded *their* sleeping bag and left the tent.

Lesson 56
Pronoun-Antecedent Agreement in Person

A **pronoun** must agree in person with its antecedent. When the antecedent of a pronoun is another pronoun, be sure that the two pronouns agree in person.

Bryan gave **his** old guitar to Jacob.   **We** want **our** money back!

▶ **Exercise 1** **Fill in the blank with the correct personal pronoun. Underline the antecedent for each pronoun.**

Juan is planning _____his_____ vacation.

1. The students in Mrs. Nakleh's social studies class discussed how _____ would spend the vacation.

2. Kristen thought her younger brothers might be frightened when _____ were close to snakes.

3. Alligators are again plentiful in the Southeast, and hunting _____ is now allowed.

4. Jason was spending the week with _____ dad in Boston, where _____ were going to watch two Celtics games.

5. Alfredo likes to be by the sea, where _____ can smell the air with _____ salty taste.

6. People can watch the seagulls swoop down to find _____ dinner in the Boston Harbor.

7. Each businessman gave _____ report at the board meeting.

8. We wanted to see _____ new apartment before moving in.

9. In the spring, the robin was busy building _____ nest.

10. Anita plays both volleyball and basketball, but volleyball is _____ favorite sport.

11. Sam and Jose, who sing duets, agree _____ need more practice before the contest.

12. Michael's father wants _____ to take geometry and accelerated English next year.

13. Cats like to relax in the sun and stretch _____ bodies.

14. Brett's nickname is "Stretch," which refers to _____ height.

15. Nathan and Elizabeth cannot go out for pizza because _____ have terrible colds.

16. That particular fish has black stripes along _____ sides.

17. I saw so many things that impressed _____ in Washington, D.C.

Grammar

18. Colleen moved to New York to work for an uncle and _____ wife.

19. We, as citizens of the United States, have to take responsibility for _____ country's

success.

20. Sidney moved to the city of Seattle and became a member of _____ city council.

▶ **Exercise 2** **Find the personal pronouns that have antecedents within each sentence or sentence group. Draw one line under the personal pronoun. Draw two lines under its antecedent. Change the personal pronoun to agree in person with its antecedent. Correct the verb if necessary.**

> her
> Katrina wants to finish his homework before dinner.

1. The first thing Mario realized when you backpacked was how heavy the pack could feel.

2. When Connor heard Rose sing, you were amazed at the high notes she could reach.

3. Barry finds it hard to concentrate when there is so much going on around you.

4. Jianming will be the first person in her family to go to college, where you plans to study medicine.

5. You can get such sore muscles when they run farther than usual.

6. The ice was so slick that with the first step I fell on your face.

7. I just love to smell fresh bread baking when you get up in the morning.

8. Sometimes I am so tired when you get off work that you fall asleep without eating my dinner.

9. I often fall asleep in the living room when you read late at night.

10. I looked and looked until you couldn't see it anymore.

11. My mom is so patient with me. You can't help but love her.

12. I studied so hard for this test that you thought you knew everything.

13. When they turn fourteen, tell them you should consider volunteer work at the hospital.

14. We visited with my grandparents, who are so active they tired you out.

15. The baby wiggled so much I thought I were going to drop him.

16. After the scouts trekked up the mountain side, it collapsed in relief when you reached the

summit.

Grammar

Lesson 57
Pronoun-Antecedent Agreement with Indefinite Pronoun Antecedents

In general, use a singular personal pronoun when the antecedent is a singular indefinite pronoun, such as *anybody, anyone, anything, each, either, everybody, everyone, everything, much, neither, nobody, no one, nothing, one, other, somebody, someone,* or *something.* If the antecedent refers to a person and the gender is not specific, it is usually most acceptable to use *he or she, him or her,* or *his or hers.*

Each of the boys folded **his** sleeping bag.   **Anyone** can bring **his or her** favorite CD.

Use a plural personal pronoun when the antecedent is a plural indefinite pronoun, such as *several, both, few,* and *many.*

Both of the runners broke **their** previous records.

Some indefinite pronouns can be either singular or plural depending on the context of the sentence: *all, any, enough, more, most, none,* and *some.*

We will play if **enough** of the students bring **their** equipment.

▶ **Exercise 1** **Write a personal pronoun that agrees with the indefinite pronoun antecedent in the sentence. Underline the antecedent.**

Few of the glee club members forgot _____their_____ music.

1. Everyone has to finish _____ assignment before Thursday.

2. Many will find that _____ uniforms from last year are now too small.

3. Does anyone disagree with me? Let _____ say so now.

4. Someone took the wrong jacket. If _____ returns it, please call me.

5. All of the computers lost _____ power.

6. Many of the graduates did not even recognize _____ classmates at the reunion.

7. Both of the contestants were nervous; _____ kept shifting their feet.

8. After gym on Monday, only one of the boys made it to _____ next class on time.

9. Everyone must pay for _____ ticket before boarding the bus.

10. One of these girls assembled _____ own computer.

11. No one should lend _____ comb to anyone else.

12. Each of the girls had to show _____ could make ten baskets in a row.

Grammar

13. Everyone who gets a ninety or better on the final can submit _____

application for the accelerated course.

14. All of the band members will be in _____ seats ten minutes before the performance.

15. Everybody can take a break whenever _____ needs one.

16. Neither of the girls made the team of _____ choice.

17. Each of the students in English class named _____ favorite author.

18. For added security, everyone must memorize _____ own combination.

19. Isn't it strange how all of our parents think _____ know just how we feel?

20. During the blackout, everyone coped in _____ own way.

21. A few of our students don't seem to understand how _____ can help.

22. Remember to put everything back in _____ place.

23. Some of our neighbors have already shoveled _____ sidewalks.

24. You can keep the money you found since nobody says it belongs to _____.

25. Several of my friends are going. _____ parents say it's okay.

26. Mike said he has something important to tell me. I wonder what _____ is.

27. We thought we had plenty of sugar, but we ran out of _____ before we finished baking.

28. Most of the trees lost _____ leaves in Saturday's storm.

29. Do any of them know the answer? It doesn't seem _____ do.

30. Since most of the volunteers signed up for another rotation, _____ must be happy

doing the work.

31. Neither of the students failed _____ test.

32. Anybody would be happy to have this album in _____ collection.

33. I will take both. Will you send _____ to me?

34. Some of the cheese has mold on _____.

35. Some of the books have very sophisticated vocabulary in _____.

36. Does anybody have a comb in _____ locker?

37. Few understand how much _____ can contribute.

38. None of the rivers in the area overflowed _____ banks.

39. Anything you can do will be appreciated. _____ is more than will be done otherwise.

40. Most of the old silver had lost _____ shine.

Lesson 58
Clear Pronoun Reference

Make sure that the antecedent of a **pronoun** is clearly stated and that a pronoun cannot possibly refer to more than one antecedent. Do not use the pronouns *this, that, which,* and *it* without a clearly stated antecedent. If a pronoun seems to refer to more than one antecedent, either reword the sentence to make the antecedent clear or eliminate the pronoun. Avoid the indefinite use of the pronouns *you* and *they.*

▶ **Exercise 1** **Rewrite each sentence to eliminate any unclear pronoun reference.**

The home team played the visiting team, and they lost the game.

The home team played the visiting team, and the visiting team lost the game.

_____

1. In the mid-1800s the best way to get a letter from New York to San Francisco was to ship it around South America, which was slow and expensive.

_____

_____

2. Clipper ships took about three months to make the trip, which was too long.

_____

3. Even after railroads began to be built, you couldn't take them across the country.

_____

4. They did not have railroad tracks between Missouri and the Pacific Coast.

_____

5. This was called the "great American desert," where they didn't live.

_____

6. Some stagecoaches crossed this land, which was very slow.

_____

7. You could get mail to Missouri, which was sent from New York in four days.

_____

8. Then the mail carriers had to cross the plains and then maneuver through the mountains, which stretched for 1,500 miles.

_____

_____

9. You could get a letter from Missouri to California in 25 days, which was almost 2,000 miles.

_____

10. Then in 1860, they created the Pony Express.

_____

11. This was a series of relay stations where fresh horses and riders waited to take the mail, which were much faster than stagecoaches.

_____

_____

12. They carried the mail 220 miles each day.

_____

13. At first, the relay stations were 25 miles apart, which was too far for them to run at full speed.

_____

14. Intermediate depots were set up every 10 to 15 miles where you could change mounts.

_____

15. Your mail got from Missouri to San Francisco in 10 days.

_____

16. The Pony Express received no subsidy from the government, which stopped operating after a year and a half.

_____

17. The Pony Express came to be one of the most colorful episodes of the American West, which was a financial disaster.

_____

_____

18. Then in 1861, the first telegraph lines were stretched across the country, which allowed you to send messages faster.

_____

_____

19. At almost the same time, the Pony Express stopped operating, which was very expensive.

_____

20. In 1869, they built the first transcontinental railroad.

_____

☑ Unit 8 Review

▶ **Exercise** **Cross out each inappropriate pronoun and write the correct word above it.**

                              her

Dominique is displaying ~~their~~ paintings in her father's office.

1. Us students decided to change our plans.

2. Choose you courses wisely. Your will only be a sophomore once.

3. Mrs. Zimmerman and Mr. Cane are great teachers. Try to get her for at least one class.

4. Who did you think we would choose?

5. Sheila generally takes longer to finish their chores than the rest of us. Do you think her likes it?

6. I try to finish some of my homework in study hall so they don't have to carry home their books.

7. My advisor suggested I try either French or Spanish for my foreign language, but you won't

    know what you like until you've tried it.

8. I try to get to school early on Thursdays, but it's hard to get yourself going in the morning.

9. Give George and Allen the homework from the classes he missed.

10. Everybody must see their advisor this week.

11. The co-presidents of the Service Club, Rashid and her, are trying to organize a food drive for
    Thanksgiving.

12. The members of the football team all celebrated the victory with its voices raised high.

13. Everyone who takes art must provide their own pastels.

14. Ginny looks so much like her sister, whom is a senior, that it is hard to tell them apart.

15. Jose's dad doesn't have to work this weekend, so they might be able to drive us to the game.

16. Whom do you think will get the soprano solo for the spring concert?

17. Our leading scorers, Ryan and him, will get trophies at the ceremony.

18. I take the bus with Sinead and Javier, but they get off before me.

19. Sonya sold more raffle tickets this year than her did last year.

20. Neither of the girls could remember just why they chose this course.

21. She, together with Rhea and I, is ready to audition now.

22. Please give the new schedules to the co-captains, Yong and he.

Cumulative Review: Units 1–8

▶ **Exercise 1** Label each word or phrase that is italicized to indicate its use in the sentence. Use these abbreviations: *subj.* (subject), *v.* (verb), *i.o.* (indirect object), *d.o.* (direct object), *p.n.* (predicate nominative), *app.* (appositive), or *p.a.* (predicate adjective).

v.   d.o.

The pilot *guided* her *plane* to the runway.

1. *Leanne,* my friend, *gave* me the *picture* on that table.

2. *Give me* your homework after school.

3. Mr. Kwan, *the class adviser,* is a *graduate* of Harvard.

4. *Karen* not only ran in the marathon but also set a personal *record.*

5. What *is* the *reason* for your tardiness?

6. The *puppy* was *frightened* but *friendly* as the visitors arrived.

7. I *passed* the *exam!*

8. My *mother* is a civil *engineer* for the government.

9. *Close* all the animal *cages* before you leave tonight.

10. The cake *tasted delicious.*

11. *Abdul missed* the *bus* and *was* late for work.

12. Joshua gave *me* a dozen *roses* for my birthday.

13. What a lousy *concert* that *was!*

14. *Sarah, our student council president,* became *speechless.*

15. *Have you* ever *traveled* down the Mississippi River by steamboat?

16. Both the *garage* and the *car were destroyed* by the storm.

17. *Franklin* was an *inventor* and a *statesman.*

18. Please *shut* the *window* because it is raining.

19. The practical *joke* was neither *clever* nor *funny.*

20. *Did* the roller coaster ride *give you* a *thrill?*

21. Mr. Sampson, *the principal, read* the morning *announcements* over the public address system.

22. The *director* shot some spectacular *footage* in the Alps.

23. Your *father gave me* this book, a *collection* of poems.

24. Stop! Your *time is* up.

▶ **Exercise 2** Draw two lines under the verb or verb phrase. In the blank, write its tense: *present,*
past, future, present perfect, past perfect, or *future perfect.* Label each personal pronoun: *nom.*
(nominative), *obj.* **(objective),** *pos.* **(possessive).**

pos.

_____**past**_____ The cat <u>slithered</u> across her owner's porch.

_____ **1.** The Iowa farmer has planted his crops.

_____ **2.** The parade will have passed the city park by noon.

_____ **3.** The insensitive people laughed loudly at my new ideas.

_____ **4.** I cheer tirelessly at our football games.

_____ **5.** Your roommate will call you soon.

_____ **6.** Mom and my sister had baked the cookies for us.

_____ **7.** Maybe we will have built our new home by then.

_____ **8.** The coach always insists on faithful attendance at our practices.

_____ **9.** The airplane landed safely after the severe storm.

_____ **10.** When will you help with mine?

_____ **11.** The math team had solved every single problem on time.

_____ **12.** Your workers have finished their duties on time.

_____ **13.** I shall always crave chocolate ice cream.

_____ **14.** The musicians' mothers made the costumes for them.

_____ **15.** The candles will have burned to nothing by tonight.

_____ **16.** Our president had opened the board meetings on time.

_____ **17.** Sometimes our thoughts turn to the upcoming weekend.

_____ **18.** Mia will graduate with academic honors.

_____ **19.** David will have waxed three cars by ten o'clock.

Grammar

_____ **20.** The other members of our tour had taken more pictures than we.

_____ **21.** Your beautiful art project will have caught their attention.

_____ **22.** At the grocery store, the flustered cashier gave her too much change.

_____ **23.** Will your parents travel to Europe?

_____ **24.** We hope for good health throughout our lives.

▶ **Exercise 3** **Correct the following sentences. Cross out any incorrect words and write the changes above them. Look for subject-verb agreement, pronoun-antecedent agreement, and correct verb tense.**

> works   her
> Susan ~~work~~ for ~~his~~ uncle after school.

1. If the teacher call your name, please respond to them.

2. Us voters will go to the polls on Tuesday to elect our government officials.

3. Golden retrievers makes wonderful family pets. It is easy to train, too.

4. Who are you inviting to your party?

5. Concert choir are my favorite class. You am often asked to sing solos.

6. No one can register for classes without their adviser's signature.

7. Jennifer work at the library. Her is always reading the latest best-seller.

8. The soybean crop have withered in the drought.

9. My most enjoyable vacation were hiking through the Rocky Mountains.

10. Frank Lloyd Wright and I.M. Pei is famous architects. His work is known throughout the world.

11. Eric know a great deal about computer programming, but he won't share its knowledge.

12. Cassie and Jess often visits Hawaii, where she can enjoy his favorite sport, surfing.

13. Gave the extra programs to Kurt and Sean. They will know what to do with it.

14. Certain members refused to pay its monthly dues.

15. When I looks at the artwork done by the seniors, we wonder if we will ever be able to do as well.

Unit 9: Using Modifiers Correctly

Lesson 59

Modifiers: Three Degrees of Comparison

Most adjectives and adverbs have three degrees: the positive, or base, form; the comparative form; and the superlative form.

The positive form of a modifier cannot be used to make a comparison. (This form appears as the entry word in the dictionary.)

The comparative form of a modifier shows two things being compared.

The superlative form of a modifier shows three or more things being compared.

Positive: The brown calf is **heavy.**
                The cat ran **swiftly.**
Comparative: The white calf is **heavier** than the brown calf.
                My dog ran **more swiftly** than the cat.
Superlative: The spotted calf is the **heaviest** calf in the herd.
                I ran **most swiftly** of all.

In general, form the comparative by adding -er and the superlative by adding -est. (In some cases a spelling change is required.)

green	green**er**	green**est**		loud	loud**er**	loud**est**
hot	hot**ter**	hot**test**		true	tru**er**	tru**est**
ugly	ugl**ier**	ugl**iest**		pretty	prett**ier**	prett**iest**

Use *more* and *most* (or *less* and *least* for the opposite) to form the degrees of comparison in the following situations:

1. adverbs that end in -*ly.*

   I see Sesto's point **more clearly** than Gabrielle's.

2. modifiers of three or more syllables.

   I think the green house is the **most attractive** house on the block.

3. whenever adding -*er* and -*est* sounds awkward.

   John was **more afraid** than Carol.

▶ **Exercise 1 Supply the comparative and superlative forms of the following modifiers.**

POSITIVE	COMPARATIVE	SUPERLATIVE
happy	happier	happiest
1. tiny	_____	_____

2. brave _____ _____

3. comfortable _____ _____

4. long _____ _____

5. icy _____ _____

6. heartily _____ _____

7. hearty _____ _____

8. hesitant _____ _____

9. big _____ _____

10. just _____ _____

11. pretty _____ _____

12. loud _____ _____

13. slow _____ _____

14. rapidly _____ _____

15. shiny _____ _____

16. loving _____ _____

17. low _____ _____

18. savory _____ _____

19. wobbly _____ _____

20. scary _____ _____

▶ **Writing Link** Write four sentences using (1) the comparative of *flat;* (2) the superlative of *keen;* (3) the comparative of *swiftly;* and (4) the superlative of *frugal.*

_____

_____

_____

_____

_____

_____

_____

_____

Lesson 60
Modifiers: Irregular Comparisons

A few modifiers form their comparative and superlative degrees irregularly. Memorizing is the most helpful way to master them.

MODIFIERS WITH IRREGULAR FORMS OF COMPARISON

POSITIVE	COMPARATIVE	SUPERLATIVE
good	better	(the) best
well	better	(the) best
bad	worse	(the) worst
badly	worse	(the) worst
far (distance)	farther	(the) farthest
far (degree, time)	further	(the) furthest
little (amount)	less	(the) least
many	more	(the) most
much	more	(the) most

▶ **Exercise 1** **Complete each sentence with the correct form of the modifier in parentheses.**

The exhausted tennis champ played _____the worst_____ match of the tournament. (bad)

1. Yosef's test score was _____ than Harold's. (good)

2. That was _____ day of my entire life. (bad)

3. Carrie was _____ patient than Eduardo. (much)

4. The Flying A was _____ ranch from town. (far)

5. She stammered _____ during her first speech. (badly)

6. *Sand, Shells and Time* was _____ photo in the contest. (good)

7. Anton had delved _____ into psychology than I had suspected. (far)

8. Clara garnered _____ votes of any candidate. (many)

9. The new roof withstood the storm _____ than the shutters. (well)

10. With five children at home, Mary had _____ free time of any member. (little)

11. Isabel was hired instead of Alan because she had _____ qualifications. (many)

12. The adoption of a baby brought Carlos and Anita _____ joy that they had ever known. (much)

13. The woman's condition was _____ than it was yesterday. (bad)

14. The school board's plan for redistricting received _____ enthusiasm than expected. (little)

15. Anna maneuvered her horse _____ of all the teenagers. (well)

16. Jorge batted _____ of all. (badly)

17. Melanie walked _____ and _____ every day. (far)

18. Doctors found that the new strain of the virus was the _____ one yet. (bad)

19. Have you ever heard a _____ speech? (bad)

20. The professor explored each topic to its _____ detail. (far)

21. Was Mickey's rendition _____ than his last one? (good)

22. Last night's storm was _____ in twelve years. (bad)

23. The old man received _____ pleasure from his radio than from his television. (much)

24. Two hundred miles was the _____ she had ever been from home. (far)

25. I bowled _____ than last week. (badly)

26. Jim put forth his _____ effort on his vegetable garden. (good)

27. "There's no sense in discussing this any _____," shouted the young man. (far)

28. Which of the two children collected _____ apples? (many)

29. Carla finished the marathon in _____ time than Sarah or Liza. (well)

30. Many landlords allot _____ money possible for maintenance. (little)

31. Charles was upset when he found there were _____ details left out of the report than were included. (many)

32. Of all the children, Rena showed the _____ concern for the missing puppy. (much)

33. Both men had an ill temper, but John's was _____. (bad)

34. Vegetables grow _____ of all in loose soil with lots of sun. (well)

35. The crops by the creek suffered _____ from the drought than the ones on the hillside. (little)

36. Ruta was embarrassed because she had behaved _____ of all the disappointed children. (badly)

37. The _____ Al carried the peat moss, the heavier it seemed. (far)

38. Holiday shopping seems to bring out the _____ tempers of the year. (bad)

39. A hurricane is _____ than a tropical storm. (bad)

40. The psychiatrist delved into the _____ recesses of the man's mind. (far)

Lesson 61
Modifiers: Double and Incomplete Comparisons

Do not make a **double comparison** by using both *-er* or *-est* and *more (less)* or *most (least)*.

Incorrect:	A redwood grows more taller than an oak.
Correct:	A redwood grows **taller** than an oak.
Incorrect:	Billie is my most closest friend.
Correct:	Billie is my **closest** friend.

Do not make an **incomplete** or **unclear comparison** by omitting *other* or *else* when you compare one member of a group with another.

Unclear:	Mercury is closer to the sun than any planet.
Clear:	Mercury is closer to the sun than any **other** planet.
Unclear:	My aunt has more pets than anyone.
Clear:	My aunt has more pets than anyone **else**.

Be sure your comparisons are between like things.

Unclear:	The head of a gorilla is larger than a chimpanzee. (The head of a gorilla is not larger than a whole chimpanzee.)
Clear:	The head of a gorilla is larger than **that of a chimpanzee.**
Clear:	The head of a gorilla is larger than **a chimpanzee's.**
Unclear:	Maria's hair is darker than Elke.
Clear:	Maria's hair is darker than **that of Elke.**
Clear:	Maria's hair is darker than **Elke's.**

▶ **Exercise 1** **Circle any double or incomplete comparisons. Write *C* in the blank if the sentence is correct.**

_____ Marcia's papers are (more neater) now.

_____ **1.** One of the most scariest rides at an amusement park is the roller coaster.

_____ **2.** Our candidate gave the most clearest answer.

_____ **3.** Leigh liked ice cream better than sherbert.

_____ **4.** Elaine finished the book sooner than anyone.

_____ **5.** Jamaal's schedule was tighter than Fred.

_____ **6.** Lazy students in my class are most likeliest to fail.

_____ **7.** Do you like pork chops better than lamb chops?

_____ **8.** Brett can type more faster than I.

_____ **9.** Seth can swim faster than anyone on the team.

_____ **10.** New York is the most largest of the four cities.

_____ **11.** The patient was feeling more better today.

_____ **12.** Four-cylinder engines get better mileage than eight-cylinder engines.

_____ **13.** A rabbit's ears are longer than a cat.

_____ **14.** A teacher spends the most largest amount of time in preparing lessons and in grading papers.

_____ **15.** The Joneses' house cost less than the Murphys'.

_____ **16.** Minneapolis is colder than any city I've lived in.

_____ **17.** My mom says that I'm the most worst procrastinator in the family.

_____ **18.** Henri likes sirloin better than any other meat.

_____ **19.** Kristen is more happier in her job than most individuals.

_____ **20.** English grammar is less consistent than Italian grammar.

_____ **21.** Janice has more better study habits than Nicole.

_____ **22.** The Irish wolfhound is the most largest dog I've ever seen.

_____ **23.** An eagle's claws are more powerful than a chicken hawk.

_____ **24.** I like the Cleveland Browns better than Los Angeles.

_____ **25.** The new catcher is a better hitter than anyone else on the team.

_____ **26.** This oak chair is more solid than any piece of furniture.

_____ **27.** That is the most tamest horse in the stable.

_____ **28.** More than any insect, ants and bees have an organized society.

_____ **29.** Elephants are larger than any land animals.

_____ **30.** Brian was more hopeful than his friend about being selected for the team.

_____ **31.** The Nile is the most longest river in the world.

_____ **32.** His house was more bigger than ours.

_____ **33.** Because he had many years of experience, Julio's knowledge was broader than that of any other beginner.

_____ **34.** Jenny was the most clumsiest gymnast on the school's team.

_____ **35.** This book is funnier than any book I've ever read.

_____ **36.** Do you think Joe Montana is a better quarterback than any football player?

Grammar

Lesson 62
Using *Good* or *Well; Bad* or *Badly*

Always use *good* as an adjective. *Well* may be used as either an adverb of manner telling how ably something is done or as an adjective meaning "in good health."

The beginning is a **good** place to start. (adjective)
You look **good** in blue. (predicate adjective)
Can you see **well** from your seat? (adverb of manner)
Aren't you feeling **well?** (predicate adjective meaning "in good health")

Always use *bad* as an adjective. Therefore, *bad* is used after a linking verb. Use *badly* as an adverb. *Badly* almost always follows an action verb.

Route 7 has **bad** curves. (adjective)
Harry's hair looks **bad.** (adjective following a linking verb)
I feel **bad** that your candidate lost the election. (adjective following a linking verb)
Carrie sings **badly.** (adverb following an action verb)

▶ **Exercise 1** **Fill each blank with the correct form of** *good, well, bad,* **or** *badly.*

It is a smart idea for a person to have a _____good_____ hobby.

1. The newly formed Riverside Writers Club was off to a _____ start.

2. Margit was elected president because she edited _____.

3. All seventeen members felt _____ about helping each other improve their skills.

4. Consuelo found that reading others' manuscripts helped her to recognize the _____ spots in her own work.

5. Receiving criticism made Sean feel _____ until he realized that such comments really helped him improve.

6. While _____ grammar plagues everyone at times, style development is also a universal concern.

7. So far, every meeting had gone _____.

8. In January, the meeting was cancelled due to a _____ winter storm.

9. Dan missed the March meeting because he was not feeling _____.

10. Knute Petersen (editor of the *Daily News*) presented a _____ overview of local free-lance opportunities.

11. One of the most popular meetings was a talk by a magazine editor discussing _____

    and _____ submissions.

Grammar

12. A writer's submission would be rejected if it did not fit in _____ with the publisher's needs.

13. In April, Robert enthusiastically announced the _____ news that he had received an assignment from *Boys' Life.*

14. He attributed the acceptance to a _____ query letter.

15. Excitement spread through the group because each member _____ coveted this new plateau.

16. As the months passed, each member found ways for _____ fellowship as well as peer help.

17. Hector's humorous stories prompted Sarah to comment, "He writes _____, but I'm

not sure he *is* _____!"

18. The Riverside Writers Club is one of many peer support groups that provide _____ needed encouragement for their members.

19. Neophyte writers generally respond _____ to peer review and encouragement.

20. If you and your friends write, forming a similar group is a _____ investment in time and effort.

▶ Exercise 2 **Circle each incorrect use of *good, well, bad,* or *badly.* Write the correct word on the blank. Write *C* if the sentence is correct.**

_____well_____   Not everyone does (good) at the same thing.

_____ **1.** Some people write bad and have no interest in writing at all.

_____ **2.** A writing club would not serve their needs very good.

_____ **3.** Kermit wanted bad to start a local theater group in his small town.

_____ **4.** He felt this would be a way to gain some good experience in his area of interest.

_____ **5.** Any hope for a successful start looked badly at first, but Kermit was determined.

_____ **6.** Soon everything looked well as more people became interested and

contributed their time and effort to the cause.

_____ **7.** The group was able to find a play that suited their needs good.

_____ **8.** Now was a good time to solicit money from local businesses to subsidize the

first performance.

_____ **9.** Space to rehearse and perform was needed bad.

_____ **10.** This was an exciting time, and it felt as if things would never go bad for the

theater group again.

Lesson 63
Double Negatives

In general, do not use a **double negative** (two negative words in the same clause). Use only one negative word to express a negative idea. Most negative words have positive forms. You can usually use positive forms to correct double negatives.

NEGATIVE	POSITIVE	NEGATIVE	POSITIVE
neither	either	none	any
never	ever	no one	any one
no	any, a	nothing	anything
nobody	anybody	nowhere	anywhere

Incorrect:	We haven't been to no concerts this year.
Correct:	We haven't been to any concerts this year.
Correct:	We've been to no concerts this year.
Incorrect:	Kathy never did nothing to justify expulsion.
Correct:	Kathy never did anything to justify expulsion.
Correct:	Kathy did nothing to justify expulsion.

Grammar

▶ **Exercise 1** **Circle each phrase containing a double negative. Rewrite the phrase correctly in the blank. Write *C* if the sentence is correct.**

would be no *or* wouldn't be any   There (wouldn't be no) opportunity for the entire team to go to camp.

_____ 1. Football camp is really nothing like summer camp.

_____ 2. There aren't no activities that are unrelated to the sport of football.

_____ 3. You don't have no reason to be there unless you truly want to play.

_____ 4. Football camp doesn't leave no opportunity to sleep late.

_____ 5. Nobody ever went to football camp to rest!

_____ 6. After breakfast, which no one ever misses, conditioning activities begin.

_____ 7. Nothing will never protect a player from injury more than conditioning.

_____ 8. There aren't no exercises that the players find easy.

_____ 9. We don't practice nothing but drills to prepare us for the actual game.

_____C_____ **10.** Players can never learn enough about the importance of

commitment.

▶ **Exercise 2** **Circle the two negative words in each double negative. Rewrite the sentence correctly in the blank. Write *C* if the sentence is correct.**

Staying at home all summer (never) is (no) fun. _Staying at home all summer never is any fun.___

1. The first time I went to summer camp, I didn't expect to have no fun. _____

_____

2. When my parents dropped me off, there wasn't no one around that I knew. _____

_____

3. Because I was the last to arrive, I didn't get no choice of bunks. _____

_____

4. I wasn't getting nowhere with making my bunk until my counselor helped me. _____

_____

5. It took a long time to fix the sheets, and I was afraid I wouldn't get no supper. _____

_____

6. In the mess hall, I sat beside Carlos, who hadn't made no friends either. _____

_____

7. I won't never forget Carlos because he became my best friend at camp. _____

_____

8. One day when there wasn't no one around, we tied the counselor's shaving gear to the rafters.

_____

9. Carlos and I promised not to play no tricks on each other. _____

_____

10. I never got bitten by no mosquitoes because I wore plenty of insect repellent._____

_____

11. When we hiked in the woods, we weren't allowed to build no fires. _____

_____

12. We looked for wild animals, but we didn't see nothing but birds and squirrels. _____

_____

Lesson 64
Misplaced and Dangling Modifiers

Place modifiers as close as possible to the words they modify in order to make the meaning of the sentence clear.

Misplaced modifiers modify the wrong word, or they seem to modify more than one word in a sentence. To correct a misplaced modifier, move the modifier as close as possible to the word it modifies.

Misplaced:	**Floating in the wind,** Hannah stared wistfully at the kite.
Clear:	Hannah stared wistfully at the kite **floating in the wind**.
Misplaced:	A **new man's** suit was in the closet.
Clear:	A **man's new** suit was in the closet.

Dangling modifiers seem logically to modify no word at all. To correct a dangling modifier, supply a word the dangling phrase can sensibly modify.

Dangling:	**Working all night long,** sleep was welcome.
Clear:	**Working all night long,** Francis welcomed sleep.
Dangling:	**After a valiant effort** the blaze still raged uncontrollably.
Clear:	**After a valiant effort** the firefighters still faced a blaze that raged uncontrollably.

If the word *only* is not placed immediately before the word or group of words it modifies, the meaning can be unclear.

Unclear:	Dan only has art on Monday.
Clear:	Dan has only art on Monday.
Clear:	Dan has art only on Monday.
Clear:	Only Dan has art on Monday.

▶ **Exercise 1** **Circle each misplaced modifying phrase and draw an arrow to the word it should modify. If the sentence is correct, place a *C* in the blank.**

_____   Ice cream was served to everyone (in a dish).

_____   **1.** Proposing new menus, healthier school lunches would be offered by the new dietitian.

_____   **2.** Standing in the cool shower, the summer heat didn't feel so intense to Danilo.

_____   **3.** Throw Mama from the train a kiss.

_____   **4.** Listening to the scanner, the accident sounded extremely serious to Kent.

_____ 5. Daydreaming quietly, Kai was reflecting on her wonderful excursion to Bermuda.

_____ 6. Climbing down from their seats, the stands seemed to sway slightly as people left.

_____ 7. Every week while doing the yard work, the mower seems to break down for Carl.

_____ 8. Nicole and Isra helped prepare for the prom, working as hard as possible.

_____ 9. Trying not to scratch herself, Lorena was miserable because of the poison ivy.

_____ 10. Two deer were spotted by the hunters licking the block of salt in the pasture.

_____ 11. Thomas developed pictures for the newspaper of the football games.

_____ 12. Climbing into bed, the tornado siren began to blow, scaring the children.

_____ 13. At noon, Karen encountered heavy traffic driving to the bank.

_____ 14. Erin must have found at least ten sources researching her term paper.

_____ 15. A delicious lunch with all the trimmings was served to the staff.

_____ 16. The president waved to the thousands of people riding in his black limousine.

_____ 17. The bears began eating their meal of ants rising from their afternoon naps.

_____ 18. With great energy, the horses entered the race track.

_____ 19. Stumbling over another player's foot, the crowd gasped as the receiver ran on for a touchdown.

_____ 20. Circling overhead, the hawk was searching for its next meal.

▶ **Exercise 2 Circle any misplaced or dangling modifier. If the sentence is correct, place a *C* in the blank.**

_____ (While rafting), the supplies had no chance of staying dry.

_____ 1. Sleeping soundly, the alarm clock startled me with its harsh ringing.

_____ 2. Walking along the beach, a shell cut Harry's foot.

_____ 3. Catching sight of our friends, we waved frantically.

_____ 4. While mowing the yard, the mail carrier's horn announced his presence.

_____ 5. Driving along the freeway, the deer ran into the woods.

_____ 6. Needing a ride to the airport, Mrs. Wiggins called a taxi.

_____ **7.** Because I was shy, I had some difficulty making new friends.

_____ **8.** After standing in line for half an hour, the clerk announced that the store was closed.

_____ **9.** A story was told to the children with a happy ending.

_____ **10.** Working at my desk, the sudden noise was startling.

_____ **11.** Gloating over his victory, Bill bored the other wrestlers with his bragging.

_____ **12.** Running home, my heel came off my shoe.

_____ **13.** Draining the radiator, I replaced the antifreeze.

_____ **14.** Lost in the woods, survival was uppermost in our minds.

_____ **15.** Lying on the couch, my snack fell to the floor.

_____ **16.** Reading intently, her entrance broke my concentration.

_____ **17.** Savoring each moment, Eileen and Tracy watched the sunset.

_____ **18.** A holiday was given to the employees with pay.

_____ **19.** Walking in the woods, a squirrel darted across Tanya's path, startling her.

_____ **20.** After smiling at his girlfriend, Achim's solo went very well.

_____ **21.** As a successful attorney, Andrea was widely sought.

_____ **22.** Tired and hungry, a meal and a bed sounded good to me.

▶ **Exercise 3** **Insert a caret (^) to show where the word *only* should be placed to match the meaning in parentheses.**

I watch cartoons on Saturday mornings. (I do nothing else on Saturday mornings.)

1. The green truck was speeding down the gravel road. (There was no other green truck.)

2. The green truck was speeding down the gravel road. (No more than one truck was speeding.)

3. The green truck was speeding down the gravel road. (There was no other gravel road.)

4. Potatoes are the main product of Idaho. (No other state has potatoes as a main product.)

5. Potatoes are the main product of Idaho. (There is no other major product from Idaho.)

6. Kerry played soccer while attending Northridge High. (Kerry participated in no other sport.)

7. Kerry played soccer while attending Northridge High. (Kerry did nothing else but play soccer while in high school.)

8. Jeanne liked to drive her convertible. (No one enjoyed driving the convertible except Jeanne.)

Grammar

9. Jeanne liked to drive her convertible. (Jeanne didn't like driving if the car was not her convertible.)

10. Esther got three books from the library. (No one got the same number of books as Esther.)

11. Esther got three books from the library. (Esther got no more than three books.)

12. Rover was Adam's pride and joy. (Rover was the one thing in which Adam took delight.)

13. Rover was Adam's pride and joy. (The other members of the family didn't care as much for Rover as Adam did.)

14. Airplanes are Linda's favorite mode of transportation for long trips. (Linda will make long trips on nothing but an airplane.)

15. Airplanes are Linda's favorite mode of transportation for long trips. (When the trip is short, Linda prefers some other form of travel.)

16. I bought Dad a screwdriver set for Christmas. (No one else got Dad a screwdriver set.)

17. I bought Dad a screwdriver set for Christmas. (I bought screwdrivers for no one but Dad.)

18. I bought Dad a screwdriver set for Christmas. (I bought one thing for Dad.)

▶ **Writing Link** **Write a paragraph about a family outing. Correctly use 2 or 3 modifying phrases and circle them. Use the word** *only* **at least once.**

_____

_____

_____

_____

_____

_____

_____

_____

_____

_____

_____

_____

_____

_____

☑ Unit 9 Review

▶ **Exercise 1** **Supply the comparative and superlative forms of the following modifiers.**

POSITIVE	COMPARATIVE	SUPERLATIVE
1. interested	_____	_____
2. true	_____	_____
3. luxurious	_____	_____
4. quick	_____	_____
5. nice	_____	_____
6. speedily	_____	_____
7. hardy	_____	_____
8. charismatic	_____	_____
9. happy	_____	_____
10. righteous	_____	_____
11. noble	_____	_____
12. clumsy	_____	_____
13. little (amount)	_____	_____
14. rapidly	_____	_____
15. grimy	_____	_____
16. caring	_____	_____
17. able	_____	_____
18. savory	_____	_____
19. calm	_____	_____
20. worrisome	_____	_____

Cumulative Review: Units 1–9

▶ **Exercise 1** **Draw two lines under the simple predicate in each sentence. Label any direct object** *d.o.* **and any indirect object** *i.o.*

                    i.o.   d.o.
Ms. Chung <u>gave</u> her students some good advice.

1. Dylan returned his library books last night.

2. Our advisor suggested the community project to the class.

3. Father will buy me a car for my sixteenth birthday.

4. Did Keshia shovel the snow from the driveway?

5. She gave the weary mail carrier a glass of water.

6. Mr. Hayashi handed the flight attendant his ticket.

7. Our house needs a new coat of paint.

8. Mai left the amiable waiter a large tip.

9. The chef promised me his recipe for moo goo gai pan.

10. Mr. Lichtenberg gave the football players a pep talk.

11. Toto's makes the best pizza in town.

12. On your vacation will you send us a postcard?

13. The scientist remembered the correct equation.

14. This year Westland High relinquished the state title.

15. The symphonic choir sang five songs at the concert.

16. Tiffany wrote her grandmother a long letter.

17. Please save me a piece of the cake.

18. The babysitter read the children a bedtime story.

19. The editor can give the writer suggestions on following the textbook guidelines.

20. The loud, screeching noise startled Tony.

Grammar

▶ **Exercise 2** **Underline the simple subject. Identify the verbal or verbal phrase in each sentence by drawing a circle around it. In the blank, write whether the verbal or verbal phrase is a gerund, a participle, or an infinitive.**

_____infinitive_____ The merry <u>carolers</u> tried (to sing together.)

_____ 1. Reading biographies is one of Kevin's favorite pastimes.

_____ 2. The heavy snowfall buried the abandoned truck.

_____ 3. A man carrying a dozen red roses walked into Miss Carter's classroom.

_____ 4. Many stuntmen were used in making this movie.

_____ 5. Li Cheng forgot to register for the computer class.

_____ 6. They hiked along the trail, over decaying logs and snarled underbrush.

_____ 7. Kim made extra money by tutoring students in math.

_____ 8. Skiing is a great winter sport.

_____ 9. It takes courage to admit our mistakes.

_____ 10. Aisha tried to wait patiently for the phone call.

_____ 11. The best place for running is the Olentangy bike trail.

_____ 12. Making costumes for the school play is a big job.

_____ 13. We achieved a victory by scoring a basket in the last minute.

_____ 14. The tuxedo was too expensive to buy.

_____ 15. Peg woke to the aroma of frying bacon.

_____ 16. Speaking before a large group isn't easy for many people.

_____ 17. My mother insisted on returning the damaged goods.

_____ 18. The homeless man discovered the deserted building.

_____ 19. The dream of the Wright brothers was to build the first successful airplane.

_____ 20. The raging wind knocked down power lines and tree limbs.

▶ **Exercise 3** **Underline the correct word given in parentheses. Draw an arrow to the word it modifies.**

Our school orchestra always performs (good, <u>well</u>).

1. The poison ivy itched (bad, badly) for at least a week.

2. What is the (taller, tallest) building in the country?

3. As the winter storm raged on, the city streets became (more icier, icier).

4. The freshly baked bread smells (good, well).

5. Randy has (many, more) baseball cards than anyone else.

6. Much to the doctor's dismay, the small child grew (worse, ill) each day.

7. The test that Mr. Rivera gave was the (most simplest, simplest) of all.

8. Mrs. Greiner cried because she felt (bad, badly) about the loss of her pet.

9. Jason has (the least, less) sales experience than Ben.

10. Wyoming is (more farther, farther) from here than Indiana is.

11. Sukey reads very (good, well) for her age.

12. We couldn't find (any, no) birdseed at the hardware store.

13. Calculus is a (more difficult, difficulter) mathematics than algebra.

14. Of the three boys, Michael is the (cuter, cutest).

15. Jeff wanted (badly, bad) to add that stamp to his collection.

16. Veronica's (badly, bad) attitude was the source of much of her discontent.

17. Our student teacher wore the (most ugliest, ugliest) dress yesterday!

18. Her father bought the (more expensive, most expensive) car on the lot.

19. Who scored (the most, more) goals during the game, Colin or Jess?

20. Of the two sisters, Carla is (the least, less) popular.

*U*sage

Unit 10: Usage Glossary

Lesson 65
Usage: *a* to *altogether*

Words that are similar are sometimes misused.

a, an Use *a* in front of words that begin with a consonant or "yew" sound. Use *an* in front of words that begin with any other vowel sound.

a house, **a** university; **an** animal, **an** honor.

a lot, alot *A lot* should always be two words or avoided completely.

There are **a lot** of new computer products on the market.

a while, awhile *A while* is made up of an article and a noun. *Awhile* is an adverb.

Let's think for **a while,** then we'll continue **awhile** with the lesson.

accept, except *Accept* is a verb meaning "to receive" or "to agree to." *Except* can be a verb, though it is often used as a preposition meaning "but."

I **accept** your explanation that footballs fly straight, **except** in high winds.

affect, effect *Affect* is a verb meaning "to influence." *Effect* can be a noun meaning "result" or a verb meaning "to accomplish."

Artificial lighting can **affect** the nutritional cycle of plants. (verb)
Artificial lighting can have an undesirable **effect** on plants. (noun)
Exposure to both daylight and darkness **effects** good health in plants. (verb)

ain't *Ain't* is unacceptable in speaking and writing unless used as a direct quote.

▶ **Exercise 1 Underline the correct term in each sentence.**

Their kitchen has (alot, <u>a lot</u>) of modern conveniences.

1. Do not use the emergency exits, (accept, except) in case of fire.

2. Blue-screen matting is a common special (effect, affect) in television and movies.

3. Mr. Chen will be coming back to his office in (a while, awhile), if you'd like to wait.

4. The track coach will not (accept, except) applications submitted after the first of the year.

5. Matthew was studying the cause and (affect, effect) of historical events.

6. We waited at the restaurant (a while, awhile) before going out into the cold.

7. Jules was working on (an, a) history paper when I called.

8. Does committing too many fouls (effect, affect) the score?

9. It (is not, ain't) incorrect to omit the leading zero on some decimal numbers.

10. It should take less than (an, a) hour to complete this test.

---

all·ready, already *All ready* means "completely ready." *Already* means "by this time."

Matthew was **all ready** to perform his gymnastics routine.
Janice was **already** capable of reading college-level textbooks.

all right, alright This should always be two words.

Any flavor of ice cream is **all right** with me!

all the farther, all the faster These are unacceptable in writing. Use *as far as* and *as fast as* instead.

Walk **as far as** you want and **as fast as** you can to build stamina.

all together, altogether *All together* means "in a group." *Altogether* means "completely."

We were **all together** for the last time at our class picnic.
Our class picnic was an **altogether** wonderful experience for everyone.

▶ **Exercise 2 Correct the word in italics. If the word is correct, write *C*.**

_____all right_____ Changing the drama club meeting to Thursday was *alright* with the
members.

_____ **1.** I was *all together* astonished at the outcome of the story.

_____ **2.** The fire had *already* raged out of control when the emergency vehicles arrived.

_____ **3.** The architect was *already* to present his design to the construction company.

_____ **4.** Is it *alright* to wear a striped necktie with a plaid shirt?

_____ **5.** The ice hockey player skated *as fast as* he could to get by the left wing.

_____ **6.** Cole had *all ready* toasted the bagels by the time his parents woke up.

_____ **7.** Hasan asked if it was *all right* to use a calculator during the exam.

_____ **8.** The band members asked, "May we go *altogether* on the same bus?"

_____ **9.** To the lake and back was *all the farther* we had to go.

_____ **10.** Will traveling by car be *alright* with Curtis?

Lesson 66
Usage: *amount* to *could of*

---

amount, **number**   Use *amount* when referring to nouns that cannot be counted. Use *number* when referring to nouns that can be counted.

The Appalachian Mountains have a vast **amount** of fog.
We have a small **number** of dictionaries in the branch library.

bad, **badly**   *Bad* is an adjective. *Badly* is an adverb.

This cold weather has been **bad** for the farmers.   The crops were **badly** damaged.

being as, **being that**   These expressions should not be used in writing. Replace them with *because* or *since*.

beside, **besides**   *Beside* means "at the side of." *Besides* means "in addition to."

My dog likes to curl up **beside** me.   There are other things in life **besides** television.

between, **among**   Use *between* to compare one person or thing with another. Use *among* to show a relationship in which more than two persons or things are considered as a group.

The sculptor had to choose **between** marble and granite.
The trees in Oregon are **among** the tallest in the Pacific Northwest.

Usage

▶ **Exercise 1** **Underline the correct word in each sentence.**

There is a large (amount, number) of fat on this steak.

1. Earth's atmosphere lies (between, among) the surface of the planet and the edge of outer space.

2. The air we breathe contains only a small (amount, number) of oxygen.

3. The atmosphere consists of different elements and layers, some portions of which have been (bad, badly) polluted.

4. (Besides, Beside) human-made pollutants, gases, steam, and ash from volcanoes contribute to air pollution.

5. A large (amount, number) of clouds reside in the lowest part of the atmosphere, the troposphere.

6. (Beside, Besides), scientists can predict weather by studying the troposphere.

7. Clouds play an important role in the earth's weather (because, being that) they contain water.

8. The water that clouds bring as rain or snow is (bad, badly) needed to sustain life.

9. Stratocumulus clouds are one of the largest types of clouds, and they contain a small (amount, number) of light and dark areas.

10. There are other by-products of clouds (beside, besides) rain; electrified regions within the cloud discharge, creating lightning.

---

borrow, lend, loan *Borrow* is a verb meaning "to take something for a limited time." *Lend* means "to give for temporary use." *Loan* is a noun.

May I borrow your pen?   **Please lend me your pen.**   **We got a loan from the bank.**

bring, take *Bring* means "to carry from a distant place to a closer one." *Take* means "to carry from a nearby place to a more distant one."

Bring your books to me.   **Take a jacket to the game tonight.**

can, may Use *can* to indicate the ability to do something. Use *may* to indicate permission to do something.

I can finish reading before dinner.   **May I finish reading after dinner?**

can't hardly, can't scarcely These expressions are double negatives. Avoid using them.

I can hardly wait for vacation.   **The driver can scarcely see through the snow.**

could of, might of, must of, should of, would of The preposition *of* is incorrect here; use the helping verb *have* instead.

The loud noise might have startled the dog.

► **Exercise 2 Correct the word in italics. If the word is correct, write C.**

___borrow___   Chris would like to *loan* that book from Tina.

_____ **1.** People *can't hardly* walk when sidewalks are covered with ice.

_____ **2.** Hot air *may* mix with cold air to cause powerful currents.

_____ **3.** Blizzards *take* with them a lot of snow, wind, and low temperatures.

_____ **4.** You *can't scarcely* imagine the total destruction a tornado can cause.

_____ **5.** Winter weather *brings* winter storms such as ice storms and blizzards.

_____ **6.** The tornado that hit Illinois in 1925 *must of* been the worst in history.

_____ **7.** There was no way this killer storm *could of* been prevented.

_____ **8.** One *may* never be safe from a tornado in a mobile home.

_____ **9.** Another type of violent storm is a hurricane, which *can* be tracked with satellites, airplanes, and radar.

_____ **10.** Before such a storm is due to hit, people *loan* each other tools and materials to board up their houses.

Lesson 67
Usage: *different from* to *regardless*

---

different from, **different than** The expression *different from* is preferred.

Although there are similarities, a clarinet is **different from** a soprano saxophone.

doesn't, **don't** *Doesn't* is used with *he, she, it* and all singular nouns. *Don't* is used with *I, you, we, they,* and all plural nouns.

She **doesn't** like cold weather.   We **don't** have a hockey team.

emigrate, **immigrate** *Emigrate* means "to go from one country to another to live."
Immigrate means "to come to a country to live."

The entire family plans to **emigrate** from Russia next year.
Most people who **immigrate** to the United States live in coastal states.

farther, **further** Use *farther* to refer to physical distance. Use *further* to refer to degree or time.

We traveled **farther** today than we did yesterday.
We will discuss this topic **further** at our next meeting.

fewer, **less** Use *fewer* to refer to nouns that can be counted. Use *less* to refer to nouns that cannot be counted.

There are **fewer** students enrolled in the city's elementary schools this year.
It takes **less** time to travel one mile in a car than on a bicycle.

▶ **Exercise 1 Underline the correct word in each sentence.**

(<u>Fewer</u>, Less) than twenty people attended the student council meeting.

1. Cleveland is (farther, further) from Columbus than is Cincinnati.

2. José (doesn't, don't) want to go to the rock concert.

3. Two families recently (immigrated, emigrated) to the United States.

4. In the 1980s, (less, fewer) Vietnamese settled in the United States than in the previous decade.

5. Ahmed (doesn't, don't) think Arizona will be any hotter than Saudi Arabia.

6. Denise and Colin (doesn't, don't) share the same opinion about the movie.

7. Los Angeles is very (different from, different than) New York.

8. The tired child could not walk any (farther, further).

9. A black hole is (different from, different than) other stars because it can't be seen.

10. I have (fewer, less) than five puppies left from the litter.

Usage

good, **well** *Good* is an adjective. *Well* is an adverb.

It was a **good** book.
The team played **well**.

had of *Of* should not be used between *had* and a past participle.

I thought I **had read** this book before.

hanged, **hung** Use *hanged* when referring to death by hanging. Use *hung* in all other instances.

In the Old West, they **hanged** people for stealing a horse.
The librarian **hung** the sign on the door.

in, **into** Use *in* to mean "inside." Use *into* to indicate movement from outside to a point within.

Meet me **in** the cafeteria.
I'm going **into** the cafeteria.

irregardless, **regardless** *Irregardless* is a double negative and should not be used. *Regardless* is the only correct usage.

The mouse tried to run across the room, **regardless** of the cat.

▶ **Exercise 2** **Correct the word in italics. If the word is correct, write C.**

_____well_____ Helena plays the guitar very *good*.

_____ 1. Our school will continue its community service projects *irregardless* of funding.

_____ 2. When my father had an aching back, he climbed *in* the bathtub very carefully.

_____ 3. Many animal species face extinction *in* the wild.

_____ 4. Tanya likes to dress *well* when she goes on a date.

_____ 5. The school drama club *hung* posters around town to advertise the school play.

_____ 6. Subway systems must be ventilated *good*.

_____ 7. The history teacher believed he *had of* explained the assignment thoroughly.

_____ 8. My guidance counselor said that *irregardless* of my grades, I should take geometry next year.

_____ 9. The mob *hung* the outlaw from a large oak tree.

_____ 10. We put our cans, bottles, and newspapers *in* the recycling bin.

Lesson 68
Usage: *this kind* to *reason is because*

---

this kind, **these kinds** Use *this* and *that* with singular words. Use *these* and *those* with plural words.

This kind of metal won't rust.　　　**These kinds** of paints are lead-free.

lay, **lie** *Lay* means "to put" or "to place." *Lie* means "to recline" or "to be positioned."

Lay your cards on the table.　　　My dog likes to **lie** in the sunshine.

learn, **teach** *Learn* means "to receive knowledge." *Teach* means "to give knowledge."

You can't **teach** an old dog new tricks unless it's willing to **learn**.

leave, **let** *Leave* means "to go away." *Let* means "to permit."

You may **leave** when you finish the test.
Don't **let** the grease settle in the pan.

like, **as** *Like* is a preposition and introduces a prepositional phrase. *As* is often a subordinating conjunction and introduces a subordinate clause.

This roller coaster feels **like** a jet!　　　We won the game **as** the final buzzer sounded.

loose, **lose** *Loose* means "free" or "not fitting tightly." *Lose* means "to have no longer" or "to fail to win."

These new shoes are too **loose**.　　　Don't **lose** your ticket.

▶ **Exercise 1 Underline the correct word in each sentence.**

(This kind, these kinds) of muffin is Crystal's favorite.

1. Our class (learns, teaches) that the animal kingdom has a well-defined social order.

2. Many animal parents (teach, learn) hunting and survival skills to their young.

3. Coyote cubs can make noises that sound (like, as) human babies crying.

4. Predatory birds won't (leave, let) their young move out of the nest until the babies have been

   prepared for life.

5. Like humans, animals quickly (learn, teach) to recognize their limitations.

6. Animals build their lives around (these kinds, this kind) of limitations because they cannot alter

   their environments.

7. A tiger may (lay, lie) its catch in a protected spot.

8. A tiger senses it should (lay, lie) in the shade of a tree on a hot day.

9. To thrive within their environments, animals have tools and instincts they cannot (loose, lose).

10. Owls have sharp eyes and strong talons to locate and capture small animals (as, like) field mice.

---

passed, past *Passed* is the past form and the past participle of the verb *to pass*. *Past* may be an adjective, a preposition, an adverb, or a noun.

We **passed** this building an hour ago!   Have you eaten any pizza this **past** week?
We drove **past** this building an hour ago!

precede and proceed *Precede* means "to go or come before." *Proceed* means "to continue" or "to move along."

Which selection will **precede** Beethoven's *Pastoral Symphony* in tonight's program?
You may **proceed** with your presentation.

raise, rise *Raise* means "to cause to move upward." *Rise* means "to go up."

Raise the flag at 7:30 A.M. sharp.
Does the sun **rise** over the eastern or western horizon?

reason is because This expression is redundant and should not be used.
The **reason** he left early is **that** he came down with a fever.
He left early **because** he came down with a fever.

▶ **Exercise 2** **Correct the word in italics. If the word is correct, write *C*.**

_____raise_____   Please do not *rise* the blind.

_____   **1.** Yesterday, Tabitha *past* a wildlife reserve while riding her bicycle.

_____   **2.** She wants to *rise* awareness of the importance of these reserves.

_____   **3.** The *reason is because* wildlife contributes much beauty, scientific value, survival value, and economic value.

_____   **4.** Scientists must *precede* with their studies of wildlife.

_____   **5.** The *reason is that* they gain valuable medical knowledge through such research.

_____   **6.** Certain animals need protection so they can *raise* every morning.

_____   **7.** The American bald eagle is the national bird of the United States and an important part of our country's *past*.

_____   **8.** Observation and study must *proceed* any action taken to remedy the wildlife situation.

_____   **9.** This *raises* the question, "Which animals, where, how, and to what extent should hunters be permitted to hunt?"

_____   **10.** In 1973 the government *past* the Endangered Species Act.

Lesson 69
Usage: *respectfully* to *where at*

---

respectfully, respectively *Respectfully* means "with respect." *Respectively* means "in the order named."

Tim **respectfully** handed the ball back to the referee.
Blue and magenta are primary and secondary colors, **respectively**.

says, said *Says* is the third-person singular of the verb *say*. *Said* is the past tense of *say*.

He always **says** he'll call.   He **said** he would call back tomorrow.

sit, set *Sit* means "to place oneself in a sitting position." *Set* means "to place" or "to put."

You may **sit** at this table.   Please **set** the table with napkins.

than, then *Than* is a conjunction. *Then* is an adverb.

Cats are more agile **than** dogs.   Layna was a young girl **then**.

this here, that there *Here* and *there* shouldn't be used after *this* and *that*. *This* and *that* should be used alone.

We like **this** song.   I don't like **that** color.

where at *At* is a preposition and should not be used after *where*.

Where is city hall?

▶ **Exercise 1 Underline the correct word in each sentence.**

After shopping, I need to (<u>sit</u>, set) for a while.

1. Thirty years ago, cars were about 25% heavier (than, then) they are today.

2. I don't know (where, where at) the new stadium is going to be built.

3. My aunt moved into (that, that there) building ten years ago.

4. Maya (respectfully, respectively) submitted her paper to her English teacher.

5. Yesterday Tim (says, said) to me that he wants to learn how to snow ski.

6. Don't (sit, set) too many boxes on the table.

7. (Where at, Where) is the lunchroom?

8. To get to the lunchroom, go through (that there, that) door and turn to your right.

9. Dan and Alta baked brownies and apple pie (respectively, respectfully) for the cast party.

10. If you need more light, (sit, set) next to the window.

▶ **Exercise 2** **Correct the word in italics. If the word is correct, write C.**

___respectively___ The band and the orchestra will play the first and second selections listed in the program, *respectfully.*

_____ 1. *Sit* that heavy package on the chair by the window.

_____ 2. Do you know *where* my school jacket is *at?*

_____ 3. George Foreman lost to Muhammad Ali in 1974; *then* twenty years later he beat Michael Moorer to regain the heavyweight championship.

_____ 4. Please take *this here* floppy disk to the computer lab.

_____ 5. *Where* is the reference section of the library *at?*

_____ 6. Let's *set* near home plate so we can watch the pitcher.

_____ 7. Our art class and our science class took tours of the art museum and underground caves, *respectively.*

_____ 8. *That there* horse is the most beautiful stallion I've ever seen.

_____ 9. A blue whale is much bigger *then* an elephant.

_____ 10. José wanted to visit the Alamo *where* Davy Crockett fought *at.*

▶ **Writing Link** **Write four sentences about your favorite season using four rules from this lesson.**

_____

_____

_____

_____

_____

_____

_____

_____

_____

_____

_____

_____

☑ Unit 10 **Review**

▶ **Exercise 1** **Underline the correct word in each sentence.**

The car had every special feature (accept, <u>except</u>) a sunroof.

1. The city library (loans, lends) books that our school library doesn't have.

2. A baboon is (different from, different than) a gorilla.

3. Rayna dragged her heavy suitcase (awhile, a while) before she stopped to rest.

4. The class enjoyed the fair because the event offered (alot, a lot) of rides, games, and exhibits.

5. I must try to (lie, lay) my keys in the same place every day.

6. Benedict Arnold's treachery did not (effect, affect) the outcome of the Revolutionary War.

7. The nonfiction of Isaac Asimov is very popular (between, among) young people.

8. Henry Ford (farther, further) improved assembly line methods to cut the cost of producing cars.

9. The elephants at the circus performed remarkably (good, well).

10. The Thanksgiving Day parade (past, passed) my uncle's apartment in New York City.

11. Nina had a (lose, loose) tooth from her fall, so she went to the dentist after school.

12. Swimming is better exercise (than, then) jogging because it doesn't hurt the knees.

13. Mark's mother asked, "Did you (bring, take) your permission slip home so I can sign it?"

14. The snowstorm in Chicago (must of, must have) caused the delays at the airport.

15. "Mr. Stewart, (can, may) I leave the room to go to speech therapy now?"

16. (Irregardless, Regardless) of the cool water, Kaveetha went swimming in the ocean.

17. Tia threw the ball (into, in) the basket to win the game for her team.

18. We (preceded, proceeded) with the lesson even though the workbooks had not yet arrived.

19. The florist (sat, set) the plant on the windowsill to absorb more sun.

20. Will your parents (leave, let) you go to the movie with me Friday night?

21. Mrs. Chang (hanged, hung) a colorful mobile over her baby's crib.

22. The choir sold bakery goods to (raise, rise) money for the field trip.

23. The cooperation (between, among) the teachers and the staff has contributed to the success of the school.

24. Recycling has (all ready, already) helped the cleanliness of the environment.

Cumulative Review: Units 1–10

▶ **Exercise 1** **Underline the pronoun in parentheses that correctly completes each sentence. Then write the type of sentence in the blank:** *simple, compound, complex,* **or** *compound-complex.*

_____complex_____ Though Gustav prepared for the worst, (she, <u>he</u>) hoped for the best.

_____ 1. Kenny is waiting for (his, their) father to give him directions.

_____ 2. Although Sonya hopes to win the scholarship, (she, he) is saving money for college.

_____ 3. The Woo family invited us to dinner, and (we, they) returned the compliment by taking them to a movie.

_____ 4. George and Rafi will perform (his, their) act at the talent show.

_____ 5. Zina liked the acrobats, but (her, his) little sister preferred the clowns.

_____ 6. A star displayed (their, its) brilliance in the night sky.

_____ 7. Isra's uncle, (who, whom) often entertains, makes a special punch with cranberry juice and sparkling water.

_____ 8. Chet (himself, itself) painted the new mural.

_____ 9. Mikasi and Poloma brought their golf clubs, even though (she, they) do not expect to have time to play more than nine holes.

_____ 10. After Grandmother went back to school, (she, they) became a reporter, and we started watching her on the news.

_____ 11. Hugh was not excited about watching the videotape of an erupting volcano because (he, it) has seen one in person.

_____ 12. Keith's older brother taught (them, him) how to guide a horse.

_____ 13. Basir's family is preparing food for (them, their) Kwanza celebration.

_____ 14. Before Marcia mails the letter, ask (her, him) to see me.

_____ 15. The person to (who, whom) Jenny wishes to speak is on vacation.

_____ 16. The setting sun cast (its, their) last rays over the horizon.

_____ 17. Ms. Ortiz planted that beautiful garden (himself, herself), yet she rarely visits it.

_____ 18. The toddler loved his well-worn coat, though (he, it) was missing two buttons.

_____ **19.** Since Mr. Conti is selling (him, his) computer, he might be selling

some of his software, too.

_____ **20.** Marcus, (who, whom) collects comic books, will send some books to

the local children's hospital.

▶ **Exercise 2 Complete each sentence by choosing the correct modifier in parentheses.**

Julian is a _____better_____ tennis player than Brad. (better, best)

1. Wilson performed _____ at the piano recital. (good, well)

2. The sun shone _____ yesterday than today. (more brightly, most brightly)

3. That was the _____ television program Nick had ever seen. (worse, worst)

4. The Spanish club had _____ refreshments at the March meeting than at the February meeting. (fewer, fewest)

5. The special effects in this movie are the _____ I have seen. (greater, greatest)

6. Katherine felt _____ because she missed her mother's birthday. (bad, badly)

7. Tony makes the _____ minestrone soup I have ever tasted. (better, best)

8. The _____ part of the entire journey occurred when Regina found the buried treasure. (more exciting, most exciting)

9. The hiking trail was _____ than the tourists expected. (more challenging, most challenging)

10. Blake selected the role with the _____ lines to learn. (few, fewest)

11. Roberto's lemon cake was _____, but his apple pie was extraordinary. (good, well)

12. Ms. Rollins felt _____ today than she did yesterday. (worse, worst)

13. This morning's balloon flight was _____ than yesterday's. (more interesting, most interesting)

14. Luigi insisted that galloping his horse through the forest was the _____ experience imaginable. (more exhilarating, most exhilarating)

15. Some critics believe the musical score was composed _____, but Dante credits the composer with inventiveness. (bad, badly)

16. Because of the misunderstanding, Julia found herself _____ informed about the current situation. (less, least)

17. Tanya and Clarice appeared _____ to volunteer their time than the other members of the club. (more willing, most willing)

18. The *Silver Arrow* is considered the _____ train in this area. (faster, fastest)

19. My father is the _____ person I know. (wiser, wisest)

20. Bonnie has been accepted into the advanced karate class even though she is _____ than the other students. (younger, youngest)

▶ **Exercise 3** **Underline the word in parentheses that correctly completes each sentence.**

The weather might (<u>affect</u>, effect) the team's chances of winning.

1. Patrick asked his sister if she was feeling (alright, all right).

2. Everyone wanted to go ice skating (accept, except) Kirsten.

3. Mr. Harper (could of, could have) given the twins a ride to the amusement park.

4. Ronda left her term paper (between, among) her notebook and her history book.

5. (Irregardless, Regardless) of the newspaper's account of the parade, ten bands marched in all.

6. My friend (emigrated, immigrated) from Italy when he was five years old.

7. The color guard will (precede, proceed) the first regiment.

8. (Lay, Lie) the basket on the shelf next to the other one.

9. First Frederica will show us the dance steps. (Than, Then) we will try them ourselves.

10. The players (respectfully, respectively) placed their hands over their hearts during the national anthem.

11. Ryan and Luisa have (already, all ready) finished their science fair project.

12. Each guest will (bring, take) one dish to the potluck dinner.

13. Dr. Carly will sit (beside, besides) Aunt Rose, and Justin will sit next to Anna.

14. The catcher (don't, doesn't) like to chase foul balls.

15. Roosevelt High School is (farther, further) from our school than Polk High School.

16. Rick (passed, past) all the necessary tests to become a lifeguard.

17. This week our cooking class will (learn, teach) how to make a soufflé.

18. Please do not (loose, lose) the concert tickets before we reach the theater.

19. The medal-winning gymnast glided through her routine (like, as) a gazelle.

20. The show choir will (raise, rise) their voices when the music indicates a crescendo.

21. (This here, This) program radiates wit and charm.

22. Grandmother used her finest china to (set, sit) the table for Thanksgiving dinner.

23. The new job had a definite (affect, effect) on Priscilla's family.

24. Delia's mother (hanged, hung) new draperies in the living room.

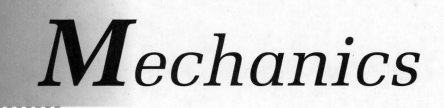

Mechanics

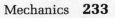

Unit 11: Capitalization

Lesson 70
Capitalization of Sentences

Capitalize the first word of every sentence, including the first word of a direct quotation that is a complete sentence.

The new barn was built to stable fifteen horses.
Kerry smiled and said, "You are the best coach in the whole school."

Capitalize the first word of a sentence in parentheses that stands by itself. Do not capitalize a sentence within parentheses if it is contained within another sentence.

Participation in soccer is growing rapidly. (Some think the growth is too slow.)
Enrico asked for an instrument (his first choice was a tenor saxophone) for his birthday.

Do not capitalize the first word of a quotation that cannot stand as a complete sentence.

The review praised the students as "caring young citizens."

Do not capitalize an indirect quotation. An indirect quotation gives the meaning of an original statement without repeating it word for word. It is often introduced by the word *that.*

The brochure said that brown bears are plentiful in the park.

▶ **Exercise 1** Draw three lines under each letter that should be capitalized. If a sentence is correct, write *C* in the blank to the left of the sentence.

_____   I looked everywhere for the book. (my dad wanted to borrow it.)

_____   **1.** the striking colors of autumn leaves are admired by nearly everyone.

_____   **2.** They come in varying shades of red, orange, and yellow. (when the sun shines on yellow leaves, they look bright gold!)

_____   **3.** those who must dispose of the fallen leaves (especially sanitation workers) seldom share the enthusiasm of mere observers.

_____   **4.** Nature's autumn array serves as a reminder that a large, recurring problem has once more arrived.

_____   **5.** Burning leaves creates a pollution problem. (all the smoke and particles fill the air.)

_____   **6.** Burning leaves is also a fire hazard. (it must be done in a well-controlled environment and watched at all times.)

Mechanics

_____ 7. Some municipalities (for these reasons) have banned the burning of leaves.

_____ 8. local governments have devised several methods of handling this annual problem.

_____ 9. mulching (chopping leaves into fine pieces) greatly reduces the volume of trash.

_____ 10. some cities require mulching before pick-up by the sanitation department.

_____ 11. One way to accomplish mulching is to use a lawn mower with a special mulching blade.

_____ 12. A local newspaper states, "mulchers save our city thousands of dollars each year."

_____ 13. trash collection costs are lowered because of the tons of leaves that do not require disposal.

_____ 14. mobile mulchers (lawn mowers) provide direct benefits, besides saving time and labor.

_____ 15. Through the process of decomposition (leaf mulch decomposes quickly), the soil becomes well fertilized.

_____ 16. A magazine article states that mulching "provides long-lasting benefits to the soil."

_____ 17. An encyclopedia (referring to mulching) explains, "it helps the soil retain water by reducing evaporation." (the encyclopedia also states that mulching helps reduce the number of weeds.)

_____ 18. the leaves are also excellent (along with coffee grounds and grass clippings) to use for compost.

_____ 19. compost makes soil more fertile to improve plant production.

_____ 20. It is best to allow compost to decay (about three to six months) before using it.

_____ 21. Karen (an avid gardener) says that she does not break up the leaves before composting.

_____ 22. Instead, she spreads the leaves over her garden for the winter. (she later tills them into the soil in the spring.)

_____ 23. She also states, "leaves make a good mulch for roses."

_____ 24. Leaf mulch also provides food for earthworms (which contribute to the growth of plants).

_____ 25. a nature magazine states that earthworms improve the soil by keeping it loose and aerated.

_____ 26. by reducing the strain on landfills and recycling the debris, everyone benefits.

_____ 27. returning the leaves to the soil changes a liability to an asset.

_____ 28. most people still use a rake (usually metal or bamboo) to rake their leaves.

_____ 29. leaf blowers, however, have become popular replacements for lawn rakes.

_____ 30. Leaf blowers can be either gas or electric (see your local hardware store).

Mechanics

Lesson 71
Capitalization of Proper Nouns

Capitalize names of individuals. Capitalize titles used before a name or in place of it. Capitalize titles that specify family relationships when they are used with a person's name or in place of it.

Vincent van **G**ogh	**C**atherine the **G**reat	**P**ope **P**ius XII
Governor **R**ichards	How do you do, **G**overnor?	Have you seen the **g**overnor?
This is **A**unt Jane.	Where is **D**ad?	This is my **a**unt.

Also capitalize these names, terms, and titles: ethnic and national groups, languages, religious terms; organizations, institutions, political parties and their members (but not the word *party*), firms; monuments, buildings, bridges, and other structures; trade names; documents, awards, laws; geographical and calendar terms, historical events and periods; planets and other heavenly bodies; compass points (but not directional words); ships, trains, aircraft; specific school courses; titles of literary and artistic works.

Native **A**mericans	**N**obel **P**rize	**S**aturn
Swahili	**A**sia	the **N**orthwest
Greek **O**rthodox	**R**hode **I**sland	west of town
Passover	**D**allas	*Titanic*
the **U**niversity of **I**owa	**N**ile **R**iver	**W**orld **C**ultures II
Republican party	**E**lm **S**treet	world history
Ford **M**otor **C**ompany	**M**onday	the *Iliad*
Empire **S**tate **B**uilding	**F**ebruary	"The Lottery"
Golden **G**ate **B**ridge	**M**emorial **D**ay	*Boston Globe*
the **M**eadowlands	**C**ivil **W**ar	"Stardust"
Kleenex tissues	**I**ron **A**ge	*The Bull from the Sea*
the **B**ill of **R**ights		

▶ **Exercise 1** **Draw three lines under each lowercase letter that should be capitalized. Strike through (B̶) each capitalized letter that should be lowercase.**

Kara's oil P̶ortraits resemble the paintings of grandma Moses.

1. The new girl's N̶ame was Althea Smithson.

2. His G̶randfather's diary told of meeting president Roosevelt.

3. Are you one of doctor Johnson's patients?

4. Alaina works after school as a V̶olunteer at mercy hospital.

5. Have you met my M̶other?

6. The ending was corny, complete with a rendition of "Home On The Range."

7. While in France, we must visit the eiffel tower.

8. Have you ever been to Yellowstone national park?

9. His accent was a musical mixture of english and italian.

10. Japan and the united States are separated by the pacific ocean.

11. When did president Lincoln issue the emancipation proclamation?

12. According to *the world book encyclopedia,* Henry Hudson explored hudson strait and Hudson bay while looking for the northwest passage.

13. Jerry's telescope is powerful enough to see the Moons of Jupiter.

14. Leonard Bernstein was a renowned conductor of the new york philharmonic.

15. Do you have señora Perez for Freshman Spanish?

16. Is the mississippi river one of the borders of Illinois?

17. Political unrest in the middle east caused great concern for the tourists.

18. Have you read the memoirs of the Native American chief Red Fox?

19. The Empire state building was once the tallest building in the world.

20. Our space program suffered a serious setback with the *challenger* mishap.

21. Joy earns outstanding grades in latin, english, and algebra.

22. Consuelo hopes to get a Basketball scholarship at the university of North Carolina.

23. The first african american to play in the american league was Larry doby.

24. I just had a visit from father Mulcahy.

25. Chariot races were regular features at circus maximus in Ancient Rome.

26. The Islamic book of holy writings is called the quran.

27. The adams high school french club meets every other thursday.

28. A favorite christmas story is *the gift of the magi.*

29. One of our gold depositories is located at fort Knox, Kentucky.

30. Many employees of the Chrysler corporation belong to the united automobile workers, one of the largest labor unions in the united states.

31. Maria and Harvey ate dinner at the olde town inn.

32. A joint session of congress includes members of both the house of representatives and The senate.

33. My cousin took astronomy 101 when she went to College in the Midwest.

34. I read an article about Sports Cars in last month's *car and driver* magazine.

35. During world war II, my Grandmother worked with the red cross in the philippine islands.

Mechanics

Lesson 72
Capitalization of Proper Adjectives

Capitalize proper adjectives (adjectives formed from proper nouns). Most proper adjectives fit into the following categories:

1. Adjectives formed from names of people

   Victorian architecture   **J**effersonian politics

   Gregorian chant   **C**linton administration

   Elizabethan poetry   **N**apoleonic era

2. Adjectives formed from specific days or holidays, place names, and names of national, ethnic, and religious groups

   Hungarian goulash   **C**hristmas decorations

   Australian folklore   **H**ispanic students

   Thursday evening   **J**ewish synagogue

▶ **Exercise 1 Draw three lines under each lowercase letter that should be capitalized. Strike through (B) each capitalized letter that should be lowercase.**

The carter Administration dealt with oil shortages, rising tax rates, and the iranian Hostage situation.

1. The book of japanese fairy tales was beautifully illustrated.

2. Jamal and Kenny always enjoyed hearing Holiday tales.

3. Many people find it quite surprising to see gregorian chants becoming popular these days.

4. Carlita is particularly fond of chinese food.

5. A tasty pizza topping is canadian bacon.

6. The stranger looked as though he had stepped out of a dickensian novel.

7. The company performed a wagnerian opera.

8. Many interesting tales are found in swedish folklore.

9. Communism was based on marxist doctrines.

10. Do may flowers really come from april showers?

11. Some holidays have Religious origins; others have secular roots.

12. The entire community looked forward to the annual italian festivities.

13. The tibetan Terrain can be treacherous.

14. There are german polkas as well as polish polkas.

15. The library at Main and Elm is a good example of georgian architecture.

16. Masaccio is credited as the founder of renaissance painting.

17. Randall Cunningham is a great american Football star.

18. The buffet menu included swedish meatballs.

19. Alice wanted to vacation on the mediterranean coast.

20. The Heritage Festival featured a thrilling demonstration of african tribal chants.

21. There are so many arthurian tales it is difficult to separate history from myth.

22. The basketball team reviews game films every monday evening.

23. Every room of the old mansion contained a franklin stove.

24. Originating on an island in the English Channel, jersey cattle provide the richest milk of all breeds.

25. My irish setter has a mahogany coat.

26. The entire family enjoyed watching disney movies.

27. What was the highlight of your caribbean cruise?

28. Forty-one democratic governors attended the conference.

29. The United States imports large amounts of colombian coffee.

30. Israeli Troops protect all residents of the country.

31. James Borland is an english Professor.

32. Tanya played a hungarian polka on her accordion.

33. We visited a Gettysburg Battlefield on our trip.

34. Molly owned recordings of all nine Beethoven Symphonies.

35. After yom kippur services at Temple Beth Shalom, we continued to fast until sundown.

36. The Dogwood tree in the backyard has beautiful white blossoms.

37. We carved our halloween pumpkin on a warm october day.

38. Luba went to her grandmother's house for thanksgiving dinner and ate turkey.

39. I would love to own a steinway Grand Piano.

40. Beverly Sills, the great american Operatic Soprano, sang with the Metropolitan Opera.

Mechanics

Name _____ Class _____ Date _____

 Unit 11 **Review**

▶ **Exercise** **Correct the capitalization in each sentence. Draw three lines under each lowercase letter that should be capitalized and a single slash (B̸) through any capital letters that should be lowercase.**

Mr. osborne, my Report on the jazz age is finished.

1. leif erikson was a norse explorer who came to north america.

2. Thick ice buries most of antarctica, the Continent that surrounds the south pole.

3. *Gone With The Wind* is a classic american novel.

4. The Postman delivered an invitation to Achim's Graduation party.

5. small in stature, mother Teresa is a giant in caring.

6. The Gotham City philatelic society meets on Wednesday Evenings. (philately is the hobby of

    stamp collecting.)

7. Rolanda had great difficulty (She loves languages) deciding whether to study german or

    spanish.

8. Karin was honored with the employee-of-the-month award.

9. Lord Byron once wrote, "the vile are only vain; the great are proud."

10. Which roman ruler was first called caesar?

11. the hiking party gave a wide berth to the Wild Boar.

12. Little John and robin hood lived in Sherwood forest.

13. The Monroe doctrine remains controversial to this day.

14. "I Want to Hold Your Hand" was a great beatles hit.

15. The first nuclear-powered submarine (the Uss *nautilus*) sailed under the ice at the North pole.

16. *ursa major* is the scientific name for the big dipper.

17. Anton studied shakespearean drama at the University.

18. At the mortgage-burning ceremony, president Masterson received the Title Deed from the vice

    president of the bank.

19. The Toyota is a Car that originated in japan.

20. There was no World Series in the Autumn of 1994 because of the Baseball strike.

Cumulative Review: Units 1–11

▶ **Exercise 1** Underline each adjective or adverb clause. Draw an arrow from the clause to the word it modifies. In the blank, write *adj.* (adjective) or *adv.* (adverb) to tell what kind of clause it is.

___adj.___   We took the highway that runs south from here.

_____ **1.** There may come a time when you will need my phone number.

_____ **2.** I shall visit Aspen, Colorado, if I can afford it.

_____ **3.** While we were gone, Mr. Salazar cared for our pets.

_____ **4.** The meeting began earlier than we had expected.

_____ **5.** The city from which I came is a large metropolis.

_____ **6.** The exchange student that you met was from Spain.

_____ **7.** Do not give your opinion unless you are asked.

_____ **8.** Sam's proudest possession was a baseball that was signed by Roberto Alomar.

_____ **9.** Our soccer team played a great defensive game although they finally lost.

_____ **10.** When you called, I was raking the leaves.

_____ **11.** Uncle Leo, to whom I told my crazy dream, just laughed and laughed.

_____ **12.** Monet is the artist whose paintings are on display.

_____ **13.** The Iowa farmer, whose place I bought, moved to southern California.

_____ **14.** Apply an ice pack if your knee begins to swell.

_____ **15.** Whenever it storms, our roof leaks.

_____ **16.** The necklace that I like is too expensive.

_____ **17.** After I do my homework, I can go to the movies.

_____ **18.** The house where my grandmother grew up was torn down.

_____ **19.** The rancher whom we asked for directions was very helpful.

_____ **20.** Hakeem, running as fast as he was able, finished the race first.

Mechanics

▶ **Exercise 2 Underline the correct word or words in parentheses.**

   Sean planned the student council meeting (good, <u>well</u>).

1. The play we saw last weekend was very (good, well).

2. The deer ran (more swiftly, most swiftly) through the open field than the fox.

3. The teacher gave the students (a, an) example to follow as they were working out the equation.

4. Simba was the (most noisiest, noisiest) puppy in the litter.

5. After little preparation, he performed (bad, badly) on the test.

6. The principal's reprimand had little (effect, affect) on the unruly student.

7. A dark and shrouded figure emerged (sudden, suddenly) from the house.

8. Of all the fresh vegetables, I like beets (less, the least).

9. Matt, our star basketball player, was taller (than, then) Mr. Cooper.

10. The abandoned building across the street is the (oldest, most oldest) in the city.

11. My elderly aunt has (a, an) honest face.

12. (Beside, Besides) soup and salad, they had a croissant.

13. The peaceful protest (proceeded, preceded) through the capital city.

14. Bananas appear to ripen more quickly than (any, any other) fruit.

15. My friend never eats (no, any) candy.

16. The crowd listened (respectfully, respectively) as the minister eulogized the hero.

17. I will (accept, except) full responsibility for my brother's actions.

18. Columbus is (further, farther) south than Cleveland.

19. These hiking boots are (cleaner, more cleaner) than yours.

20. Mrs. Ichiko (immigrated, emigrated) to the United States in 1968.

21. Yesterday, it snowed so hard we (couldn't hardly, could hardly) see the highway.

22. (Irregardless, Regardless) of what my opponents say, I am (a, an) avid supporter of the school levy.

▶ **Exercise 3 Draw three lines under each lowercase letter that should be capitalized. For each italicized word write in the blank *com.* (common noun) or *prop.* (proper noun).**

<u>com.</u>   Two famous *landmarks* in Washington, D.C., are the <u>l</u>incoln <u>m</u>emorial and the <u>c</u>apitol.

_____ 1. While in the west, our family climbed *pikes peak* in rocky mountain national park.

_____ 2. In american history *class* we are studying world war II.

_____ **3.** because of the baseball *strike,* the world series wasn't held in 1994.

_____ **4.** great changes took place during the *industrial revolution.*

_____ **5.** The boat navigated the ohio river from *Cincinnati* to Louisville.

_____ **6.** I read an *article* about martin luther king jr. in last sunday's newspaper.

_____ **7.** The fourth of july is an american *holiday.*

_____ **8.** When in *chicago,* we went to the top of the sears tower.

_____ **9.** on our *flight* from san francisco to sacramento, we flew over yosemite national park.

_____ **10.** the metropolitan museum of art is located in *new york city.*

_____ **11.** For thanksgiving dinner we took grandma and grandpa to a *restaurant.*

_____ **12.** On *may* 20, 1927, charles lindbergh touched down near paris, france.

_____ **13.** tutankhamen reigned as *king* of egypt from about 1347 B.C. to 1339 B.C.

_____ **14.** My most difficult *courses* in school are geography and spanish.

_____ **15.** *india,* a country in southern asia, was once a british colony.

_____ **16.** linus pauling, an american chemist, received two *nobel prizes.*

_____ **17.** My sister's favorite *book* is by laura ingalls wilder.

_____ **18.** The navajo are the largest Native American group in the *united states.*

_____ **19.** the indianapolis 500 automobile *race* is held every memorial day weekend.

_____ **20.** The massive *steamboat* rolled lazily along the mississippi river.

_____ **21.** *pope john paul II* met with the President at the white house.

_____ **22.** The *brooklyn bridge* spans the east river from Brooklyn to manhattan island.

Mechanics

Unit 12: Punctuation, Abbreviations, and Numbers

Lesson 73
End Punctuation: Period, Exclamation Point, and Question Mark

Use a period at the end of a declarative sentence and at the end of a polite command.

Declarative Sentence: The computer room is at the end of the hall.
Polite Command: Please close the door when you leave the room.

Use an exclamation point to show strong feeling and indicate a forceful command.

Oh, my gosh!   What a great jacket!   Watch out!   Jump!

Use a question mark to indicate a direct question.

Who knows the answer to the riddle?   Is this the right bus stop?

Do not place a question mark after an indirect question (one that has been reworded so that it is part of a declarative sentence).

Jason wondered whether he would be accepted into the program.
She asked if she could hand in her paper early.

▶ **Exercise 1** **Place a check in the blank next to each sentence that has correct end punctuation.**

___✓___   Where are we going after the game?

_____ **1.** Most people have heard of the Nobel Prize.

_____ **2.** Six prizes are given each year to outstanding people in various fields!

_____ **3.** The six fields are physics, medicine or physiology, literature, chemistry, peace, and economics.

_____ **4.** Do you know which one is the most recently created.

_____ **5.** The economics prize was awarded for the first time in 1969!

_____ **6.** The other prizes have been given for more than 90 years?

_____ **7.** The prizes were created by a Swedish industrialist and inventor named Alfred Nobel!

_____ **8.** Nobel, who lived from 1833 to 1896, became fascinated by explosives when he was working in his father's factory in Russia.

_____ **9.** The young Alfred invented a process in which an explosive called *nitroglycerine* could be exploded in a controlled situation?

Mechanics

_____ 10. Even though he was a gifted inventor, Nobel never attended a university.

_____ 11. In fact, he attended school for only one year!

_____ 12. Nitroglycerine proved to be a dangerous material to work with, and several explosions in Nobel's factories caused many deaths?

_____ 13. Among the people who died in a factory in Sweden was Alfred's younger brother, Emil.

_____ 14. Eventually he discovered a way to mix nitroglycerine with a kind of sandy clay!

_____ 15. The clay made the nitroglycerine more stable and less likely to explode unexpectedly?

_____ 16. The new blasting product was put to many peaceful uses, such as mining, road construction, and tunnel building.

_____ 17. Nobel's invention, which he called *dynamite,* also became a weapon of war!

_____ 18. The inventor wondered if he could do something to promote peace and good will among people to make up for the deadly uses of his invention?

_____ 19. A very rich man at the time of his death, Alfred Nobel decided his money should be used to create prizes for those who had helped the world's people.

_____ 20. In this amazing way, the inventor of a deadly explosive honors people who have saved lives!

▶ **Exercise 2 Complete each sentence by adding a period, an exclamation point, or a question mark as needed.**

I can't believe I'm going to Europe !

1. Sweden, the homeland of Alfred Nobel, is an interesting and beautiful country

2. Do you have any idea how far north this country is

3. Many North Americans are surprised to learn that Sweden is as far north as Hudson Bay

4. In spite of its northerly location, Sweden has a temperate climate

5. Winters are long and cold, but the summers can be quite warm

6. In northernmost Sweden during the winter, the sun never rises above the horizon

7. How would twenty-four hours of darkness affect you

8. Many Swedes who live above the Arctic Circle combat the gloom by lighting candles

9. This desire to spread light in the darkness of winter is the basis for the holiday honoring Saint Lucia, which charms each year's Nobel Prize winners

10. Because of the tilt of the earth, a summer day in northern Sweden lasts for twenty-four glorious hours

11. Swedes celebrate the warm weather and bright days on the country's most beloved holiday

12. June 24, *Midsommardag*—Midsummer Day—is a glorious festival of merrymaking

Lesson 74
Colons

Use a colon to introduce a list, especially after a statement that uses words such as *these*, *the following*, or *as follows*.

Denise has lived in these three cities: Albuquerque, Sacramento, and Boulder.

The following students should report to the guidance counselor's office: Dwight Robinson, Angela Martinez, Michael Byrne, and Li Chen.

Do not use a colon to introduce a list if the list immediately follows a verb or a preposition.

Among the prizes offered were a camera, a calculator, and a radio.
The people at the next table ordered their pizza with green peppers, onions, black olives, and anchovies.

Use a colon to introduce a long or formal quotation. A formal quotation is often preceded by words such as *this, these, the following*, or *as follows*.

The governor repeated the following words of Motavato, chief of the Southern Cheyennes: "Although wrongs have been done to me, I live in hopes. I have not got two hearts."

Use a colon between the hour and minute of the precise time, between the chapter and verse in biblical references, and after the salutation of a business letter.

| 1:25 P.M. | Job 6:1–8 | Sir or Madam: |
| 8:57 A.M. | Leviticus 4:22–27 | Dear Ms. Rayburn: |

▶ **Exercise 1 Insert a colon where necessary. If the sentence is correct, write *C* in the blank.**

_____ You will need the following tools:a hammer, a screwdriver, and a wrench.

_____ **1.** The school bus came every morning at about 745.

_____ **2.** The animals I liked best at the zoo were the elephants, the giraffes, the electric eels, and the baboons.

_____ **3.** Many people remember President John F. Kennedy's famous statement from his inaugural address "Ask not what your country can do for you; ask what you can do for your country."

_____ **4.** Don't forget the following items: a bathrobe, soap, slippers, a towel, and a washcloth.

_____ **5.** I'll pick you up at 7:30 sharp.

_____ **6.** The most popular sports in the United States are football, basketball, and baseball.

_____ **7.** Try to deliver the package between 1145 and 1215.

Mechanics

_____ 8. I'll never forget his final words "Don't look back—something might be gaining on you."

_____ 9. To whom it may concern:

_____ 10. The following are the main steps in booting up the computer 1. turn the unit on; 2. log on; 3. select the software program you want.

_____ 11. Their study group had written a song using Hamlet's famous speech: "To be or not to be; that is the question."

_____ 12. A tin-roof sundae is made from vanilla ice cream, chocolate syrup, peanuts, and whipped cream.

_____ 13. This morning's reading is from the book of Luke 7:15–22.

_____ 14. Make sure you follow this advice Neither a borrower nor a lender be.

_____ 15. Ms. Richardson asked if we knew who the author of the novel was.

_____ 16. The essay for the contest had to be on the following subject former House Speaker Thomas "Tip" O'Neill's saying that all politics is local.

_____ 17. The last three people in line were Jason, Mary-Margaret, and Dawn.

_____ 18. Our presentation consisted of the following a report, a bulletin board, an audiotape, and a fashion show.

_____ 19. The following books were chosen by the group: *Middlemarch, The Old Man and the Sea, Song of Solomon, Wuthering Heights,* and *The Scarlet Letter.*

_____ 20. When it's 1100 in the morning in New York, it's 400 in the afternoon in London.

_____ 21. The fencing club's poster had a picture of a fencer, followed by the caption: "Fencing—try it once and you'll get the point!"

_____ 22. My dad's favorite song has this line "Life's a hotel at best; you're here as a guest."

_____ 23. To make popcorn, follow these instructions: 1. add the oil to the pan; 2. pour in the popcorn; 3. shake the pan over the heat as the popcorn pops.

_____ 24. These are the magazines she read regularly *Time, Newsweek, Sports Illustrated,* and *People.*

_____ 25. The children's favorite vegetables were corn, broccoli, peas, and carrots.

_____ 26. The police officer took the 6:15 train to Haverford.

_____ 27. Angela's parents grew these crops soybeans, corn, wheat, and oats.

_____ 28. The following streets will be closed for curb repair Main Street, Broad Street, High Street, M.L. King Drive, Southwest Boulevard, and Northern Lights Avenue.

Mechanics

Lesson 75
Semicolons

Use a **semicolon** to separate main clauses that are not joined by a coordinating conjunction (*and, but, or, nor, yet,* and *for*).

She can't play the saxophone, but I know she'd like to learn.
She can't play the saxophone; I know she'd like to learn.

Use a semicolon to separate main clauses joined by a conjunctive adverb (such as *however, therefore, nevertheless, moreover, furthermore,* and *subsequently*) or by an expression such as *for example* or *that is.* In general, a conjunctive adverb or expression such as *for example* is followed by a comma.

Some people in our group refused to take the assignment seriously; therefore, we received a *D* on our project.

Use a semicolon to separate the items in a series when the items contain commas.

Italians have created an almost unlimited number of pasta shapes and sizes, among them *orecchiete,* which means "little ears"; *capellini,* or "angel hair"; and *orzo,* which look like small grains of rice.

Use a semicolon to separate two main clauses joined by a coordinating conjunction when the clauses already contain several commas.

The book was very long, almost six hundred pages, and contained more than seventy-five characters, which made keeping track of them difficult; but I loved it anyway and would recommend it to anyone.

▶ **Exercise 1** **Place a check on the blank next to each sentence that is correct.**

___✔___ Kristy, who finished first, won the trophy; however, Marla won the award for most improved.

_____ **1.** Nobel Prizes are awarded each year in six areas; which are physics, chemistry, physiology or medicine, literature, peace, and economics.

_____ **2.** The prizes were created by Swedish inventor Alfred Nobel; they are administered by various organizations in Sweden and Norway.

_____ **3.** Five of the six prizes are given by Swedish organizations for example, the physics, chemistry, and economics prizes are awarded by the Royal Academy of Sciences.

_____ **4.** The sixth prize, for peace, is awarded by a committee appointed by the Norwegian parliament; how it came to receive this duty is an interesting story.

_____ **5.** During Alfred Nobel's life, Norway belonged to Sweden; and the inventor stated in his will that Norway should award the peace prize.

Mechanics

_____ 6. Today, even though Norway and Sweden are separate and independent countries, which came about early in this century, the Norwegians have kept the right to award the peace prize, it is a source of pride to all Norwegians.

_____ 7. Winners of a Nobel Prize receive a cash award from Alfred Nobel's estate; the award is currently worth about $950,000.

_____ 8. Up to three people may share the prize, for example, the prizes in science and peace are often awarded to several people.

_____ 9. Winners of the different prizes are usually announced in October or November; late in the year.

_____ 10. Winners receive their prizes in a ceremony on December 10, the anniversary of Alfred Nobel's death; these include a gold medal, a diploma, and a check.

_____ 11. During Nobel week in Sweden, many festivities take place; that is, banquets, dances, parties, and receptions.

_____ 12. Nobel week takes place at the same time as the Swedish holiday honoring Saint Lucia; consequently, prizewinners are serenaded by groups of young girls who also take part in a pageant on December 13.

_____ 13. One young girl, wearing the traditional costume of a white robe and a crown of candles, represents the saint; others dress as her attendants.

_____ 14. Prizewinners also give lectures during Nobel week; their only obligation.

_____ 15. Many famous scientists, writers, and world political figures have won Nobel Prizes; however, many others have not.

_____ 16. The decisions of the various committees are often criticized, no one can make a perfect decision every time.

_____ 17. Some of the greatest writers of this century were passed over by the Swedish Academy, the committee that awards the prize in literature; for example, Virginia Woolf, Marcel Proust, and James Joyce.

_____ 18. Some peace prizes have also gone to controversial figures; these include Henry Kissinger, U.S. secretary of state, and Yasir Arafat, leader of the Palestine Liberation Organization.

_____ 19. In setting up the prizes; Alfred Nobel wrote only that the prizes should go to those who have "conferred the greatest benefit" on the world's people.

_____ 20. The roster of Nobel Prize winners contains some of the greatest figures in the scientific, literary, and diplomatic life of the last hundred years; no other award is held in higher regard.

Mechanics

Lesson 76
Commas and Compound Sentences

Use **commas** between the main clauses in a compound sentence. Place a comma before a coordinating conjunction (*and, but, or, nor, yet,* or *for*) that joins two main clauses.

The members of the choir went to the concert, and the artists' group went to the museum.

Many tourists visit Miami in the summer, but most people go during the colder months.

You may omit the comma between very short main clauses that are connected by a coordinating conjunction unless the comma is needed to avoid confusion.

Dad raked the leaves and I washed the car. (clear)
I went to English class and gym comes next. (confusing)
I went to English class, and gym comes next. (clear)

▶ **Exercise 1 Add commas where necessary. Cross out commas used incorrectly using the delete symbol ( ). Some sentences may be correct.**

On Saturday we visited Capitol Hill,and tomorrow we want to visit the monuments.

1. Many important discoveries in the field of science are the result of work done by women and the achievements of Dorothy Crowfoot Hodgkin are no exception.

2. Dorothy Crowfoot was born in Egypt and moved to England when she was a child.

3. Her parents were English educators living in Cairo and Dorothy spent the first four years of her life in the Egyptian city.

4. Her father was interested in archaeology and her mother shared his interest by collecting unusual plants and studying ancient methods of weaving cloth.

5. While at school in England, Dorothy first learned about the science of chemistry and her interest was to lead her to a scientific career.

6. She became fascinated by the study of crystals, and even set up a small laboratory in her family's home when she was 14.

7. Certain natural substances are actually made up of tiny crystals but many people do not know that even aspirin is crystalline.

8. Substances made of crystals can look quite different yet all crystals share important characteristics.

9. All crystals are solid, and have regular shapes.

10. Patterns in crystals repeat themselves over and over and crystals with flawless repetition are said to be perfect.

11. Dorothy finished high school and she decided to attend Oxford University.

12. Dorothy studied at Oxford for four years but then she received an offer to be an assistant to a famous chemist at the University of Cambridge.

13. She became familiar with a research technique called X-ray diffraction and this method became one of the foundations of her career as a scientist.

14. Later she returned to Oxford to teach and do research.

15. She received a laboratory space in which to work and continued her studies of crystals but another element soon appeared in her life.

16. She met a young man named Thomas Hodgkin and the couple was married a short time later.

17. World War II began shortly after her marriage but Dorothy's work was not interrupted.

18. The war led to Dorothy's first major scientific success and her discovery was to have far-reaching consequences.

19. A British scientist named Alexander Fleming had several years earlier discovered a special mold, that could destroy harmful bacteria.

20. The mold was called penicillin and it grew naturally.

21. Doctors knew that penicillin could cure diseases caused by bacteria yet it was available in such small quantities that it could not be used in widespread applications.

22. It was a medical dream to learn to "grow" penicillin artificially in a laboratory for then it could be manufactured in large quantities.

23. Dorothy started to work on this problem but it proved to be very difficult to crystallize the penicillin molecules.

24. Dorothy and her assistants analyzed the structure of penicillin using the X-ray diffraction technique and the discoveries they made changed the history of medicine.

25. Penicillin and similar drugs can now be manufactured in large quantities but this breakthrough could not have been achieved without the work of Dorothy Crowfoot Hodgkin's team of scientists.

Lesson 77
Commas in a Series and Between Coordinate Adjectives

Use commas to separate three or more words, phrases, or clauses in a series.

Josh caught the pass, dodged a tackler, and sprinted for the goal line.

No commas are necessary when all of the items are connected by conjunctions.

She was the kindest and wisest and gentlest person I have ever known.

Nouns that are used in pairs (*bread and butter, sweet and innocent, bacon and eggs*) are usually considered single units and should not be separated by commas. If such pairs appear with other nouns or groups of nouns in a series, they must be separated from the other items in the series.

The storm is expected to cause *thunder and lightning,* heavy rains, and gusting winds.

Place a comma between coordinate adjectives that precede a noun. Coordinate adjectives modify a noun equally. To determine whether adjectives are coordinate, try to reverse their order or put the word *and* between them. If the sentence still sounds natural, the adjectives are coordinate.

The sergeant ordered a slow (and) cautious (and) orderly approach.
The sergeant ordered a slow, cautious, orderly approach.

▶ **Exercise 1** **Add commas where necessary. Delete (Ɣ) unnecessary commas. Some sentences may be correct.**

The weather today will be warm,sunny,and windy.

1. Her pen rolled off her desk onto the floor and under the cabinet.

2. Sheep cattle poultry and swine are all raised in Ohio.

3. My mouth is watering just thinking about those big juicy tomatoes!

4. Darnay wanted to borrow my best, red pen for the interview.

5. Would you like mashed potatoes, or baked potatoes, or scalloped potatoes?

6. The audience loved the movie cheered at the end and left happy and satisfied.

7. The Montinis have just put in a new, wooden deck.

8. He often said that people could either lead follow or get out of the way.

9. The little, brown house on Adams Street is for sale again.

10. Logging, cattle farming, and mining all pose a threat to the Amazon basin's rain forest.

11. Rita looked out on the playground saw the child fall and ran out to help him.

12. Thomas enjoys both hiking, and fishing.

13. The man had a black, and blue bruise on his leg a cut on his forehead and a scratch on his hand.

14. Don't eat the food, don't drink the water, and don't breathe the air—then you'll be fine!

15. My dad put the new lamp in our, dining room.

16. The spring beauty is a little, pink, and white flower that blooms in early March.

17. Alaska is the biggest state Rhode Island is the smallest and California has the most people.

18. The character was pictured as a rough-and-ready ornery, and argumentative frontiersman.

19. Her favorite vegetables are carrots, green beans, and zucchini.

20. Raymont was having a hard time choosing between the Toyota, and the Mercury, and the Pontiac.

21. They took a trip to Vermont to see the beautiful, fall colors.

22. The woods echoed with the sounds of birds, insects, and different, kinds of small mammals.

23. We went on the roller coaster, the Ferris wheel, and the bumper cars.

24. The strange bird we saw was yellow, and blue.

25. He had never been on an airplane a bus, or a train!

26. Wait in this line get your ticket and take it to the cashier.

27. My birthday was a cold and drizzly and miserable day.

28. He yelled that he was sick, and tired of the way they treated their cat.

29. The bus stopped in Dayton Springfield Columbus and Zanesville.

30. I presented my report, asked if there were any questions, and then turned the meeting over to the president.

31. It was so hot that we took off our shoes and socks hats and jackets.

32. The people of the community are its most valuable important resource.

33. The political candidate solicited money, bought TV time and ran newspaper ads, for his campaign.

34. The members of the Spanish club always served ham and bean chicken and noodle and vegetable beef soups on election night.

35. The red, velvety coals from the campfire were glowing in the dark.

36. The long winding steep trail was the cause of a hot dusty and exhausting hike.

37. Teri wanted the small spotted puppy, but her sister liked the big golden retriever.

38. That new restaurant makes the juiciest, and tastiest, and biggest hamburgers in town.

Mechanics

Lesson 78
Commas and Nonessential Elements

Use **commas** to set off nonessential participles and infinitives and their phrases (see Lesson 19, pp. 91–92, and Lesson 21, pp. 95–96). Do not set off essential phrases.

Waving, the man came toward us. (nonessential)
The man **waving to my mother** is my uncle. (essential)
Her goal, **to become a doctor,** has finally been achieved. (nonessential)
To win is her goal. (essential)

Use **commas** to set off nonessential adjective clauses (see Lesson 26, pp. 107–110). Do not set off essential clauses.

Bangkok, **which is the capital of Thailand,** is an intriguing city. (nonessential)
People **who live in glass houses** shouldn't throw stones. (essential)

Use **commas** to set off nonessential appositives (see Lesson 20, p. 94). Do not set off essential appositives.

My brother, **Bill,** loves cars. (nonessential—The writer has only one brother.)
My brother **Bill** loves cars. (essential—The writer has more than one brother.)

Use **commas** to set off interjections (such as *oh* and *well*) and parenthetical expressions (such as *on the other hand* and *without a doubt*).

Oh, I can hardly believe it!
Last year, **on the other hand,** you could have taken journalism.

▶ **Exercise 1** Insert commas where necessary. Delete (⌦) unnecessary commas. Some sentences may be correct.

John went to the restaurant⌦to eat lunch.

1. Just thinking about the test, made her nervous.

2. Abraham Lincoln an Illinois congressman was born in Kentucky.

3. An old bicycle battered and rusted lay in the creek.

4. The actress went to school in Nashville the capital of Tennessee.

5. Robert breathing heavily ran an extra lap around the track.

6. OK you win.

7. Franklin's father, to be honest, is not interested in baseball.

8. Walking to school, is good exercise.

9. Russell walking to school wondered how the tryouts would go.

10. To save enough money to buy a pair of in-line skates, was his goal.

Mechanics

11. The performance, which we rehearsed for two months, was a smashing success!

12. The car, that the drunk driver hit, was totally demolished.

13. The little dog with the jeweled collar was behaving badly.

14. Oh I suppose you're right about that.

15. Disappointed by his performance Harry left the room.

16. Someone who is really interested in animals, should get the job at the zoo.

17. To grow cactuses at home is not easy.

18. To prevent computer damage many people use surge protectors.

19. I have the strangest feeling, that something peculiar is about to happen.

20. Our tour guide the young man in the safari hat is a native of Kenya.

21. All students will of course, be responsible for their own lunches.

22. Animals that are active at night are said to be nocturnal.

23. It was obvious that the man, getting off the plane, was her father.

24. Colorado Springs where I was born is in central Colorado.

25. That coat is without a doubt the warmest one I have ever owned.

26. Yes, I now understand the assignment.

27. A coyote howling sadly, added a lonely feeling to the fall evening.

28. Melissa, who loves all sports also finds writing poetry enjoyable.

29. To be a loyal friend, is an admirable quality.

30. You would enjoy Mesa Verde National Park a place I have visited.

31. Our committee will have the list of nominees tomorrow by the way.

32. Is the young lion, standing on that ledge, one of the zoo's new animals?

33. The Statue of Liberty is a symbol that represents opportunity.

34. The woman, sitting on the bench, is my aunt.

▶ Writing Link **Write a paragraph about your favorite entertainer. Use one adjective clause, one interjection, and one parenthetical expression.**

_____

_____

_____

_____

Mechanics

Lesson 79
Commas and Introductory Phrases

Use a **comma** after a short introductory prepositional phrase (see Lesson 18, pp. 89–90) only if the sentence would be misread without it. (However, a comma setting off a short introductory prepositional phrase is not incorrect.)

For the children inside, the playhouse seemed like a magical world. (comma needed to prevent misreading)

During the winter the building is drafty. (comma not needed)

Use a **comma** after a long prepositional phrase or after the final phrase in a succession of phrases.

During the exciting game's final three minutes, the fans began to cheer wildly.

In the middle of the night on the stroke of twelve, the man's eyes opened wide, and he stared into the darkness.

Do not use a comma if the phrase is immediately followed by a verb.

In the middle of the train station stood the famous writer.

Use **commas** to set off introductory participles and participial phrases. (See Lesson 19, pp. 91–92.)

Growling, the dog advanced toward the wolf.
Appealing to the jury, the lawyer made her final remarks.

▶ **Exercise 1** **Place a check in the blank next to each correctly punctuated sentence.**

___✔___   Moving cautiously, the little boy climbed the tree.

_____ **1.** In baseball gloves are used by the fielders.

_____ **2.** During the commercial after this one, I'll try to telephone Andrew.

_____ **3.** By the railing was the captain's special telescope.

_____ **4.** Seeing the crash we ran out to see if we could help.

_____ **5.** Inside the calzone, were sausage, cheese, and onions.

_____ **6.** Standing behind the man in the blue suit, DeJuan looked impatient.

_____ **7.** In the small space above the closet was a frightened and mewing Mimi.

_____ **8.** Behind the dairy cows grazed in a pasture.

_____ **9.** Smiling, the man behind the desk motioned us to come forward.

_____ **10.** At the wheel of the sleek red sports car, was none other than my dad!

_____ **11.** At the insistence of her parents she decided to attend.

_____ 12. Laughing she handed me the photograph.

_____ 13. From the mouth of the cannon flew the Great Stromboli!

_____ 14. After the game boys thanked the referee.

_____ 15. Gazing intently at the scar on the stranger's face, the sheriff stood up slowly.

_____ 16. At the beginning of the race through the downtown area, sat the timekeepers.

_____ 17. To those in need of help from the Red Cross, the plane was the best sight they had ever seen.

_____ 18. On the edge of the pond scum covered the reeds.

_____ 19. Catching a glimpse of the rescue team's light the trapped miners let out whoops of happiness.

_____ 20. Beneath the cold water of Lake Superior, lay the wreck of the *Edmund Fitzgerald*.

▶ **Exercise 2 Insert commas where necessary. Delete (⅄) unnecessary commas.**

After two hours of tennis‚the players cooled off by swimming.

1. Curling up in her favorite chair with a new book Regina felt happy and calm.

2. Under the Egyptian sand, lay ancient temples, statues, and buildings.

3. For us children are never a nuisance.

4. At the mouth of the river on the edge of the jungle, lay the village.

5. Spotting a familiar face in the crowd the nervous performer seemed to relax a little.

6. In the middle of the night she was awakened by a strange tapping sound at the window.

7. After the ridiculously expensive dinner guests were astonished to be asked to leave immediately.

8. Spying a fish the seagull dived straight down into the ocean.

9. Crying the lost child could not be comforted.

10. Looking under the porch I spotted a raccoon.

11. By the photograph of the pig farmers signed their names.

12. After twelve hours of nonstop hiking we finally came to the campsite.

13. Muttering the man returned to the bench.

14. Settling itself on a high branch the osprey carefully scanned the surface of the inlet.

15. To her parents were both friends and teachers.

16. Underneath the piano, lay the missing string of pearls.

Lesson 80
Commas and Adverb Clauses and Antithetical Phrases

Use commas to set off all introductory adverb clauses. Use commas to set off internal adverb clauses that interrupt the flow of the sentence.

Before you sign that agreement, make sure you read it carefully.
Most people, if they eat too much, will get indigestion.

In general, do not set off an adverb clause at the end of a sentence unless the clause is parenthetical or the sentence would be misread without the comma.

Don't come to the show unless you really want to see it. (comma not needed)

Use commas to set off an antithetical phrase. An antithetical phrase uses a word such as *but*, *not*, or *unlike* to qualify what precedes it.

She, not Michael, should have been elected class president.
Sheep, unlike cows, do not cause heavy damage to a pasture or a field.

▶ **Exercise 1 Add commas where necessary. Delete (⅄) unnecessary commas. Some sentences may be correct.**

The juror, not the detective, leaked the news⅄to the press.

1. If you have never heard the name of Agnes Gonxha Bojaxhiu you're not alone.

2. Although Agnes may be the most famous person in the world few know her original name.

3. Agnes was born where people of several nationalities lived.

4. Although both Orthodox churches and Muslim mosques were plentiful in Agnes's town her family was Catholic.

5. After her father died young Agnes became increasingly involved in the church.

6. She attended meetings about missionary programs whenever she could.

7. While she was attending one meeting Agnes learned of the Sisters of Loreto.

8. These nuns performed missionary work in foreign countries, but especially in India.

9. After she expressed her interest in the Loreto nuns' activities a priest told her to wait until she was older.

10. When she became eighteen Agnes decided she wanted to join the missionary nuns.

11. The main headquarters of the Loreto nuns was in Dublin, Ireland not India.

12. Agnes's family reacted differently when she told them she had decided to become a nun.

Mechanics

13. Her brother Lazar after he heard the news was shocked.

14. Since Agnes was so full of fun he felt a nun's life would be unsuitable for her.

15. Her mother was proud but sad.

16. She knew she might never see Agnes again if Agnes went to India.

17. To her family, it would be, almost as if their Agnes had died.

18. In 1928 Agnes went to Dublin to join the Sisters of Loreto.

19. After two years the Loreto sisters sent Agnes to India where she started her new life.

20. When she took her vows to become a nun, Agnes Gonxha Bojaxhiu became Sister Teresa.

▶ **Exercise 2 Draw one line under each adverb clause. Then add necessary commas.**

<u>When she became principal</u>,Ms. Jansen began to change the rules.

1. So that she could better serve God Sister Teresa promised to remain in poverty, to take no pay for her work, and to own only a few things.

2. Although nuns cannot marry in the ordinary sense many consider themselves to be brides of Jesus.

3. Sister Teresa would wear the special robe and head covering, called a habit, of the nuns wherever she went.

4. After she visited Darjeeling near the Himalayan Mountains Sister Teresa was sent to Calcutta.

5. In 1937 Sister Teresa took her final vows so that she could consecrate her life to her faith.

6. Although her first job was teaching at a Catholic girls' school in a middle-class section of Calcutta Sister Teresa became aware of the poverty and misery of many residents of the city.

7. Then one day in 1946 when the regular food delivery failed to arrive at her convent Sister Teresa went into the city to buy supplies.

8. Although she knew Calcutta had some of the worst living conditions in the world Sister Teresa was shocked at the things she saw.

9. Although convent life was peaceful the streets of Calcutta were frightening and strange, with starving beggars and unsanitary conditions.

10. Sister Teresa after she had this powerful experience felt that God wanted her to work with the poor of Calcutta.

Mechanics

Lesson 81
Commas with Titles, Addresses, and Numbers

Use commas to set off titles when they follow a person's name.

Sylvia Chang, Ph.D.
Walter Jackson, mayor of Toledo
Christina Lundgren, M.D., will give the opening speech.

Use a comma after each part of an address, a geographical term, or a date.

Mason, Ohio, is the location of King's Island.
Graham's new address is 622 Van Buren Street, Richmond, Indiana 47374.
On Thursday, May 24, 1994, she received notification about the loan.

In a letter use commas as follows:

622 Van Buren Street
Richmond, IN 47374
November 11, 1996

Do not use commas if only the month and the day or only the month and the year are given. Do not use a comma between a state and a zip code.

July 12   January 1993   Columbus, Ohio 43210

Use commas to set off the parts of a reference that direct the reader to the exact source.

The quotation about overcoming oneself is from the *Lao Tzu*, Book One, Chapter 33.
Ariel, the airy spirit, makes his first appearance in Act I, Scene ii, of *The Tempest* by Shakespeare.

▶ **Exercise 1** **Add commas where necessary. Delete (⸋) unnecessary commas. Some sentences may be correct.**

Her Korean pen pal's birthday was⸋ August 9, 1980.

1. Please welcome our speaker tonight, Angelina Thomas senator from New Mexico.

2. The Nobel Prize in physics is presented each year in Stockholm Sweden.

3. However, the Nobel Peace Prize is awarded in, Oslo Norway.

4. All the Nobel Prizes are awarded in a gala ceremony on December, 10 of each year.

5. Did you know there is a Kansas City Missouri, and a Kansas City Kansas?

6. The return address on the envelope was Christine Lundgren M.D., 622 Van Buren Street

   Richmond, Indiana 47374.

7. When he gave his birth date as December 3 1951, I knew he couldn't be telling the truth.

Mechanics

8. Richard and Sarah's address until September is 1892 Sunshine Drive Arlington Heights Illinois 60005.

9. It looks as if the game on March 4 will decide the conference title.

10. The archaeology lecture will be given by Leopold M. Steinhauer Ph.D., a noted Egyptian explorer.

11. A notice in the newspaper said that the classes would begin on Monday September 12 1996.

12. The group's concert tour includes performances in Saginaw Michigan and Wausau Wisconsin.

13. I think you'll find the answer to that question in Act III Scene ii of *The Merchant of Venice.*

14. My sister joined the navy in October, 1992.

15. The dentist handed him a card that read "Dr. Ariella Blubaugh D.D.S."

16. You can redeem the coupons by sending them to, P.O. Box 398 Blacksburg Virginia 24063.

17. The masquerade takes place in Act I Scene iii of the second part of Goethe's *Faust.*

18. Stephen's pen pal lives in Quito, Ecuador.

19. Please have your applications in by March, 21.

20. I have a recommendation from Anthony Wheeler director of the Wheeler Institute.

21. Danielle's brother in the army is stationed in Frankfurt Germany.

22. The letter introduced the new priest as Father Jeffrey Rhoades S.J.

23. The sweepstakes entries have to be postmarked by midnight on, April 30.

24. Send the entries to Contest, 1112 Northridge Avenue Minneapolis Minnesota 55401.

25. Until, September 1 1985 the *Titanic,* a grand but tragic ship, sat in total darkness two miles beneath the Atlantic Ocean.

26. A demonstration of CPR will be given in the auditorium by Elaine Hollister R.N. head of nursing at Memorial Hospital.

27. The new tape and CD store is at 505, Butler Avenue.

28. Her little brother started school on September 1 1990.

29. Marcelina Lopez is a, city councilwoman.

30. The address on the form read 901 Old Mill Road, Salida, Colorado 81201.

31. The last day of band camp is Friday August 3.

32. I ordered my hiking boots from a Portland Maine company.

Mechanics

Lesson 82
Commas and Direct Address and in Tag Questions and Letter Writing

---

Use **commas** to set off words or names used in direct address.

Robin, have you ever been to the zoo?
Yes, sir, we can have lunch together this week.
Don't forget to turn in your books, class.

Use commas to set off a tag question. A **tag question** (such as *Do you?* or *Can I?*) emphasizes an implied answer to the statement preceding it.

You don't like raisins, do you?
You've read *The Outsiders,* haven't you?

Place a comma after the salutation of an informal letter and after the closing of all letters.

Dear Ruben,
Sincerely,

▶ **Exercise 1** **Add commas where necessary. Cross out commas used incorrectly by using the delete symbol (ͷ). Write *C* in the blank if the sentence is correct as written.**

_____   Carlos, hand me my books.

_____ **1.** No my friend I don't think we shall ever meet again.

_____ **2.** We've never been to Nebraska have we?

_____ **3.** Dear Brian

_____ **4.** You'll try to get some sleep before the test won't you?

_____ **5.** Excuse me ma'am the sign says not to feed the animals.

_____ **6.** Don't forget to call me on Saturday Lena.

_____ **7.** He knows about the deadline next week doesn't he?

_____ **8.** Very truly yours, Ms. Julia Pataky

_____ **9.** That's the bus to Little Rock, isn't it?

_____ **10.** Dad you're the greatest!

_____ **11.** Yes Your Honor I am prepared for trial today.

_____ **12.** This shirt, doesn't make my hair look orange does it?

_____ **13.** I guess I am disappointed Mom but I'll get over it.

_____ **14.** Listen folks, and I'll let you in on a little secret.

_____ **15.** They don't really believe that do they?

_____ **16.** Dear Grandpa

_____ **17.** That's not a very smart thing to do is it?

_____ **18.** Whoa Brandy! Down girl!

_____ **19.** Those are Kerry's gloves aren't they?

_____ **20.** No, Officer, I did not see the flashing lights.

_____ **21.** Jenny and Jillian didn't already leave for the pool did they?

_____ **22.** All right you guys the party's over!

_____ **23.** Yes Your, Majesty the ambassador from Persia has arrived.

_____ **24.** I don't think Deanne left a forwarding address did she?

_____ **25.** Yes Madame Chairman I am happy to second the motion.

_____ **26.** Miguel won first place in the judo contest, didn't he?

_____ **27.** You're not paying attention people.

_____ **28.** Ricky you shouldn't walk down the stairs with a sucker in your mouth.

_____ **29.** He won't tell anyone will he?

_____ **30.** Dear, Mom and Dad

_____ **31.** Attention students.

_____ **32.** She shouldn't be messing around with that fuse box, should she?

_____ **33.** All right Bobcats, let's go out and play our best game!

_____ **34.** Electricity can be dangerous if you don't know what you're doing can't it?

_____ **35.** Here Mittens come get your dinner.

_____ **36.** Your friend Anthony

_____ **37.** The news story about us will be next won't it?

_____ **38.** Good evening, sir. My name is Tom and I'll be your waiter tonight.

_____ **39.** I couldn't have seen Tyrone at the play could I?

_____ **40.** Dear, Todd and Trevor

_____ **41.** Orange juice is a lot better for you than soda pop isn't it?

_____ **42.** Go team! Beat Washington High!

Mechanics

Lesson 83
Commas in Review

▶ **Exercise 1** **Add commas where necessary. Delete commas used incorrectly using the delete symbol ( ).**

To my surprise, Aunt Mary, bought tickets to the concert for Tony, Miguel, and me.

1. Jenny and I were planning to go to the parade but when it started to rain we decided to stay at her apartment and listen to music.

2. Although the other team had a big lead at halftime we were barely able to eke out a victory.

3. Uncle Mervyn likes to work in his flower garden and Aunt Jane spends most of her time spinning wool on her spinning wheel.

4. By the time we got to town we found that the shoe store the sporting goods store and the clothing store were all closed.

5. Before they could play volleyball players had to sign up for the team.

6. Among the sites we visited on our trip to New York was the Statue of Liberty which was so crowded we couldn't go to the top.

7. We also saw the Museum of Modern Art my favorite spot of all.

8. Her grandparents celebrated their 50th wedding anniversary on May 3 1994.

9. The author, whose books I like best, is Walter Dean Myers.

10. Dad took a picture of Max and Mimi asleep on his favorite, red, easy chair.

11. Mr. Graves ran out of the house in a hurry slipped on a patch of ice and wound up in the emergency room with a broken wrist.

12. Sigrid Undset a Norwegian novelist won the Nobel Prize in 1928.

13. James Joyce on the other hand never won the Nobel Prize in literature.

14. Joyce, Ireland's best-known novelist lived most of his life outside the country.

15. Ben went to visit his cousins in Highland Park a town outside Chicago.

16. Anyone, playing around with her food, is likely to make a mess.

17. The word *smorgasbord,* came into the English language from Swedish.

18. Well I don't think there's anything more we can do about it now.

19. Along the sheer rocky cliff hanging over the crashing waves she crept along carefully never daring to look down.

Mechanics

20. The actor's favorite speech was in Shakespeare's *Much Ado About Nothing,* Act IV Scene ii.

21. In order to be considered healthy foods should not be too high in fat or sugar.

22. You're not serious about it are you?

23. Could I have your schedule form please?

24. Randall will have to study harder or he'll be in danger of losing his B average.

25. Can't you try one more time, to reach her?

26. Hey wait a minute!

27. Learning to downhill ski, is not as hard as you might think.

28. To create a sound that offers good stereo speakers should be placed at least eight feet apart.

29. To become a member of the band, had been her goal for three years.

30. Sarah did you mail a package to 522 Van Buren Street Richmond Indiana 47374?

31. Oh I didn't realize this was your magazine.

32. I can't remember the last time I read such an exciting electrifying novel!

33. Could you tell me, how to get to the city attorney's office?

34. The group of weary explorers trudged on through the jungle yet many had already given up hope of ever being found.

35. Breathing a sigh of relief the coach shook hands with his assistant.

36. Ladysmith Black Mombazo a famous choir from South Africa has recorded many albums of religious and traditional music.

37. She won't go along with our plan nor will she try to think of a better one.

38. Anyone, who wants to go to the Spanish play, should sign up in advance with the club advisor.

39. That girl, reading the newspaper by the cafeteria door just moved here from Seattle.

40. Kristy missed the penalty kick I'm sorry to say.

41. With this software program you don't need to save your work every few minutes.

42. Chad was looking for the office of Janet Montgomery M.D.

43. You are requested to appear in court on Thursday August 18 1996 to give testimony on the case.

44. Inside the tumbledown and ramshackle old mansion we found the evidence we were looking for.

45. You might still be able to sign up for the trip if you hurry.

Mechanics

Lesson 84
Dashes to Signal Change and to Emphasize

Use a **dash** to set off an abrupt break or change in thought within a sentence.

The owl's excellent sight—a valuable complement to its astounding ability to turn its head 270 degrees—makes it a master hunter, even at night.

Dashes may also be used to set off and emphasize supplemental information or parenthetical comments.

Melanie finished reading the book—the best she had ever read.
When Melanie finished reading the book—the best she had ever read—she had tears in her eyes.

▶ **Exercise 1** **Insert dashes where necessary. If the sentence is correct as written, write *C* on the blank.**

_____ Born in Wapakoneta a small western Ohio city Neil Armstrong became the first man to set foot on the moon.

_____ **1.** The slight woman she smiled shyly and curtsied was Nelly Sachs.

_____ **2.** Nelly Sachs the story of her life reads like a modern fairy tale was awarded the Nobel Prize for literature.

_____ **3.** Born in 1891 in Berlin the capital and leading city of Germany Nelly Sachs was the daughter of a well-to-do manufacturer.

_____ **4.** The Sachses lived in the most fashionable neighborhood in Berlin; who could have imagined what horrors this city would experience over the next half-century?

_____ **5.** The Sachses like many other middle-class and well-to-do Germans of the early twentieth century were Jewish.

_____ **6.** As a teenager, Nelly decided to try to develop her talent for writing abandoning her early interest in dance and began to compose stories and poems.

_____ **7.** Her first poems based on her observations of nature and on her reading Nelly collected in a book.

_____ **8.** In the 1920s Berlin was a cultural capital of Europe; many artists, writers, and musicians called it home.

_____ **9.** The Sachs family unaware of the violent storm building in their homeland lived a quiet, respectable life.

Mechanics

_____ 10. Looking out the windows of her home, Nelly might have seen organizers for a new political party the National Socialists, or Nazis.

_____ 11. In 1929 the economy of Germany and of all the industrialized world fell apart.

_____ 12. This period of economic hardship it was known as the Great Depression frightened people all over the world.

_____ 13. In Germany, many people believed that the leader of the Nazi party he was an Austrian who believed that power and might were Germany's rightful future had the answers to Germany's devastating economic problems.

_____ 14. The confusion, fear, and economic hardships of the German people led many to become followers of the Nazis and their leader, Adolf Hitler.

_____ 15. Hitler had a simple explanation for all of the country's problems "The Jews," he claimed, "are poisoning Germany."

_____ 16. Like poison, Hitler's beliefs spread through German society, and in 1934 the Nazi leader became the country's ruler.

_____ 17. The Nazis they now had total control of the country were prepared to enforce their will by imprisoning or murdering those who opposed them.

_____ 18. A series of laws they were known as the Nuremberg Laws and decreed that Jews were no longer citizens gradually eliminated the rights of Germans who were Jewish.

_____ 19. A brutal secret police force known as the Gestapo enforced the laws against Jews.

_____ 20. As the campaign became more intense, Nazi police prevented people from dealing with Jewish doctors, lawyers, or retailers; Jews understood that the situation would only grow worse.

_____ 21. Thousands of Jews left Germany, although thousands more remained.

_____ 22. In the meantime, Nelly Sachs's poetry because of its rhyme and subject matter had begun to be published.

_____ 23. As the Nazis moved closer to the Jews who remained many of whom were still loyal to their country Nelly and her mother were forced to move from their home.

_____ 24. Taking only a few of their possessions, they moved to a poorer neighborhood of Berlin.

_____ 25. In spite of the reduced circumstances she found herself in, Nelly tried to continue with her writing and other parts of her old life.

Mechanics

Lesson 85
Parentheses

Use parentheses to set off material that is not important enough to be considered part of the main statement.

The Dead Sea, at 397 meters (1,302 feet) below sea level, is the lowest spot on the earth's land surface.

A complete sentence within parentheses is not capitalized and needs no period if it is contained within another sentence. If a sentence in parentheses is not contained within another sentence, both a capital letter and a period are needed.

In 1940 Nelly Sachs (she was almost fifty years old) was forced to flee Nazi Germany.

If a comma, a semicolon, or a colon is required, place it *after* the closing parenthesis.

During the year of Grandma's birth (1939), many important historical events took place.

Place a necessary question mark or exclamation point inside the parentheses if it is part of the parenthetical expression.

I saw your brother Tim (or was it Tom?) at the game.

▶ **Exercise 1** **Rewrite the sentences in the space provided, adding parentheses and punctuation where necessary. If a sentence is correct, write *correct* on the line.**

Mr. Fox my biology teacher needs three volunteers to help with the field trip.

Mr. Fox (my biology teacher) needs three volunteers to help with the field trip.

1. If my cousin comes to visit I really hope he does, I'm sure he'll bring his banjo.

_____

2. Peugeot and Renault neither is sold in the United States are both French automobiles.

_____

3. The TV show will air at 9:00 P.M. Eastern Standard Time 8:00 P.M. Central.

_____

4. Giuseppe Verdi the Italian composer became popular during Italy's drive for independence.

_____

_____

5. Can you imagine close your eyes and try staying at a hotel that doesn't have electricity?

_____

Mechanics

6. If you like that idea, then LeConte Lodge in Tennessee is for you!

_____

7. Racing bicycles yes, I know you have a mountain bike are very efficient machines.

_____

8. Gina told me you lost her denim jacket.

_____

9. A person should eat two to four servings from another food group fruit is a good one.

_____

10. One source of ascorbic acid Vitamin C is orange juice.

_____

11. Peter Gabriel he was once in the band Genesis has performed solo for almost twenty years.

_____

12. When you get a letter from your pen pal I hope you get it soon, let me know right away.

_____

13. I'm applying for a pen pal myself.

_____

14. It sounds like fun to write to someone in a foreign country.

_____

15. Birds flying south migrating is one unmistakable sign of fall.

_____

16. My grandfather always talks about his favorite baseball player, Stan the Man Musial.

_____

17. African elephants they're rightly feared by many people differ from Asian elephants.

_____

18. At birth a typical Asian elephant weighs about 260 pounds about 118 kilograms!

_____

19. His parents left on a tour of Scandinavia Norway, Finland, Sweden, and Denmark.

_____

20. Did you hear that Luis he's my brother's friend was accepted at Harvard?

_____

Mechanics

Lesson 86
Quotation Marks for Direct Quotations

Use **quotation marks** to enclose a direct quotation. Separate introductory or explanatory remarks from the quotation with a comma.

The man looked at Angie and said, "I believe you are to blame for this."

Do not use a comma after a quotation that ends with an exclamation point or a question mark.

"What are you doing here?" the police officer asked.

When a quotation is interrupted by explanatory words such as *she said*, use two sets of quotation marks.

"An aged man is but a paltry thing," wrote the Irish poet William Butler Yeats, "a tattered coat upon a stick."

Do not use quotation marks in an indirect quotation.

Father said the train was running late.

Use single quotation marks around a quotation within a quotation.

"I heard the announcer say, 'You win a new car,'" he explained excitedly.

In writing dialogue, begin a new paragraph and use a new set of quotation marks every time the speaker changes.

Little Crow asked quietly, "Are you ready for the ceremony?"
"I don't know," White Wing replied, not daring to look at the older man.

▶ **Exercise 1** **Rewrite the sentences in the space provided, adding or deleting quotation marks and other punctuation where necessary. Some sentences may be correct.**

"Fools need advice most" Ben Franklin wrote, but wise men only are the better for it.

"Fools need advice most," Ben Franklin wrote, "but wise men only are the better for it."

1. The poster read, It's 11:00. Do you know where your kids are

_____

2. My reply he explained, was I would never do that _____

3. Rehearsals start on Monday announced the director. I hope everyone will be on time

_____

4. Everybody get down the woman screamed when the car exploded.

_____

5. The scarecrow told Dorothy that some folks went this way and others went that way.

_____

6. The school nurse asked Charlie, Are you feeling better now?

_____

7. Ms. Wallinchek assigned Patrick Henry's speech" said Annie.

_____

8. The one in which he says Give me liberty or give me death asked Tonya.

_____

9. May I help you asked the girl behind the counter.

_____

10. We got our history tests back yesterday, Matt explained."

_____

11. I got a B plus he added proudly. _____

12. The woman walked up to my mother and asked Do you know me

_____

13. William boasted "that he had read *The Scarlet Letter* in one night."

_____

14. We have a problem said Grandpa with a worried look a big problem

_____

15. The forecast for tonight said the meteorologist is snow

_____

16. Christina Rossetti is my favorite poet declared Megan.

_____

17. The clerk explained how the radio worked. _____

18. Lincoln warned "that a house divided against itself could not stand."

_____

19. Did the announcement say, Only sophomores need report at 3:30

_____

20. When Jose mentioned "that he might be going to the chess club meeting," I asked Do you mind
if I come along

_____

_____

Lesson 87
Quotation Marks with Titles of Short Works, Unusual Expressions, and Other Marks of Punctuation

Use **quotation marks** to enclose titles of short works, such as stories, poems, essays, newspaper and magazine articles, book chapters, and songs.

"The Tell-Tale Heart" (short story)
"Self-Reliance" (essay)

Use quotation marks to enclose unfamiliar slang and unusual expressions.

Jamal explained that in football a "pick" is a pass interception.

Place commas and periods inside closing quotation marks.

"I Like to See It Lap the Miles," a poem by Emily Dickinson, is about a train.

Place a colon or semicolon outside closing quotation marks.

This is my opinion of Emily Dickinson's "Because I Could Not Stop for Death": it's one of the greatest poems ever written.

Place a question mark or an exclamation point outside the closing quotation marks when it is part of the entire sentence but inside if it refers only to the quoted matter.

Did the caller say, "Drop the ransom money behind the big oak tree"?
Suzi asked, "What is your favorite poem?"

▶ **Exercise 1 Rewrite the sentences in the space provided, adding quotation marks where necessary. If a sentence is correct, write *correct*.**

The Necklace is a famous story by Guy de Maupassant.

"The Necklace" is a famous story by Guy de Maupassant.
_____

1. Ouch! yelled Clarissa.

_____

2. Mom likes to listen to Michael Feinstein sing Isn't It Romantic?

_____

_____

3. In tennis a score of zero is called love.

_____

Mechanics

4. Which of these poems by Edgar Allan Poe do you prefer—The Bells or The Raven?

_____

_____

5. I'm going to call my essay How to Proceed to Succeed.

_____

6. Never, shouted Morgan, will I agree to such terms!

_____

7. Am I Blue? was a popular song in my great-grandmother's youth.

_____

_____

8. Did Stephen Crane write a short story called The Open Boat?

_____

_____

9. For my report I read an article titled Unidentified Flying Objects—Fact or Fiction?

_____

_____

10. Can you quote the first line of the patriotic poem Concord Hymn?

_____

_____

11. For homework Ms. Ruiz assigned Chapter 22, The Great Depression.

_____

_____

12. Do you know what a gofer is?

_____

13. Do you know who wrote the nonsense poem Jabberwocky?

_____

_____

14. The Bear is probably William Faulkner's most famous short story.

_____

_____

Mechanics

Lesson 88
Italics

Titles of books, long poems, plays, films, television series, works of art, and long musical compositions are printed in italic type. Names of newspapers, magazines, ships, trains, airplanes, and spacecraft are also printed in italics. It is common practice not to italicize the article preceding the title of a newspaper or a magazine. In handwriting, use underlining to indicate italics.

the ***Washington Post*** (newspaper)   ***The Marriage of Figaro*** (musical work)

Italicize (underline) foreign words and expressions that are not used frequently in English.

In Italy, we spent a lot of time at the ***stazione ferroviaria,*** or train station.

Italicize (underline) words and letters used to represent themselves.

The word *carols* comes from the Greek word *choraules.*

▶ **Exercise 1** **Underline each word or phrase that should be italicized. Not every sentence has words that should be italicized.**

Tamara will read <u>The Return of the Native</u> for her book report.

1. Selma Lagerlof's best-known novel is The Story of Gosta Berling.

2. Lagerlof was the first woman to win the Nobel Prize in literature.

3. There is an article in National Geographic about Lagerlof's homeland.

4. The music club went to see a production of the opera Billy Budd.

5. The opera is based on a story by Herman Melville, author of the novel Moby-Dick.

6. Semper paratus—"Always prepared"—is the motto of the U.S. Coast Guard.

7. Sarah's dad made us a delicious dinner with bulgogi and kimchee.

8. My sister hung in her room a poster of Edward Hopper's painting Nighthawks.

9. Ich dien is the motto of the Prince of Wales.

10. Lianna didn't have any idea how often she said the word whatever.

11. Matt felt proud that he had earned all A's and B's.

12. We read the early edition of the Cleveland Plain Dealer.

13. One of the best places to get a galette is Rennes, France.

14. He was suffering from weltschmerz, a German word for "world-weariness."

15. My mom's favorite album of all time is the Police's Ghost in the Machine.

Mechanics

16. However, her favorite song is Aretha Franklin's "Respect."

17. The drama club is presenting Thornton Wilder's play Our Town next weekend.

18. Which movie did you like better: Home Alone or Home Alone II?

19. The word smee plays an important role in A.M. Burrage's story of the same name.

20. Whenever it's my turn to cook a meal for the family, I always make spaghetti.

21. It's fun to look through old Life and Look magazines.

22. Mahpiua-luta was a famous chief of the Dakota people.

23. The Broadway musical My Fair Lady is based on Pygmalion, a play by George Bernard Shaw.

24. My grandparents sent me a postcard of Michelangelo's statue David.

25. "The sequels to Gone with the Wind aren't as good as the original movie," she said.

26. The h on his computer keyboard didn't work.

27. My favorite story in the book Twice-Told Tales is "The Gray Champion."

28. We rode aboard the Delta Queen, a remodeled steamboat.

29. Roberto made a delicious Puerto Rican dish called monfongo con caldo.

30. Jennifer's mom, a carpenter, appeared on the television series This Old House.

31. Whitman was in tune with the zeitgeist, or "spirit of the times," of the 1850s.

32. Bach's Mass in B Minor is a great choral work.

33. Achilles, the great warrior, is a main character in the poem.

34. We traveled on the Highland Belle through northern Scotland.

35. I looked at the poster and realized I'd left out the c in dance!

36. You can make Ethiopian injera bread with wheat flour.

37. Our film club rented the movies Citizen Kane and Ben-Hur.

38. Rachel read the novel Pride and Prejudice in two days.

39. Dad christened his new boat Daybreak.

40. One of my favorite paintings is called Luncheon of the Boating Party.

41. My little sister is dancing to selections from The Nutcracker Suite.

42. Arthur says watching Sesame Street helped him learn to read.

43. Jerome's grandmother suggested that he mind his p's and q's.

44. Jazz great Charlie Parker was nicknamed "Bird."

Lesson 89
The Apostrophe

Use an apostrophe and -s to form the possessive of a singular noun, even one that ends in -s. Use an apostrophe alone to form the possessive of a plural noun that ends in -s. Use an apostrophe and -s to form the possessive of a plural noun that does not end in -s.

Doris's car　　boys' bicycles　　the children's room

Put only the last word of a compound noun in the possessive form.

the secretary of state's home　　her brother-in-law's car

If two or more partners possess something jointly, use the possessive form for the last partner named. If two or more partners possess something individually, put each one's name in the possessive form.

Laurel and Hardy's comedies　　Boeing's and Lockheed's airplanes

Use an apostrophe in place of letters omitted in contractions. Common contractions combine a subject and a verb or a verb and an adverb.

he's (he is, he has)　　won't (will not)　　it's (it is, it has)

Use an apostrophe in place of the omitted numerals of a particular year.

the class of '97　　the '96 election

▶ **Exercise 1** Add an apostrophe where necessary. Delete (⋎) apostrophes used incorrectly.

Cara's ski club is borrowing our⋎ room for their meeting.

1. Among Nobel Prize winners, Barbara McClintocks name stands out in many ways.

2. For example, this world-famous scientist doesnt own a telephone, so when she won the Nobel Prize in medicine in 1983, the Nobel committee couldnt call her!

3. She's not a teacher as so many other winner's of the award have been.

4. Barbaras childhood was unusual.

5. Barbaras father, a doctor, insisted that his children not be given any homework.

6. He wanted them to have free time to enjoy the wood's and outdoor activities.

7. Barbara chose to study at New Yorks Cornell University.

8. At Cornell Barbara made many friend's and was elected president of the womens freshman class.

9. Although she worked hard on her' studies, she was able to find time to play the banjo in a student jazz band.

10. At Cornell Barbara became interested in genetics and the study of heredity—the passing on of a parents characteristics to his or her offspring.

11. Genetic's as a science was still in it's youth when Barbara began to study it.

12. The pioneer in genetics' research was an Austrian monk named Gregor Mendel.

13. Mendel experimented with plants in his monasterys garden.

14. Mendels discoveries' about how the plants passed on certain characteristics to their offspring became the foundation of modern genetics.

15. However, it took scientists several decades to accept Mendels theories.

16. By the time Barbara McClintock was studying genetics at Cornell, scientists had confirmed the existence of genes, hereditys building blocks.

17. Genes, which transmit organisms messages to their offspring, are carried on chromosome's, tiny rods present in the cells of all living things.

18. Youd be surprised to learn about the methods of pioneers in the study of genetics.

19. Mendel studied pea plants while other's studied fruit flies.

20. Barbara McClintocks favorite organism was a type of corn called maize.

21. Maize is the multicolored corn youd use as a decoration in the fall.

22. The colors of the kernels indicate the genetic makeup of the corns chromosomes.

23. The early scientists research was difficult because of the small size of chromosome's.

24. The future Nobel Prize winners first major breakthrough was the identification of a corn kernels individual chromosomes.

25. During her year's at Cornell, Barbara met many other's interested in genetics.

26. In later years they would benefit greatly from each others research.

27. Barbara and another young scientist, Harriet Creighton, discovered that a cells chromosomal message's are exchanged during meiosis.

28. Meiosis is the process of a cells reproduction by division.

29. After several years at Cornell, Barbara accepted the National Research Councils offer of a fellowship to study and teach.

30. Over the next forty years, Barbara made many discoveries' about the nature of chromosomes, genes, and heredity.

Mechanics

Lesson 90
The Hyphen

Use a **hyphen** after any prefix joined to a proper noun or proper adjective (see Lesson 2, pp. 49-50, and Lesson 8, pp. 61–62). Use a hyphen after the prefixes *all-, ex-,* and *self-* joined to any noun or adjective. Use a hyphen after the prefix *anti-* joined to a word beginning with a vowel, and use a hyphen after the prefix *vice-,* except in *vice president.*

trans-Africa   **all-state**   **anti-inflation**

Use a hyphen in a compound adjective that precedes a noun. Do not use a hyphen if one of the words is an adverb ending in *-ly.*

a twelve-year-old boy *but* **The boy is twelve years old.**   **softly spoken words**

Hyphenate any spelled-out cardinal or ordinal compound number up to *ninety-nine* or *ninety-ninth.* Hyphenate a fraction used as an adjective.

twenty-two   **one-half tablespoon** *but* **one half of a tablespoon**

Words are generally hyphenated at the ends of lines between syllables. In general, if a word contains two consonants occurring between two vowels, divide the word between the two consonants. If a suffix has been added to a complete word that ends in two consonants, divide the word after the two consonants. Use a dictionary when in doubt.

moun-tain   **ask-ing**

▶ **Exercise 1 Add hyphens where necessary. Delete (⅄) unnecessary hyphens. Some sentences may be correct.**

The seasoned reporter removed a well-worn suitcase from the trunk of her car.

1. Ashok finished twenty first out of ninety seven runners.

2. When Torrie found out she had made the all conference team, she was ecstatic.

3. Babies are certainly tiny when they're three-weeks-old.

4. Oscar Robertson is one of basketball's all time greats.

5. Use one fourth teaspoon of cinnamon in this recipe.

6. The evening sky was an unbelievable shade of dark-blue.

7. Our ex babysitter's photograph was in the paper because she won an award.

8. Of all the teachers in our school, Ms. Sanchez is probably the most-popular.

9. The horse had to run the race with a sixteen pound weight on his saddle.

10. The concerto was well performed.

11. Sean's self confidence rose when he won second prize in the art show.

Mechanics

12. The teacher said she could tell our report was thoroughly-researched.

13. Excuse me, but are these tulips the late blooming variety?

14. The members of the anti poverty group were meeting in the auditorium.

15. The recipe called for three-quarters of a pound of butter or margarine.

16. This is definitely a mouth watering dish.

17. Steven eats only well done hamburgers.

18. Virginia's blue green outfit did not look good with her bluish purple hat.

19. Congratulations to the fifty ninth graduating class of Roosevelt High.

20. That was a back breaking job.

▶ **Exercise 2** **Show where each word would be hyphenated at the end of a line by drawing a vertical line (l) at the spot.**

sum|mer

1. thinking

2. chicken

3. highest

4. banquet

5. spokesperson

6. stomping

7. million

8. thoughtless

9. mistake

10. longest

11. hollow

12. doctor

13. announce

14. salvage

15. thankful

16. possessive

17. football

18. otherwise

19. balloon

20. friendship

▶ **Writing Link** **Write a paragraph describing an outfit you might wear to a costume party. Use at least two compound adjectives and two prefixes in your description.**

_____

_____

_____

_____

_____

_____

Mechanics

Lesson 91
Abbreviations

Use all capital letters and no periods for **abbreviations** that are pronounced letter by letter or as words. Exceptions are U.S. and Washington, D.C., which do use periods.

NBC   **PIN**   **AMA**   **NASA**   **NAACP**   **AIDS**   **NATO**

In ordinary prose, spell out state names and words that refer to streets, such as *Street, Road,* and *Boulevard*. On envelopes only, use the postal abbreviations for state names. Also on envelopes only, you may abbreviate words that refer to streets, such as *Street, Road,* and *Boulevard*.

AL Alabama   **MI** Michigan   **IL** Illinois
St. Street   **Rd.** Road   **Blvd.** Boulevard

Use the abbreviations A.M. (*ante meridiem*, "before noon") and P.M. (*post meridiem*, "after noon") for exact times. For dates, use B.C. (before Christ) and, sometimes, A.D. (*anno Domini*, "in the year of the Lord," after Christ.)

9:12 A.M.   11:20 P.M.   A.D. 1200   10,000 B.C.

Personal titles, such as *Mrs.* and *Jr.,* are almost always abbreviated. Titles of government and military officials and of clergy members are often abbreviated when used before the full name. This kind of abbreviation always ends with a period.

Ken Griffey **Jr.**   **Gen.** Dwight Eisenhower   **Sen.** Bruce Johnson

Units of measure are abbreviated when used with numerals in technical or scientific writing but are not abbreviated in ordinary sentences. The abbreviation is the same for both plural and singular units. Metric abbreviations do not take periods.

ENGLISH SYSTEM   METRIC SYSTEM
ft. foot   **cm** centimeter

▶ **Exercise 1** **Choose the word or abbreviation in the parentheses that correctly completes each sentence and write it on the blank.**

Tomorrow I will run one _____kilometer_____ farther than I ran today. (km, kilometer)

1. Marlene missed her goal shot by two _____. (feet, ft.)

2. _____ Ted Kennedy was the name on the office door. (Sen., Sen)

3. Saudi Arabia is one of the members of _____. (OPEC, O.P.E.C.)

Mechanics

4. Martin Luther King _____ was born in January. (Junior, Jr.)

5. At 11:45 _____ the balloon touched down behind the school. (A.M., *ante meridiem*)

6. _____ is one of the major television networks. (A.B.C., ABC)

7. _____ Robert E. Lee led the South during the Civil War. (Gen., GEN.)

8. Three _____ of the fabric cost $5.40. (yd., yards)

9. Around 8000 _____ the wooly mammoth died out. (B.C., before Christ)

10. When we toured the Space Center, a _____ official was our guide. (N.A.S.A., NASA)

11. The steak weighed about two _____(lb., pounds) on the butcher's scale.

12. In _____ 476 the Roman Empire finally came to an end. (A.D., *anno Domini*)

13. Step 4 of the lab instructions says, "Cut a segment 3 _____ long." (cm., cm)

14. Did the bus arrive before or after 4:00 _____? (*post meridiem*, P.M.)

15. My friend Spencer lives in Long Branch, _____. (NJ, New Jersey)

16. Mom sent me to the grocery store to buy one _____of bacon. (lb., pound)

17. The tire pressure measured thirty-five _____. (cc, cubic centimeters)

18. The story's main character is a lovable giant who is nine _____ tall. (ft., feet)

19. The _____ will see you tomorrow at noon. (Dr., doctor)

20. _____ is the abbreviation for the North Atlantic Treaty Organization. (N.A.T.O., NATO)

▶ **Exercise 2** **Rewrite the following addresses as if they would appear on envelopes, using the acceptable abbreviations.**

Maria Lopez   _____

1557 Westchester Boulevard   _____

Detroit, Michigan 13799   _____

Rachel Goldberg   _____

375 Andrews Street   _____

Huntsville, Alabama 10227   _____

Michael Lee   _____

879 Meander Road   _____

Chicago, Illinois 11337   _____

Mechanics

Lesson 92
Numbers and Numerals

Use **numerals** in charts and tables. In sentences, spell numbers that begin a sentence or that can be written in one or two words. Use numerals for those requiring more than two words.

An acre equals **43,560** square feet.
Five hundred fifty-five students attended the exhibit.
Mitch was the **twenty-second** person in the long ticket line.

Use numerals to express decimals, percentages, and amounts of money involving both dollars and cents. Write out amounts of money that can be written in one or two words.

2.2 liters   70 percent $17.95   seventy-five cents

Use numerals to express the year and day in a date and to express the precise time with the abbreviations A.M. and P.M. Spell out expressions of time that are approximate or that do not use A.M. or P.M.

November 11, 1918   8:15 A.M.   eight o'clock

Use numerals for numbered streets and avenues over ten and for all house, apartment, and room numbers.

202 East 44th Street   Apartment 34B   305 First Avenue

Use numerals to express page, line, act, and scene numbers.

page 101   lines 4–20 of the poem   Act 2, Scene 3, *or* Act II, Scene iii

▶ **Exercise 1** **Write in the blank the expression shown in parentheses that correctly completes the sentence.**

The candidate collected _____ one thousand _____ signatures. (1,000; one thousand)

1. On page _____ I found information about the Crusades. (42, forty-two)

2. On November _____, 1095, Pope Urban II gave a speech that launched the Crusades. (27, twenty-seventh)

3. The Crusades occurred between 1096 and _____. (twelve hundred seventy, 1270)

4. About _____ crusaders fought in the First Crusade. (thirty thousand; 30,000)

5. _____ of these crusaders were knights. (4,000; Four thousand)

6. The store at 349 West _____ Street has many books about history. (47th, forty-seventh)

7. There I purchased a biography of Franklin D. Roosevelt for _____. (sixteen dollars and ninety-five cents, $16.95)

Mechanics

8. The store also has a large table of bargain books that are priced from _____ cents to three dollars. (25, twenty-five)

9. The library sells used books for _____ each. ($1.00, one dollar)

10. More than _____ percent of all library users check out videos. (seventy, 70)

11. The average number of books checked out by each user is _____ per visit. (five point five, 5.5)

12. Jane lives on _____ Avenue between Ninth Street and 11th Street. (10th, Tenth)

13. At _____ feet, Nanga Parbat is one of the highest peaks in the Himalayas. (twenty-six thousand, six hundred; 26,600)

14. The country of Sweden covers _____ square miles. (170,250; one hundred seventy thousand two hundred fifty)

15. Chapter 3 begins on page _____ . (76, seventy-six)

16. The meeting will be held Tuesday at _____ P.M. (eight fifteen, 8:15)

17. More than _____ people attended the rally. (500, five hundred)

18. In Act 1, Scene _____, a farmer and his wife are discussing how they will make ends meet after a drought has destroyed their crops. (1, one)

19. In lines _____ of the scene, the oldest daughter explains why she has decided to leave the farm. (66–72, sixty-six to seventy-two)

20. The daughter, one of _____ children, longs for a job in the city. (4, four)

21. The whale-watching boat leaves from this dock at _____ o'clock. (six, 6)

22. The _____ state to join the United States was Alaska. (49th, forty-ninth)

23. Arnette was one of _____ students who were recognized for outstanding effort in cleaning up the park. (twelve, 12)

24. _____ percent of our students graduate from high school. (Eighty-five, 85)

25. The judge fined the company _____ a day until they stopped releasing chemicals into the lake. ($30,500; thirty thousand five hundred dollars)

26. The art museum is at 600 _____ Avenue. (Second, 2nd)

27. The university library owns more than _____ books. (nine million three hundred thirty-nine thousand five hundred sixty; 9,339,560)

28. On election day the polls will open at _____ A.M. (7:00, seven)

29. Jana knocked on the door of Apartment _____. (3, three)

30. He was the _____ player chosen in the draft. (25th, twenty-fifth)

Mechanics

✓ Unit 12 **Review**

▶ **Exercise** **Add all necessary punctuation marks. Underline words or phrases that should be in italics.**

Jane Austen,who wrote the novel <u>Emma</u>,is one of my favorite authors.

1. Among authors who have won the Nobel Prize for literature is Gabriela Mistral the Chilean poet who wrote the collection Sonnets of Death

2. Her haunting early poems often reflect the sadness of her childhood and youth which she spent as a schoolteacher in the Chilean countryside

3. Her later poems are concerned with the joys of motherhood social justice and the plight of the poor campesinos rural people of Latin America

4. What prizewinning author is known for her portrayals of life in the Middle Ages

5. Sigrid Undset who won the Nobel Prize in literature in 1928 is the author of Kristin Lavransdatter an epic story of life and love in medieval Norway

6. The winner of the 1938 Nobel Prize in literature was American Pearl Buck whose famous novel The Good Earth is based on her experiences living in China.

7. The Good Earth which tells the story of Chinese peasants very much like the ones Pearl Buck lived with in the 1920s and 1930s has been translated into at least sixty five different languages.

8. Another American winner of the Nobel Prize in literature is Toni Morrison her rich absorbing novels such as The Bluest Eye reveal both beauties and tragedies of African American life.

9. In the category of peace one indeed in which women have won a large number of Nobel Prizes two American women have been honored.

10. Perhaps best known as the founder of Hull House a famous community center in Chicago Jane Addams won the Nobel Peace Prize in 1931.

12. The name of Emily Balch unlike Jane Addams's is not familiar to most Americans.

13. Throughout her ninety four years Emily Balch was a tireless worker for the rights of women and for international peace.

14. Her efforts were rewarded in 1946 with the Nobel committees decision to award her the Nobel Peace Prize

Cumulative Review: Units 1–12

▶ **Exercise 1** Label each adjective clause *adj. clause* and each adverb clause *adv. clause*. Write the kind of sentence in the blank using these abbreviations: *dec.* (declarative), *imp.* (imperative), *int.* (interrogative), or *exc.* (exclamatory).

adj. clause

_____dec._____ The player who scores the most points will win a prize.

_____ 1. Did you leave your skates in the garage?

_____ 2. After Katie joined the soccer team, she gave us tickets to the first game.

_____ 3. Look how high that skier jumped!

_____ 4. Ivan's family still lives in the house that his grandfather built.

_____ 5. Because he did not practice, Jake did not make the team.

_____ 6. Don't break the antique glasses that Aunt Emily gave me.

_____ 7. Where is the map that shows the best route to take?

_____ 8. Brigitta joined us as soon as she could.

_____ 9. What an incredible story we heard!

_____ 10. Our coach, who usually walks to practice, drove her car today.

_____ 11. Bring me the letter that the mail carrier delivered.

_____ 12. Who wants to claim the hat that was left on the chair?

_____ 13. Although we both shopped for an hour, Claire visited twice as many stores as I did.

_____ 14. I will wait until Suzy is finished painting the fence.

_____ 15. Cora will play the melody while An Li plays the harmony.

_____ 16. Why did the puppy hide when Sebastian appeared?

_____ 17. Look for the person who is in charge of volunteers.

_____ 18. Those special effects were fantastic!

_____ 19. Who ate the dessert before I served dinner?

_____ 20. She chose a time when the park was deserted for our picnic.

_____ 21. The car which Kurt purchased can travel thirty miles on a single gallon of gas.

_____ 22. Help me hang the portrait that Linda painted.

Mechanics

Name _____ Class _____ Date _____

▶ **Exercise 2** Complete each sentence by writing the form of the verb listed in parentheses. Cross out each pronoun that does not agree with its antecedent and write the correct pronoun above it.

their

Angela and Tim _____worked_____ on ~~its~~ science fair project. (past tense of *work*)

1. Karla _____ to give their old clothes to charity. (present tense of *want*)

2. Steve and Lauren _____ its car to Dallas. (past tense of *drive*)

3. The team _____ for next year; she starts practice again next week. (future tense of *wait*)

4. Ms. Sanchez _____ all the food in his own kitchen. (past tense of *prepare*)

5. The thunderstorm _____ her mark on the small town. (past tense of *leave*)

6. The astronauts _____ the space shuttle in five minutes. (present tense of *board*)

7. I _____ to the store for milk and will be home soon. (present perfect tense of *go*)

8. These books can be checked out, so _____ it to Sabrina to place on the shelves. (present tense of *give*)

9. This department store _____ both men's and women's fragrances, though

   his selection is rather limited. (present tense of *sell*)

10. The artist _____ their canvas in bold strokes of red and blue. (past tense of *paint*)

11. Michael _____ the boat into the lake, then she photographed the swans. (past tense of *sail*)

12. The mirror might break if we _____ him. (present tense of *drop*)

13. Wildflowers _____ prettiest when growing in its natural habitat. (present tense of *be*)

14. Before leaving for practice, Jennifer _____ her ball and glove. (past tense of *grab*)

15. Several tourists _____ to visit the museum, and he hope to see the new

   monument as well. (present progressive tense of *hope*)

16. Aunt Sylvia _____ us at the fabric store when they finishes talking to Darla. (future tense of *meet*)

17. Uncle Antonio _____ us bowling last Tuesday. (past tense of *take*)

18. The mysterious castle _____ his secrets locked inside. (past tense of *keep*)

19. Claude _____ the hill quickly, but Lawrence took its time. (past tense of *climb*)

20. We _____ six miles when we reach their destination. (future perfect tense of *walk*)

21. George _____ Susan before remembering they was out of town. (past perfect tense of *invite*)

22. Kyle _____ jewelry out of everyday objects and gives it to his friends. (present tense of *make*)

▶ **Exercise 3** Draw three lines under each letter that should be capitalized. Add the correct end mark to each sentence. Delete (⸦) each unnecessary comma, semicolon, or colon.

george is traveling to Connecticut, for thanksgiving.

1. When is the independence day celebration going to start

2. The following, plays were written by William shakespeare: *Romeo and Juliet, Twelfth Night,* and *othello*

3. Two chemistry students will be selected; to participate in the demonstration

4. look at those: incredible acrobats

5. Leave your books on the table next to the letters, and the box of stamps

6. My american history class will take a field trip to ford's theater next week

7. Why, do you look so confused, kristen

8. That television show was fantastic

9. kimberly, jerome, and juanita will sing selections from: *Grease*

10. My friend and i want to learn; how to play lacrosse

11. mr. bennet, who collects antique clocks, can tell you how much grandfather's present is worth

12. Do you know, how to get to Chelton street

13. Open the kitchen window, victor

14. wave to Susie, from the train

15. Two of the contestants arrived early; however, jack arrived late because his car had a flat tire

16. Tabitha's grocery list included, bread, milk, eggs, and apples

Vocabulary and Spelling

Unit 13: Vocabulary and Spelling

Lesson 93

Building Vocabulary: Learning from Context

Clues to the meaning of an unfamiliar word can be found in its context, the other words and sentences surrounding it. As a reader, you can analyze a passage both for specific clues and for general context.

CLUE WORDS

that	like	also	but	because
in other words	for example	likewise	on the other hand	since
or	such as	similarly	on the contrary	therefore
also known as	for instance	resembling	unlike	as a result
which means	including	identical	however	consequently

INTERPRETING CLUE WORDS

Type of Context Clue

Definition: The meaning of the unfamiliar word is stated in the sentence.
Meteorology, or the science of weather forecasting, has become Todd's favorite subject.

Example: The meaning of the unfamiliar word is explained through one familiar case.
Fran loves to study mammals such as kangaroos.

Comparison: The unfamiliar word is similar to a familiar word or phrase.
Dissension closely resembles disagreement.

Contrast: The unfamiliar word is the opposite of a familiar word or phrase.
Constructive criticism can be helpful; however, criticism without foundation can be harmful.

Cause and effect: The unfamiliar word describes a cause in a sentence in which the effect is understood.
Garret had to fly stand-by; therefore, he was not sure he would get a seat on the five o'clock flight.

▶ **Exercise 1** Underline the specific clue word or words. Using the context of the italicized word, define the word.

Unlike Michiko, who always wore colorful and fashionable clothing, Myra dressed in a

nondescript manner. lacking distinctive or interesting qualities

1. The story is an *allegory* like the tale of the tortoise and the hare. _____

Vocabulary and Spelling

2. Though both of the senators were opposed to the bill, one seemed willing to reconsider but the other was *adamant*. _____

3. Although he delayed his research for a week, Miguel finally started to work seriously when he realized his group might get an "incomplete" for the project as a result of his *dilatory* practices. _____

4. The *itinerant* farmers were concerned their children would not have the advantage of a good education because they changed schools with each move. _____

5. The fashion museum was filled with styles that were the *vogue* during different eras. For example, mini-skirts and knee-high boots from the sixties were on display. _____

6. Jackie usually talks only when she has something important to say. Armand, on the other hand, is often rather *garrulous*. _____

7. David had been fascinated with insects since he was a child. Consequently, no one was surprised when he chose *entomology* as his major in college. _____

8. Since the project involves much detail, we need a very *meticulous* person to manage it. _____

9. The *facade* of the building is very ornate, unlike the interior, which is almost austere. _____

10. Jeannie felt challenged by *profound* ideas such as the meaning of existence and the origin of the universe. _____

11. Sam really is a *flamboyant* dresser; likewise, Judy enjoys wearing bright colors and unusual styles. _____

12. Harriet is *zealous* in her efforts to preserve the environment. However, she finds few people who share her enthusiasm. _____

13. My diagnosis as *hypertensive,* which means my blood pressure is higher than it should be, was all I needed to control my diet. _____

14. I expected my classmates to have a *plethora* of ideas for community service projects. Therefore, I was surprised when only a few offered suggestions. _____

Vocabulary and Spelling

Lesson 94
Building Vocabulary: Word Roots

The main part of a word is its root. When this is a complete word, it is called a base word. A root is often combined with a prefix (a part attached to the beginning), a suffix (a part attached to the end), or another root. Prefixes and suffixes often change the direction of a word's meaning. The chart below lists some word roots and their meanings.

Roots	Meanings
arch	rule, govern
ben	good
ced	go
dic, dict	say, speak
fac, fact	make
gen	class, start
hydr	water
man	hand
port	carry
sci	know
string, strict	bind
trac	draw, pull
viv	live, alive

▶ **Exercise 1** **Underline the root of each word. Using a dictionary when needed, define each word. If there is more than one definition, use one that emphasizes the meaning of the root.**

generic _characteristic of a whole group_____

1. monarch _____

2. matriarchy _____

3. hierarchy _____

_____

4. benefit _____

5. benefactor _____

6. benevolence _____

7. procedure _____

8. precede _____

9. antecedent _____

10. dictate _____

11. predictable _____

Vocabulary and Spelling

12. syndicate _____

_____

13. valedictory _____

14. manufacture _____

15. fact _____

16. genesis _____

17. generation _____

18. homogeneous _____

19. hydraulic _____

20. anhydrous _____

21. rehydration _____

22. manacles _____

23. manicure _____

_____

24. portage _____

_____

25. portfolio _____

26. transport _____

27. conscious _____

28. conscientious _____

29. prescient _____

30. constrict _____

_____

31. restrict _____

32. astringent _____

33. tractor _____

_____

34. distract _____

35. survive _____

36. vivid _____

Lesson 95
Building Vocabulary: Prefixes and Suffixes

Prefixes are syllables attached before a root to alter or enhance its meaning. For example, the prefix *un-* gives the opposite meaning to any word to which it is attached.

PREFIX	MEANING	PREFIX	MEANING
circum-	around, about	*il-, im-, in-, and ir-*	not
de-	from, down	*mis-*	do badly, hate
dis-	not	*pre-*	before
hyper-	excessive	*sub-*	beneath, less than

Suffixes can be added to root words to create new words with new meanings. Suffixes also have grammatical functions and can change, for example, an adjective like *deaf* into a noun like *deafness* with the addition of a suffix like *-ness.* Note that the spelling of the root can change when a suffix is added.

SUFFIXES	MEANING	PART OF SPEECH FORMED
-able, -ible	capable of, able to be	adjective
-ant, -ent	one who does an action	concrete noun
-en	to become	verb
-hood	condition, state	abstract noun
-ist	one who	concrete noun
-ly	in the manner or way of	adverb
-ous	full of	adjective
-sion, -tion	the state of being something	abstract noun

▶ **Exercise 1** Underline the prefix in items 1 through 10 and the suffix in items 11 through 20. Using the meanings of the prefixes and suffixes listed above, write the meaning of the word. Check your answers in a dictionary.

illegal __not legal_____

1. devaluate _____

2. misrepresent _____

3. circumnavigate _____

4. disrespectful _____

5. hyperactive _____

6. subtotal _____

7. illogical _____

8. improper _____

9. prehistoric _____

10. irregular _____

11. exportable _____

12. student _____

13. likelihood _____

14. servant _____

15. normally _____

16. confusion _____

17. famous _____

18. humorist _____

19. toughen _____

20. flexible _____

▶ **Exercise 2 Underline at least one prefix or suffix in each word. Write the meaning of the word. Check your answers in a dictionary.**

improper ___not proper_____

1. disagreeable _____

2. descendant _____

3. subcommittee _____

4. motherhood _____

5. artist _____

6. imbalanced _____

7. circumscribe _____

8. decongestant _____

9. hypercritical _____

10. sensitively _____

11. disadvantage _____

12. cancerous _____

13. absorption _____

14. preoperative _____

15. adoption _____

16. unpopular _____

17. stiffen _____

18. misbehave _____

19. tension _____

20. incompressible _____

Vocabulary and Spelling

Lesson 96
Basic Spelling Rules I

SPELLING *IE* AND *EI*

The *i* comes before the *e,* except when both letters follow *c* or when both letters are pronounced together as an *ā* sound. However, many exceptions to this rule exist.

ach**ie**ve (*i* before *e*)   rec**ei**ve (*ei* after *c*)   sl**ei**gh (*a* sound)   s**ei**ze (exception)

SPELLING *-CEDE, -CEED,* AND *-SEDE*

The *sēd* sound at the end of a word is usually spelled *-cede. Supersede, succeed, proceed,* and *exceed* are exceptions.

ac**cede**   con**cede**   inter**cede**   pre**cede**

SPELLING UNSTRESSED VOWELS

An unstressed vowel is a vowel sound that is not emphasized when the word is pronounced. For example, in *or-i-gin* the second syllable, *i,* is unstressed. To determine how an unstressed syllable is spelled, think of a related word in which the syllable containing that vowel sound is stressed. For *origin* think of *original.*

▶ **Exercise 1** Write each word, adding *ie* or *ei* where necessary. Items 1 through 15 follow the rules; items 16 through 20 are exceptions to the rules.

ch—f *chief* _____

1. f—nd _____
2. s—ge _____
3. br—f _____
4. pr—st _____
5. repr—ve _____
6. r—gn _____
7. sl—gh _____
8. b—ge _____
9. v—n _____
10. h—nous _____

11. dec—t _____
12. rec—pt _____
13. perc—ive _____
14. misconc—ve _____
15. imperc—vable _____
16. d—ty _____
17. h—r _____
18. effic—nt _____
19. kal—doscope _____
20. h—fer _____

▶ **Exercise 2 Fill in the missing letter or letters in each word.**

trag___e___ dy

1. succe_____
2. interce_____
3. pre_____de
4. proc_____d
5. super_____de
6. med_____cine
7. fall_____cy
8. col_____ny
9. sed_____tive
10. dram_____tist

11. re_____
12. se_____
13. ex_____
14. con_____
15. ac_____
16. com_____tose
17. com_____dy
18. magn_____tize
19. comb_____nation
20. crit_____cism

SUFFIXES AND THE SILENT *E*

When adding a suffix that begins with a consonant to a word that ends in silent *e*, keep the *e*. When adding a suffix that begins with a vowel or *y* to a word that ends in silent *e*, drop the *e*. When adding a suffix that begins with *a* or *o* to a word that ends in *ce* or *ge*, keep the *e* so the word will retain the soft *c* or *g* sound. When adding a suffix that begins with a vowel to a word that ends in *ee* or *oe*, keep the *e*.

plac*ement* (*e* + suffix)   **excit*able*** (drop *e,* add suffix)
chang*eable* (*e* + suffix)   **se*eing*** (*e* + suffix)

When adding a suffix to a word that ends in a consonant + *y*, change the *y* to *i*. Do not change the *y* to *i* when the suffix begins with *i*. When adding a suffix to a word that ends in a vowel + *y*, keep the *y*.

tr*i*ed (*y* changed to *i* + suffix)   **cop*ying*** (*y* + suffix)   **jo*yous*** (*y* + suffix)

▶ **Exercise 3 Use the spelling rules in this lesson to spell the words indicated.**

reuse + -able ___reusable___

1. dose + -age _____
2. degrade + -able _____
3. guide + -ance _____
4. replace + -able _____
5. salvage + -able _____

6. notice + -able _____
7. courage + -ous _____
8. foresee + -able _____
9. tiptoe + -ing _____
10. accompany + -ed _____

Vocabulary and Spelling

Lesson 97
Basic Spelling Rules II

DOUBLING THE FINAL CONSONANT

Double the final consonant before adding a suffix that begins with a vowel to a word that ends in a single consonant preceded by a single vowel.

tip**ping**   submi**tting**   rese**tting**

ADDING -*LY* AND -*NESS*

When adding -*ly* to a word that ends in a single *l*, keep the *l*. If a word ends in a double *l*, drop one *l*. If a word ends in a consonant +*le*, drop the *le*. When adding -*ness* to a word that ends in *n*, keep the *n*.

real**ly**   hil**ly**   horri**bly**   mea**nness**

FORMING COMPOUND WORDS

When joining a word that ends in a consonant to a word that begins with a consonant, keep both consonants.

day**b**reak   sun**s**et

▶ **Exercise 1** **Use the spelling rules in this lesson to spell the words indicated.**

drop + -ing _dropping_____

1. sled + -ing _____
2. numerical + -ly _____
3. slip + -age _____
4. modern + -ness _____
5. clan + -ish _____
6. rebel + -ion _____
7. book + keeper _____
8. offset + -ing _____
9. full + -ly _____
10. camp + site _____
11. dismal + -ly _____
12. agreeable + -ly _____

13. underbid + -ing _____
14. shrill + -ly _____
15. card + board _____
16. lean + -ness _____
17. prefer + -ing _____
18. ear + ring _____
19. humble + -ly _____
20. critical + -ly _____
21. knot + -ed _____
22. chill + -ly _____
23. able + -ly _____
24. night + time _____

25. stern + -ness _____

26. broken + -ness _____

27. especial + -ly _____

28. lamp + post _____

29. admirable + -ly _____

30. near + -by _____

GENERAL RULES FOR FORMING PLURALS

Most nouns form their plurals by adding -*s* or -*es*. However, nouns that end in -*ch, -s, -sh*, -*x,* or -*z* form their plurals by adding -*es*. If the noun ends in a consonant +*y*, change *y* to *i* and add -*es*. If the noun ends in -*lf*, change the *f* to a *v* and add -*es*. If the noun ends in -*fe*, change the *f* to a *v* and add -*s*.

books   lun**ches**   fol**lies**   shel**ves**   li**ves**

SPECIAL RULES FOR PLURALS

To form the plural of proper names and one-word compound nouns, follow the general rules for plurals. To form the plural of hyphenated compound nouns or compound nouns of more than one word, make the most important word plural.

D'Albertos   Jones**es**   blueberr**ies**   mother**s**-in-law

Some nouns have the same singular and plural forms.

series   deer

▶ **Exercise 2 Write the plural of each word.**

mess _messes_

1. church _____

2. patio _____

3. donkey _____

4. self _____

5. desk _____

6. city _____

7. proof _____

8. cuff _____

9. fox _____

10. Gomez _____

11. waltz _____

12. lieutenant governor _____

13. all-star _____

14. thrush _____

15. sheep _____

16. festival _____

17. basketball _____

18. wife _____

19. business _____

20. teammate _____

21. calf _____

22. bunch _____

23. Chin _____

24. knife _____

Vocabulary and Spelling

☑ Review: Building Vocabulary

Nowadays the term "Creole cuisine," a relatively recent American food interest, *conjures up* images of blackened fish and overbearing spices. *Natives* of southern Louisiana, who have enjoyed Creole delights at their dinner tables for generations, know their *culinary tradition* is rich and complex. It is a popular *misconception* to consider the terms "Creole" and "Cajun" *interchangeable.* While there are similarities, the two styles are *distinctly* different. The *inhabitants* of New Orleans created Creole *cuisine* over many years with the *influence* of many cultures. The French, Spanish, Africans, Native Americans, Cajuns, Chinese, and Germans all contributed to the *genuine* Creole cuisine enjoyed in homes in southern Louisiana. The Cajuns, who *emigrated* from Nova Scotia in the eighteenth century and settled in the more *remote* areas of the Louisiana countryside, *improvised* with ingredients readily available in the swamps and bayous. While Cajun cooking *features* the fresh food that the wetlands *bountifully* provide, Creole cuisine *developed* over the centuries, changing to accommodate the needs and tastes of each new group that came to Louisiana to settle.

▶ **Exercise 1** **Circle the letter of the word or phrase that best defines each italicized word in the above passage.**

_____c_____ images
   a. eras
   b. dreams
   c. concepts
   d. formulas

_____ **1.** nowadays
   a. soon
   b. at the present time
   c. rarely
   d. occasionally

_____ **2.** conjures up
   a. calls to mind
   b. performs magic
   c. confuses
   d. brings together

_____ **3.** natives
   a. people born in the area
   b. senior citizens
   c. inborn
   d. visitors

_____ **4.** culinary
   a. holiday
   b. char-broiled
   c. community
   d. of cooking

_____ **5.** tradition
   a. beliefs
   b. customs
   c. vocabulary
   d. subjects

_____ **6.** misconception
    a. mistaken idea   **c.** belief
    b. understanding   **d.** pregnancy

_____ **7.** interchangeable
    a. the same size   **c.** having the same meaning
    b. from the same source   **d.** movable

_____ **8.** distinctly
    a. vaguely   **c.** ordinarily
    b. definitely   **d.** separate

_____ **9.** inhabitants
    a. visitors   **c.** people who live in a place
    b. people who have moved to the city   **d.** original settlers of a place

_____ **10.** cuisine
    a. kitchen appliances   **c.** decor
    b. style of cooking   **d.** stored food

_____ **11.** influence
    a. authority   **c.** effect
    b. bias   **d.** motivate

_____ **12.** genuine
    a. real   **c.** counterfeit
    b. sincere   **d.** recent

_____ **13.** emigrated
    a. moved from   **c.** descended from
    b. cared about   **d.** changed names

_____ **14.** remote
    a. pointless   **c.** outlying
    b. public   **d.** private

_____ **15.** improvised
    a. made do   **c.** made better
    b. fake   **d.** wrong

_____ **16.** features
    a. qualities   **c.** portrays
    b. highlights   **d.** fastens

_____ **17.** bountifully
    a. charitably   **c.** meagerly
    b. abundantly   **d.** reluctantly

_____ **18.** developed
    a. became stronger   **c.** evolved
    b. became more available   **d.** faded away

Vocabulary and Spelling

Name _____ Class _____ Date _____

☑ Review: Basic Spelling Rules

▶ **Exercise 1** **Underline the word that is spelled correctly.**

1. In medieval warfare, castles were put under (siege, seige) for many months.

2. Truly, I can not (percieve, perceive) any difference.

3. Queen Victoria was the (reigning, riegning) monarch of England for sixty-four years from 1837 to 1901.

4. South Carolina was the first state to (sesede, secede, seceed) from the nation in 1860.

5. The highway patrol mounted a campaign urging motorists not to (exsede, excede, exceed) the speed limits.

6. Jacob couldn't remember the (combination, combenation) to his lock.

7. The wrappings on this package are all (biodegradeable, biodegradable).

8. Anne's scar is hardly (noticeable, noticable) now.

9. (Providing, Provideing) child care in the workplace has significantly reduced the absenteeism among parents of young children.

10. This order is wrong. I know I (specifyed, specified) the color as blue.

11. We can't decamp yet. The tent is still (driing, drying) in the sun.

12. Even though I was (annoyed, annoid), I remained calm and collected.

13. Miguel hasn't yet decided what courses he will take to meet the language (requirement, requirment) for college admission.

14. Wong enjoys (struming, strumming) his guitar while thinking about other things.

15. The racquetball (rocketed, rocketted) off both walls before Ian could hit it again.

16. I am already (regreting, regretting) my decision.

17. The detectives were (investigateing, investigating) the mysterious disappearance of the mayor.

18. The school is (scheduling, scheduleing) parent-teacher conferences for Tuesday.

19. The (preferred, prefered) dress code for ushers is white shirts and black slacks.

20. I wouldn't mind (repeatting, repeating) if I thought you had listened the first time.

21. To reduce the fat content of your diet, look for (leaness, leanness) in the cuts of meat you buy.

22. Ryan was really excited to have Geoffry as a (teammate, teamate).

23. Stacey didn't enjoy the movie even though it was (critically, criticaly) acclaimed.

24. A sixty-degree temperature in August seems (chily, chilly).

25. Mrs. Reed (humbly, humblely) accepted the award.

▶ **Exercise 2** **Write the plural form of each noun.**

bike _bikes_ _____

1. bench _____

2. video _____

3. turkey _____

4. bookshelf _____

5. sister-in-law _____

6. activity _____

7. belief _____

8. staff _____

9. duplex _____

10. topaz _____

11. Gonzalez _____

12. Rand _____

13. kickoff _____

14. brush _____

15. leaf _____

16. library _____

17. monkey _____

18. life _____

19. bus _____

20. holiday _____

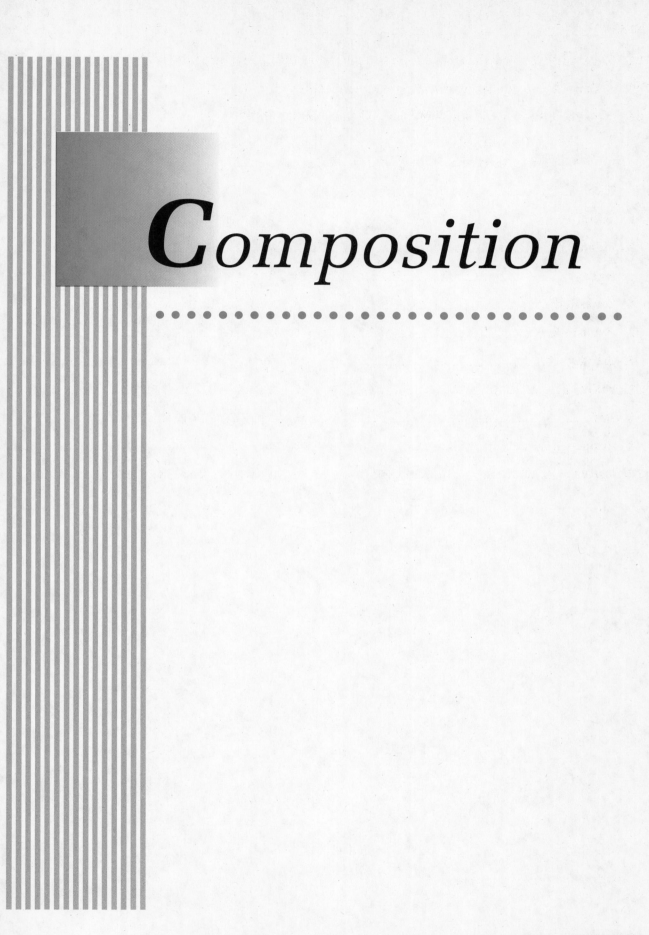

Composition

Unit 14: Composition

Lesson 98
The Writing Process: Prewriting

Before you begin writing anything, there are several factors that you must determine about what you are going to write. The topic is the subject about which you will write. You can determine the topic by *freewriting,* writing anything that comes to mind; *collecting,* gathering information from various sources; *making lists* about one key word or idea; and *asking general questions.* After a topic is chosen, determine the purpose, which is the reason for writing. One piece can have more than one purpose. The purpose is a narrowed form of the topic. Finally, you must determine the audience, or who is intended to read the piece. The overall nature of the piece will be different if it is intended for your best friend as opposed to the President. Knowing your audience will tell you how much they know about the topic, what writing style is needed, and what level of vocabulary is necessary. All of these factors will color your writing differently. Basically, you will determine *what* you want to say (topic), *how* you want to say it (purpose), and *to whom* you want to say it (audience).

▶ **Exercise 1** **Spend 10 minutes prewriting, using any of the techniques listed above.**

_____

_____

_____

_____

_____

_____

_____

_____

_____

_____

_____

_____

_____

_____

Composition

_____

_____

_____

_____

_____

▶ **Exercise 2** **Choose five specific topics that can be found in your prewriting from the previous exercise.**

_____

_____

▶ **Exercise 3** **Identify the purpose and topic of each topic sentence given below.**

Has the food in the cafeteria ever tasted worse? _topic: cafeteria food; purpose: to persuade_

the reader that the cafeteria food is bad

1. Currently, legislators are debating whether or not to increase the legal driving age. _____

_____

2. Annette is clearly the best candidate for mayor. _____

_____

3. The violins began the piece the orchestra played. _____

_____

4. This town has a ten o'clock curfew. _____

_____

5. Did you hear the one about the three-legged dog? _____

6. The earth is in grave danger from our constant pollution. _____

_____

7. The locker, standing as tall as I, is painted red. _____

_____

8. If you have not tried fly-fishing, you are really missing out on some great fun. _____

_____

9. The television show began with a fade-in before the credits. _____

Composition

_____

10. Many endangered species could become extinct within our lifetime.

_____

_____

▶ **Exercise 4** **Write a sentence that conveys both the topic and the purpose listed below.**

topic: books; purpose: to inform the reader of new titles available _Twenty new books are now_

displayed in the window of the bookstore.

1. topic: job; purpose: to persuade an employer to hire _____

_____

2. topic: fast food; purpose: to inform the reader of the different styles of fast food

_____

_____

3. topic: movie; purpose: to amuse a friend with a funny scene from a film _____

_____

4. topic: family; purpose: to describe your family to a stranger _____

_____

5. topic: entertainment; purpose: to persuade a friend to join you with that entertainment

_____

6. topic: the solution to a mystery; purpose: to describe the events of the case _____

_____

7. topic: money; purpose: to inform a manufacturer that you want a cash refund _____

_____

8. topic: sporting event; purpose: to narrate a commentary of the event _____

_____

9. topic: military action; purpose: to inform a soldier of the next mission _____

_____

10. topic: clothes; purpose: to persuade someone to buy you an article of clothing as a present

_____

Composition

▶ Exercise 5 **Write a brief paragraph about the controversy for each audience listed.**

Controversy: Whether or not to put a soda pop vending machine in the cafeteria.

1. audience: the student body

_____

_____

_____

_____

_____

_____

2. audience: the office

_____

_____

_____

_____

_____

_____

3. audience: parents

_____

_____

_____

_____

_____

_____

4. audience: the custodial staff

_____

_____

_____

_____

_____

_____

Composition

Lesson 99
The Writing Process: Drafting

After prewriting, you can begin drafting, or writing the piece in paragraph form. From the topic and the purpose you can develop a theme, the point the piece is trying to make. This theme should be stated in a thesis statement in the first paragraph. A paragraph consists of a topic sentence, which states a main idea related to the theme, and related sentences that support the main idea with details. Depending on the audience, theme, and purpose, you may choose to adopt a different style or voice, which gives the writing its "feel."

▶ **Exercise 1** **State a theme that is consistent with the topic and the purpose given. Use a complete sentence.**

topic: glaciers; purpose: inform _Glaciers are slow-moving blocks of ice travelling over our planet._

1. topic: castles; purpose: describe _____

2. topic: basketball; purpose: narrate _____

3. topic: airplanes; purpose: inform _____

4. topic: smoking; purpose: inform _____

   _____

5. topic: cars; purpose: persuade _____

6. topic: languages; purpose: describe _____

   _____

7. topic: the Vietnam War; purpose: narrate _____

   _____

8. topic: painting; purpose: describe _____

9. topic: politics; purpose: persuade _____

10. topic: AIDS; purpose: inform _____

11. topic: fashion; purpose: describe _____

12. topic: singing; purpose: amuse _____

13. topic: computers; purpose: describe _____

   _____

14. topic: weddings; purpose: narrate _____

Composition

15. topic: giraffes; purpose: amuse _____

_____

16. topic: apartments; purpose: describe _____

17. topic: school; purpose: amuse _____

18. topic: celebrities; purpose: persuade _____

19. topic: situation comedies; purpose: narrate _____

20. topic: math; purpose: inform _____

▶ **Exercise 2 Write a complete thesis statement from the theme given below.**

theme: the danger of being an astronaut _Although being an astronaut can be exciting, much danger_

is involved.

1. theme: the significance of the invention of the telephone _____

_____

2. theme: the beauty of wintertime _____

_____

3. theme: the exhilaration of horseback riding _____

_____

4. theme: the impact of photography on journalism _____

_____

5. theme: the excitement of skiing _____

6. theme: the unique quality of rap music _____

7. theme: the plight of Native Americans _____

8. theme: the high-quality acting in a play _____

9. theme: the hardships of the American frontier _____

_____

10. theme: the variety of events in track and field _____

_____

11. theme: the joys of woodworking _____

12. theme: the events leading the world into World War II _____

13. theme: the humor found in reading certain comic strips _____

_____

Composition

14. theme: the vastness of the oceans _____

15. theme: the accomplishments of the Aztecs _____

_____

16. theme: the health benefits of dancing _____

17. theme: the importance of rain forests for new medicines _____

_____

18. theme: the suspected causes of cancer _____

19. theme: the chain of command below the President. _____

_____

20. theme: the many different species of birds _____

▶ **Exercise 3** **Write four related sentences that provide details to support the topic sentence below.**

1. Martin Luther King Jr. accomplished much for the American civil rights movement.

_____

_____

_____

_____

2. Japanese culture seems exotic and mysterious to some. _____

_____

_____

_____

_____

3. A variety of career opportunities await me after I finish school. _____

_____

_____

_____

_____

4. Different families celebrate holidays differently. _____

_____

_____

_____

Composition

5. Finding the right hairstyle requires a little thought. _____

_____

_____

_____

_____

▶ Exercise 4 **Draft a brief one-paragraph piece concerning the following theme. Be sure to incorporate a proper voice and style.**

1. theme: thanking a friend for a gift _____

_____

_____

_____

2. theme: urging a politician to vote a certain way on an issue _____

_____

_____

_____

3. theme: requesting a day off from your employer _____

_____

_____

_____

4. theme: demanding a formal apology for a public insult _____

_____

_____

_____

5. theme: informing your family about your vacation. _____

_____

_____

_____

_____

Composition

Lesson 100
The Writing Process: Revising

Revise, or improve, your writing after completing a draft. Revising a paper allows you to improve the quality of the sentences and paragraphs. As you revise, check for three things. First, check for meaning. Make sure the piece is stating the intended theme. Then, check for unity. Make sure the organization is logical and the necessary details support the topics. Finally, check for coherence. Make sure the writing flows and the communication is clear.

▶ **Exercise 1** **Reorganize each paragraph for meaning, unity, and coherence.**

1. Earvin "Magic" Johnson played professional basketball for the Los Angeles Lakers. He went to Michigan State to play college basketball. Earvin Johnson was born in 1959. Recently, he contracted HIV and retired from playing professional basketball. He was nicknamed "Magic"

because of a spectacular basketball game he played in high school. _____

_____

_____

_____

_____

_____

_____

2. The Battle of the Bulge included an unsuccessful attempt by the Germans to make the Allies retreat. It was one of the next major military steps after D-Day in July 1944. The Battle of the Bulge, also called the Battle of the Ardennes, raged from December 16, 1944, to January 16, 1945. It got its name from Winston Churchill, who said that the Germans drove a "bulge," or wedge, into the Allied lines. _____

_____

_____

_____

_____

_____.

_____

_____

Composition

3. Clearly, pronghorns are built for blazing speed. They are similar to deer and antelope. Pronghorns, the fastest of all American mammals, can easily outrun their enemies. Their huge windpipes, lungs, and hearts accommodate sudden bursts of energy. _____

_____

_____

_____

_____

_____

▶ **Exercise 2** **Revise and rewrite the paragraph below.**

1. The idea of a computer has been around for a very long time. Microprocessors make modern computers very fast. Much faster than early computers like ENIAC. I have a computer at home. In 1944, Howard Aiken of Harvard built an early digital computer. It was Mark I. In 1642, Blaise Pascal of France built a calculating machine. It used rotating toothed wheels. In 1946, J. Presper Eckert Jr. and John W. Mauchly built ENIAC (*E*lectronic *N*umerical *I*ntegrator *A*nd *C*omputer.) It was 1,000 times faster than Mark I. In 1930, Vannevar Bush made a "differential analyzer," a machine to perform calculus. Transistors made computers faster and smaller. So did integrated circuits. _____

_____

_____

_____

_____

_____

_____

_____

_____

_____

_____

_____

_____

Composition

Lesson 101
The Writing Process: Editing

After revising your work, you can **edit** and clarify your ideas in writing. While you edit, look for the following items: correct word usage, subject-verb agreement, correct verb tenses, clear pronoun references, run-on sentences, and sentence fragments. When editing, cross out words and write new words in margins and spaces. **Proofreading** entails checking for spelling, punctuation, and capitalization errors. Use the following proofreading marks:

MARK	MEANING	EXAMPLE
∧ (caret)	insert	sould
⅄ (dele)	delete	thje
#	insert space	hockeypuck
⌒	close up space	over use
≡	capitalize	texas
/	make lowercase	Mine
⬭ sp	check spelling	recieve
∿	switch order	you me or
¶	new paragraph	...how I felt. Just then....

▶ **Exercise 1** **Edit the sentence for clarity and correct grammar.**

is   player
The best football guy, he be it.

1. She are the starling of the team.

2. Gary asked Ken why he should do that.

3. Boy did we work for Over five hours!

4. My brother run to the store yesterday.

5. I bought some bread came home quickly.

6. Looking at the *Lone Ranger* movie are fun.

7. Dogs and cats makes great pets.

8. The coach not know why I left practice.

9. Two friends of mine Kenji and Jose.

10. That instructor reallyknows the Subject

Composition

▶ **Exercise 2 Edit the paragraph for clarity and correct grammar.**

Yesterday, I had to give my first aural report ever since. I don't know how I did it I was so nervous. I was so nervous that the back of my knee caps was sweating. But I did it I'll never know. I guess I could of did as good without worrying as much as I had. Went great. This is the kinda report where you speak.

▶ **Exercise 3 Proofread each sentence for spelling, punctuation, and capitalization errors.**

I was (nervus) when I moved from ontario, canada.

1. he returned from scalling the mountains;.

2. Ana saw a pod of dolfins swiming off the florida coast.

3. Jack considered mr. Han, his Algebra teacher among his personal heros.

4. My bike roored over the hill.

5. Struggling the majician freed hisself.

6. Because this Bandage keeps falling off this cut will never heel.

7. I bought the new albumn at zany's, that new record store.

8. They visited the great Smoky Mountains.

9. space travvel is dream a of the future.

10. Jane and leanne wattered the poinsetas.

▶ **Exercise 3 Proofread the paragraph for spelling, punctuation, and capitalization errors.**

The Special Effects in motion pitures ofen addto the realisium of a film. Some times movies are mad simply to showoff; some effects special. This part ofthe movie-making prosess has often contribeuted to enormus budgets for certainfilms. With new technology, in Computer Animation, movie makers can bring The Impossible to Life! A process knownas "morphing" can visually change one image toanother. who knows the limit of this technolgy?

Composition

Lesson 102
The Writing Process: Presenting

After completing a piece of writing, you may want to present, or share your work with others. The idea of presentation can come as early as the prewriting stage. Knowing the audience often defines the market for your work. Many times, the nature of the material also defines the market. Several different outlets exist for writing composed by ninth graders. Some markets include school forums, which include school newspapers and classroom presentations; community forums, which include community groups and local community papers; contests, which are often offered by magazines; and open-market forums, which include professional magazines and periodicals. Carefully examine your writing and determine the audience. Then search for a market that serves that audience. You may find the *Market Guide for Young Writers,* available at libraries, very useful. Some outlets, like classroom presentations, exchange groups, and community productions, offer a chance for an oral presentation. In this case, prepare visual aids to add to your presentation.

▶ **Exercise 1 Suggest a market for the writing described below.**

an essay on model-making __a hobby magazine or newsletter or a school assignment_____

1. a short romance story _____

2. an original song composition _____

3. a review of a movie or play _____

4. an anecdotal essay about your childhood _____

5. an opinion piece concerning the school's curriculum _____

_____

6. a brief biography of your favorite actor or actress _____

7. a humorous year in review of your freshman class _____

8. a poem about nature _____

9. a report on a recent scientific development _____

10. an analysis of one of Shakespeare's plays _____

▶ **Exercise 2 Suggest two visual aids to increase the effectiveness of the writing piece listed.**

a speech about the ozone layer __photos of the ozone hole and models of the chemicals involved__

1. a research paper on economics _____

2. a short play _____

Composition

3. a music composition _____

4. a review of a film or television show _____

_____

5. an informative speech about history _____

_____

6. a poem about nature _____

7. an anecdotal speech about your vacation _____

8. an explanation of the sports teams in your school _____

_____

9. a speech to the student body about your running for student council _____

_____

10. a plea to the community to donate to a wildlife fund _____

_____

▶ **Exercise 3** **Prewrite on any topic desired. Write a short piece with a specific audience in mind. Then, explain how and to whom you might present this piece.**

_____
_____
_____
_____
_____
_____
_____
_____
_____
_____
_____
_____
_____
_____
_____

Composition

Lesson 103
Outlining

Outlining is a method used to organize the information in a piece of writing. Because prewriting can often be a jumble of words and phrases, it makes sense to organize that information before starting the drafting process. One method of constructing an outline is to put all your prewriting information on index cards. These cards can then be arranged by main topics and the details supporting that topic. To write your outline, indicate your main topics with Roman numerals. Put supporting details, or subtopics, beneath each topic with capital letters. These subtopics can have subdivisions as regular numbers. However, if you subdivide a topic or subtopic, at least two subdivisions must be named. For example, an outline of an audition for the school play might look like this:

I. Trying Out for the School Play
   A. First time trying out
      1. I was nervous and excited
      2. I did not think that I would remember my lines
      3. I had to audition for Ms. Hendrix, the drama teacher

   B. The role I wanted
      1. Hero of a romantic comedy
      2. Character is handsome and charming
      3. I had pictured myself in a role like this
II. Performing In the School Play

▶ **Exercise 1 Evaluate the outline below.**
   I. Jets
      A. Effects on warfare
         1. Non-stop bombing flights
      B. Helicopters used in Korean and Vietnam Wars
   II. Balloons
      A. Used to observe troop movements
      B. Blimps
         1. Hindenburg was one
         2. Filled with hot air or gas
   III. Airplanes

_____

_____

_____

_____

_____

_____

Composition

▶ **Exercise 2** **Organize the following topics and details into an outline of the biography of Howard Hughes.**

Became a millionaire; Born 1905 in Houston, TX; Business Life; Companies controlled; Controller of Trans World Airlines; Died in 1976; Dropped out of society in the 1950s; Early Life; Father died in 1924; Hughes Aircraft Company; Inherited Hughes Tool Company upon father's death; Later Life; Never seen in public; Refused to be photographed; RKO Pictures Corporation

_____

_____

_____

_____

_____

_____

_____

_____

_____

_____

_____

_____

_____

_____

▶ **Exercise 3** **Prewrite on any topic desired. Then, construct an organized outline about that topic.**

_____

_____

_____

_____

_____

_____

_____

_____

_____

Composition

Lesson 104
Writing Effective Sentences

When you tell a story out loud, you can raise or lower your voice to emphasize a passage. You can also control how fast you read, slowing down if you want to be solemn and speeding up if you want to show quick action. When you write, sentences do the work of your voice.

The hardest working sentence in a paragraph is the topic sentence. A topic sentence states the main idea of a paragraph. Write a clear, strong topic sentence. Use supporting details to develop the main idea. Supporting details prove, clarify, or give more information about the main idea. Emphasis and pace are determined by where you place the supporting details in the sentence and by the number of details you choose to include. Long sentences have a slower pace than short sentences. Change the pattern of a topic sentence to add emphasis to a word or group of words.

You can draw attention to the subject by moving it to the end of the sentence. For example, "Over the horizon rose a ship's mast." This sentence would also be correct with the subject stated first: "A ship's mast rose over the horizon." Notice that whether the subject comes first or last, its verb remains the same.

The action verb is in the active voice when the subject of a sentence performs the action. When the action is performed on the subject, the action verb is in the passive voice. Use the passive voice when you do not want to emphasize the subject or when you do not know who is performing the action.

▶ **Exercise 1** **Combine the four sentences into an effective topic sentence, or write a topic sentence accompanied by one or more supporting details.**

    a. Many youngsters go without food.
    b. This happens every day.
    c. We should help them.
    d. They are very needy.

    Because many youngsters go without food each day, we should help feed needy children.

1. a. We will perform the play on Friday.
    b. We need more rehearsals.
    c. It will be a huge hit if we rehearse.
    d. People will talk about it for weeks afterwards.

Composition

2. a. Elephants are enormous.
   b. They are also very gentle.
   c. They will pluck a peanut right from your hand.
   d. The elephants at the zoo fascinate me.

_____

_____

3. a. My favorite skater took the ice.
   b. She had an excellent routine.
   c. The jumps were amazing.
   d. I was excited.

_____

_____

4. a. You are very negative.
   b. That behavior is unpleasant.
   c. You may lose friends over this.
   d. Stop being negative.

_____

_____

5. a. Ernie sells hot dogs.
   b. He is weird, yet lovable.
   c. Everyone in town knows and likes him.
   d. He is part of what makes our town interesting.

_____

_____

6. a. The night was hot.
   b. The night was wet.
   c. Our air conditioner broke.
   d. We were miserable that night.

_____

_____

7. a. The balls fly.
   b. The players stumble.
   c. The pace of volleyball is very fast.
   d. Volleyball is very exciting.

_____

_____

Composition

8. a. Jules Verne lived in the nineteenth century.
    b. He wrote *20,000 Leagues Under the Sea.*
    c. The book has sold well to this day.
    d. It predicted the use of submarines.

_____

_____

9. a. I went to the football game.
    b. The home team won.
    c. The score was close.
    d. The game went into overtime.

_____

_____

10. a. Tyrannosaurus rex was the largest meat-eating dinosaur.
    b. It stood eighteen feet tall.
    c. It lived during the Cretaceous period.
    d. Only a small number of Tyrannosaurus fossils have been found.

_____

_____

▶ **Exercise 2 Explain whether the verb voice used in the sentence is the best choice. If the verb voice needs to be changed, rewrite the sentence.**

The pie was eaten by Chen. __Chen ate the pie._____

1. The dance contest was won by Sabrina. _____

2. The money was stolen from the register. _____

3. The rival teams were evenly matched. _____

4. The actors were given scripts by the director. _____

5. The actors auditioned for the director. _____

6. This ticket must be presented at the door. _____

7. The dog was covered with mud. _____

_____

8. The dog frolicked in the mud. _____

9. That portrait was painted by Koto. _____

10. The design was approved by Ana. _____

Composition

▶ **Exercise 3** **Rewrite the paragraph below with effective sentences.**

I am amazed at the sight of the enormous roller coaster. The group waiting to board the roller coaster is joined by me. I watch the bright red cars grind to a halt. The riders seem exhausted but happy. The riders spring out of their seats. The riders head for the next ride. I sit in one of the cars when my turn comes. I buckle myself in. I take a deep breath. The roller coaster starts to move. It moves at a deceptively slow pace. It moves with more force up a steep incline. It reaches the top of the steel hill. At this time I can see the entire park. The park is spread out before me like a colorful quilt. The roller coaster suddenly begins to move downward. Whoosh! I feel like I'm plummeting to the ground! But I am not plummeting to the ground. I am safely inside a car. The car is following a track. The track is carefully placed. The ground is never reached by me. Instead, I am led up another steel hill. This hill is taller. But this time I am prepared. Here I go!

_____

_____

_____

_____

_____

_____

_____

_____

_____

_____

_____

_____

_____

_____

_____

_____

_____

_____

_____

Composition

Lesson 105
Building Paragraphs

The supporting details in a paragraph can be arranged in different ways. Chronological order places events in the order that they happened. Spatial order is the way objects appear. Compare/contrast order shows similarities and differences.

For example, this note from a friend makes use of compare/contrast order in the first paragraph, spatial order in the second, and chronological order in the third.

You must try the East Side Grill! It is bigger and better than the restaurant we went to last week. The servers and hosts at the East Side Grill are much friendlier. Also, the bill at the East Side Grill was a lot less expensive!

When you walk into the East Side Grill, you might think the place is run-down and old. But the dark hallway opens into a bright, modern dining room with windows on the ceilings. There is a jukebox against one wall and a grand piano against another.

The food at the East Side Grill is great! First, we had huge salads filled with crisp vegetables. Then we had thick, hot soups. Next, we had main courses of roast beef and potatoes. We finished our meals with slices of homemade pie for dessert.

▶ **Exercise 1** **Number the following sentences in chronological order.**

_____ Then I cut two slices from a tomato.

_____ I place the tomato slices atop the cheese and ham.

_____ I always make my favorite sandwich a certain way.

_____ To complete my creation, I put the mustard-covered slice of bread atop the loaded slice of

bread.

_____ First, I place two slices of whole wheat bread on a plate.

_____ Next, I put one slice of Swiss cheese on top of the ham.

_____ Finally, I enjoy!

_____ I put mayonnaise on one slice of bread and mustard on the other.

_____ Then I lay three pieces of ham on the mayonnaise-covered slice.

Composition

▶ **Exercise 2** **Revise the following paragraph in chronological order, then rewrite the paragraph.**

First we hiked up a steep grade, but the trail was clear and easy to follow. We had to climb over nearly a dozen felled trees to get to the halfway point. Our six-mile hike to the river thoroughly exhausted us. We began our hike from Pine Grove Park early in the morning. At the two-mile mark, we spotted a family of deer. We found the stream that marked the end of the fifth mile and followed it to the river. We got lost, wandered in a circle, and ended up doing the fourth mile twice! Finally, we fell asleep under a giant tree.

_____

_____

_____

_____

_____

_____

_____

_____

_____

_____

_____

_____

_____

_____

_____

_____

_____

_____

_____

_____

_____

Composition

► **Exercise 3** **Write the following paragraph in spatial order.**

At the stop sign, a boy and a girl jumped rope. Across the street from the Garzas' house, a mail carrier made a delivery. At the Wittenauers' house across the street from ours, sprinklers noisily sprayed water onto the grass. From my front step, I looked from one end of the street to the other. The mail carrier moved to the next house, where Mrs. Meyer and her two sons were playing basketball. In the driveway of the first house on the right, Mr. Garza washed his car. Our street was buzzing with activity on Saturday morning. At the end of our street, my friend Jerry was trying to teach his puppy to sit.

_____

_____

_____

_____

_____

_____

_____

_____

_____

_____

_____

_____

_____

_____

_____

_____

_____

_____

_____

Composition

▶ **Exercise 3** **Use compare/contrast order to write a paragraph about one of the following topics:**

your best friend

what has made this school year interesting

the way your bedroom looks

_____

_____

_____

_____

_____

_____

_____

_____

_____

_____

_____

_____

_____

_____

_____

_____

_____

_____

_____

_____

_____

_____

_____

Composition

Lesson 106
Paragraph Ordering

Revising a first draft includes checking the unity and coherence of paragraphs. You need to make sure that each paragraph is unified; that is, it opens with a topic sentence (a sentence that states the main idea of the paragraph) and the supporting details are related to that topic sentence. To make sure the comparisons are clear, or coherent, you must check chronological, spatial, and compare/contrast details. (See Lesson 105.) Finally, you need to make sure that ideas are properly linked by transitions.

▶ **Exercise 1** **Revise the following paragraphs for unity and coherence.**

I had been watching and admiring the ragged puppy from my porch for about an hour. My dog Emma was a stray when I found her. Her "home" was the cold concrete under a car in front of my house. She was thinner and dirtier, but what made me fall in love with her were her ears, of all things. I could just tell that beneath all that grime was the pet I'd always wanted.

I had to figure out a way to get her. She would venture out from under the car only when she was sure no humans were near. As soon as I approached her, she would scurry back under the car. She would creep up to the sidewalk and give me a look that seemed to say that she wanted to be friends. One ear pointed straight up, and the other flopped down. When I looked under the car, she whimpered. I could tell that she needed me as much.

I had an idea, and I was glad that my mother wasn't home so I could put my plan into action. I went into our house and got my mother's leftover beef stew. I brought out a big bowl and placed it beside the car so the dog would have to come out to eat.

Slowly, she inched toward the bowl. I could hear her sniffing, so I knew that she was smelling a better meal. She stuck her head out from under the car and looked up at me with those big brown eyes. I didn't grab her when she began eating. I stroked her head slowly, to let her know I was her pal. When she was finished, I picked her up and carried her home. She couldn't have weighed more than ten or fifteen pounds. I've had her ever since. I had to bathe her three times to get the engine oil off her.

Composition

▶ Exercise 2 **Rewrite the paragraphs, based on your revisions.**

_____

_____

_____

_____

_____

_____

_____

_____

_____

_____

_____

_____

_____

_____

_____

_____

_____

_____

_____

_____

_____

_____

_____

_____

_____

_____

_____

Composition

Lesson 107
Personal Letters

A **personal letter** is often a letter to a friend or relative. In a personal letter, you describe recent events in your life and ask the recipient questions about his or her life. A personal letter can also be an invitation or a thank-you note.

These letters are usually written in indented form. Each paragraph is indented, as well as each line in the heading and the signature (see Handbook page 20).

▶ **Exercise 1** **Read the following personal letter. Answer each question.**

951 Pleasantville Drive
Sunnydale, Illinois 60000
May 15, 1996

Dear Chris,
    You won't believe what a great month I've had! I couldn't wait to write you. First of all, I finally made the swim team. All that extra practice has paid off. My first meet is Monday. I'm a little nervous, but I'll be all right once I get in the water.
    The time I've spent mowing lawns and cleaning garages is paying off, too. I'm using the money I've earned to buy the mountain bike I told you about in my last letter. The next time you come for a visit, you can try it out.
    Did you buy the bike you had your eye on? Write soon and tell me all about it. Tell me what else you've been doing, too. I miss you.

Your friend,
Taylor

1. Who is Chris? _____

2. Why is Taylor writing to Chris? _____

3. How is this a good example of a personal letter? _____

_____

_____

_____

4. What might Chris include in a response to Taylor's letter? _____

_____

_____

_____

_____

Composition

Name ______________________ Class ________ Date ____________

▶ **Exercise 2** **Write a personal letter to a friend.**

Different situations call for different kinds of personal letters. You would probably use a different tone and style in writing to an adult relative than you would in writing to your best friend. Your letter to your relative would probably be more formal, while you might make use of secret code words and slang in your letter to your friend.

You would also write differently to an author you admire than you would to a friend who has just performed in a play. While you would certainly be gracious in both letters, your letter to the author might express stronger feelings about how art affects life.

▶ **Exercise 3** **Write a letter thanking an adult relative for a gift or discussing a recent visit. On the last three lines of the answer space, explain why you chose the style you used.**

_____

_____

_____

_____

_____

_____

_____

_____

_____

_____

_____

_____

_____

_____

_____

_____

_____

_____

_____

_____

Composition

▶ **Exercise 4** **Write a letter to an author or performer you admire. On the last three lines of the answer space, explain why you chose the style you used.**

_____

_____

_____

_____

_____

_____

_____

_____

_____

_____

_____

_____

_____

_____

_____

_____

_____

_____

_____

_____

_____

_____

_____

_____

_____

_____

_____

_____

Composition

Lesson 108
Business Letters: Letters of Request or Complaint

A letter of request is a letter that asks for information or service. When writing a letter of request, you should be clear and courteous. Explain what information you need and why you need it. Include any information the receiver may need to answer your request.

Business letters are usually written in block form or semiblock form. In block form, everything is lined up with the left margin. In semiblock form, the heading, complimentary close, and signature are placed on the right-hand side of the page (see Handbook, pages 19–20).

▶ **Exercise 1** **Read the following letter. Is this a good example of a letter of request? Why or why not?**

_____

_____

_____

_____

Dear Ms. Ling:
I am a freshman at Polk High School. I am currently working on a science-fair project concerning methods of weather forecasting. Since I am planning to be in New York next week, I was wondering if I could tour your meteorological facility and ask you some questions. I hope so.

Sincerely,

Paul Thornton

▶ **Exercise 2** **Think of a situation in which you would need to ask someone for information. Perhaps there is a certain camp you are interested in attending or a service program you would like to join. Write some ideas for your letter on the lines below. Then write your letter on a separate piece of paper and send it to the person who can answer your questions. Be sure to use proper business-letter format.**

_____

_____

_____

_____

_____

Composition

A **letter of complaint** is a letter informing someone of a problem or concern and sometimes a request for action. It should be clear, concise, and rational. Never let your anger get the best of you. Begin your letter by stating the problem and telling how it happened. Then use supporting details as evidence of your problem. End your letter by explaining what you want done. Be reasonable, and avoid insults and threats.

▶ **Exercise 1** **Describe any problems that exist in the letter of complaint below. Suggest how to correct any errors.**

Dear Customer relations manager,

You're umbrellas stink! I just bought one and it fell apart as soon as I walked out the door. First of all it leaked then it ripped when the wind blew. Dont you know umbrelas are supposed to protect us from things like that. I got soaked when I walked home and its all you're stupid fault! I don't want another of you're lousy umbrellas, all I want is my money back now. If you dont give me a full refund I promise, you will be sorry!

Angrily,
Bill Higgins

_____

_____

_____

_____

_____

_____

_____

▶ **Exercise 2** **Revise and rewrite the letter of complaint above.**

_____

_____

_____

_____

_____

_____

_____

_____

_____

_____

Composition

Lesson 109
Business Letters: Résumés and Cover Letters

A **résumé** is a summary of your work experience, school experience, talents, and interests. It is used in applying for a job or for admittance into a school or academic program.

You want your résumé to be clear, concise, and expressive. In describing your accomplishments, use action verbs *(won* the award, *taught* the children). Because a résumé is a summary, it is not necessary to use complete sentences. However, you do want to use a consistent format, as in the following example:

Frank Garcia
2210 Victory Parkway
Cincinnati, Ohio 45210
(513) 555–5555

Objective:	Admission into the Future Teachers of America Young Scholars Program
Education:	Central High School, September 1994–present. 4.0 grade-point average Eastern Junior High School, September 1989–June 1992. 4.0 grade-point average.
Work Experience:	Camp counselor, Camp Lookout, Cincinnati, Ohio, June–August 1994.
Responsibilities:	Tutored third graders in math and English.
References:	John McGraw, teacher, Central High School (513) 555–5555 Marla Quincy, manager, Camp Lookout (513) 555–5555

▶ **Exercise 1   Answer the following questions about Frank Garcia's résumé.**

1. How might the headings (Objective, Education, etc.) of his résumé be ordered if Frank were applying for a job? Why? _____

_____

_____

2. In what order should entries for education and experience be listed? _____

_____

_____

3. The headings Frank used are not the only ones you can use on a résumé. Name at least two other

appropriate headings. _____

_____

_____

_____

4. Whom should you use for references? Why should you get their permission first?

_____

_____

_____

_____

_____

▶ **Exercise 2 You are applying for one of the following:**

• a summer job as a camp counselor

• a job teaching a musical instrument to children

• a job coaching a children's sports team

• an academic honors society

Freewrite for ten minutes about the information you want in your résumé.

_____

_____

_____

_____

_____

_____

_____

_____

_____

_____

_____

_____

_____

Composition

▶ **Exercise 3** **Write your résumé. Pay close attention to structure.**

_____

_____

_____

_____

_____

_____

_____

_____

_____

_____

_____

_____

_____

_____

_____

_____

_____

_____

_____

_____

_____

_____

_____

_____

_____

_____

_____

_____

Composition

A cover letter is a brief letter of introduction that usually accompanies a résumé. A cover letter states what you are applying for and where you can be contacted, and it refers the reader to your résumé for additional information. It may also briefly state why you feel you are well-suited for the position.

The following is an example of a well-formatted, concise cover letter. Note that the letter follows business letter style rules and that it is directed to a specific person.

Frank Garcia
2210 Victory Parkway
Cincinnati, Ohio 45210

Future Teachers of America
Young Scholars Program
c/o Barbara Jeffers
106 Vine Street
Cincinnati, Ohio 45216

Dear Ms. Jeffers:
As a hard-working honors student at Central High School, I am interested in becoming a member of the Young Scholars Program. My dedication to education makes me a worthy candidate for membership in your organization.

Enclosed is a copy of my résumé. I hope you will find that I am a well-qualified student. Please feel free to contact me if you have any questions. I hope to hear from you soon.

Sincerely,
Frank Garcia
Frank Garcia

▶ **Exercise 1** **Write a cover letter based on the position you applied for in the résumé activity.**

_____
_____
_____
_____
_____
_____
_____
_____
_____
_____
_____

Composition

*I*ndex

Index

subject, 6, 85
Complete predicates, defined, 6, 77
Complete subjects, defined, 6, 77
Complex sentences, defined, 7, 105
Compound elements
   numbers, hyphens in, 17, 279
   predicates, 6, 80
   prepositions, 5, 69
   sentences, 7, 103
   subjects, 5, 79, 103, 171
Compound-complex sentences, 7, 105
Concrete nouns, defined, 2, 50
Conjunctions, defined, 5, 71
   conjunctive adverbs, 5
   coordinating, 5, 71
   correlative, 5, 71
   list, 71
   subordinating, 5, 71, 101
Continual, continuous, 12
Conversations, punctuating, 15 –16, 271
Coordinate adjectives, 15, 44, 253
Coordinating conjunctions, 5, 71
Correlative conjunctions, 5, 71
Could of, might of, must of, should of, would of, avoiding, 12, 222

D

Dangling modifiers, avoiding, 10, 38–39, 209
Dates, punctuating, 15, 261, 283
Declarative sentences, defined, 8, 119
Degrees of form (comparison), 9–10, 67, 199, 201
Demonstrative pronouns, 2, 53
Dependent (subordinate) clauses, 7, 101
   See Also Adjective clauses, Adverb clauses, Noun clauses
Diagraming
   sentences with clauses, 133
   simple sentences, 129
   simple sentences with phrases, 131
Different from, different than, 12, 223
Direct address, 15, 263
Direct objects, defined, 6, 83
Doesn't, don't, 12, 223
Double comparisons, avoiding, 10, 203
Double negatives, avoiding, 10, 207, 222
Drafting, 18, 311
   style, voice, 311

theme, 311
thesis statement, 311
topic sentence and related sentences, 311

E

Each, agreement with, 8, 29, 171
Editing, 18, 317
   proofreading, 317
Effect, affect, 11, 219
Either, agreement with, 8, 28, 171
Elliptical clauses, 111
Emigrate, immigrate, 12, 223
Emphatic verbs, defined, 4, 152
Except, accept, 11, 219
Exclamation points, 121, 245
   and quotation marks, 16, 273
Exclamatory sentences, defined, 8, 121

F

Farther, further, 12, 223
Fewer, less, 12, 223
Fragments, sentence, defined, 22–23, 123

G

Gerund phrases, 7, 93, 209
Gerunds, defined, 7, 93
Good, well, 12, 205, 224

H

Had of, avoiding, 12, 224
Hanged, hung, 12, 224
Hardly, in double negatives, 11, 222
Helping (auxiliary) verbs, 3, 59
Hyphens, rules, 16, 279

I

Illusion, allusion, 11
Immigrate, emigrate, 12, 223
Imperative mood, verbs, 4
Imperative sentences, defined, 8, 119
In, into, in to, 12, 224
Incomplete comparisons, avoiding, 10, 203
Indefinite pronouns, defined, 2, 53, 175
   agreement with verb, 8, 29, 175
   list, 53, 175
Independent (main) clauses, 7, 101
Indicative mood, verbs, 4
Indirect objects, defined, 6, 84
Indirect quotations, 235, 271
Infinitive phrases, 7, 95
   comma after, 42
Infinitives, defined, 7, 95

as adjectives, 7, 95
as adverbs, 7, 95
as nouns, 7, 95
Inquiry, letters of, 20, 337
Inside addresses in letters, 19
Intensive pronouns, 2, 51
Interjections, 5, 72
Interrogative pronouns, 2, 53
   list, 53
Interrogative sentences, defined, 8, 121
Into, in, 12, 224
Intransitive verbs, defined, 3, 55
Inverted order in sentences, 8, 26–27, 167
Irregardless, avoiding, 12, 224
Irregular verbs, 3–4, 143
Italics, 16, 275
Its, it's, 41, 277

L

Lay, lie, 12, 225
Learn, teach, 12, 225
Leave, let, 12, 225
Lend, borrow, loan, 11, 222
Less, fewer, 12, 223
Letter writing, 19–20, 333, 337–339, 342
   business, 19–20, 337–339, 342
      block and semiblock forms, 19, 337
      cover letters, 20, 342
      letters of request, 20, 337–338
      résumés, 20, 339
   personal, 19–20, 333
   See also Business letters; Personal letters
Lie, lay, 12, 225
Like, as, 12–13, 225
Linking verbs, 3, 57
Loan, borrow, lend, 11, 222
Loose, lose, 13, 225

M

Main (independent) clauses, 7, 101
May, can, 11, 222
Modifiers
   adjective clauses, 7, 42, 107, 255
   adjectives, 4–5, 9–10, 61
   adverb clauses, 7, 111, 259
   adverbs, 5, 9–10, 63
   comparisons, degrees, 9–10, 67, 199, 201
   comparisons, double and incomplete, 10, 203
   comparisons, irregular, 10, 201

misplaced or dangling, 10, 38–39, 209

Moods of verbs, 4

N

Negative words as adverbs, 10, 63

Negatives, double, avoiding, 10, 207

Neither, with compound subjects, 5, 79

Nominative case, pronouns, 2, 8–9, 181, 183, 185

Nor, with compound subjects, 5, 79

Noun clauses, 7, 115

Nouns, defined, 2, 47, 49–50
    abstract, 2, 50
    as appositives, 6, 94
    collective, 2, 47
    common and proper, 2, 49
    concrete, 2, 50
    as direct objects, 83
    as gerunds, 7, 93
    as indirect objects, 84
    as infinitives, 7, 95
    as objects of prepositions, 6, 69
    plurals, 2, 47
    possessive, 2, 277
    proper, 2, 13–14, 49, 237
    singular, 2, 47
    as subjects, simple and compound, 75, 79

Number, amount, 221

Numbers and Numerals, 16, 17, 283
    and hyphens, 16, 17, 279

O

Object complements, 5–6, 86

Objective case, pronouns, 2, 9, 181, 183, 185

Objects of prepositions, defined, 6, 69, 89

Of, misused for *have,* 12, 222, 224

Only, placement of, 10, 38, 209

Outlines, writing, 19, 321

P

Paragraphs, building, 18, 327
    chronological order, 18, 327
    compare/contrast order, 18, 327
    spatial order, 18, 327

Paragraphs, ordering, 18, 331
    coherence, 18, 331
    unity, 18, 331

Parentheses, 15, 269
    punctuation with, 15, 269

Participial phrases, defined, 7, 91
    comma after, 42, 91

Participles, defined, 7, 91

Passed, past, 13, 226

Passive voice, 4, 155, 323

Past, passed, 13, 226

Periods, rules, 14, 245

Personal letters, 19–20, 333

Personal pronouns, defined, 2, 51, 181
    cases, 2, 8–9, 181, 183
    first person, 2, 51
    intensive, 2, 51
    list, 2, 51, 181
    nominative, 2, 8–9, 181, 183, 185
    objective, 2, 9, 181, 183, 185
    possessive, 2, 9, 41, 51, 61, 181
    reflexive, 2, 9, 51
    second person, 2, 51
    third person, 2, 51

Phrases, defined, 6–7, 89, 91, 93–95, 97
    See also Appositive phrases, Gerund phrases, Infinitive phrases, Participial phrases, Prepositional phrases, Verbal phrases

Plural nouns, 2, 47

Plurals, spelling of, 18, 300

Positive form, modifiers, 9–10, 67, 199, 201

Possessive apostrophes, 16, 40–41, 277

Possessive case, pronouns, 2, 9, 51, 61, 181

Possessive nouns, 2, 16, 61, 277

Precede, proceed, 13, 226

Predicate adjective, 6, 85

Predicate nominative, defined, 6, 85

Predicates
    complete, 6, 77
    compound, 6, 80
    simple, 6, 75

Prefixes, 17, 295
    and hyphens, 16, 279

Prepositional phrases, defined, 6, 69, 89
    as adjectives, 6, 89
    as adverbs, 6, 89
    object of the preposition, 6, 89

Prepositions, defined, 5, 69
    compound, 5, 69
    list, 5, 69

Presentation, of writing, 18, 319

Prewriting, 18, 307
    choosing a topic, 18, 307
    determining the audience, 18, 307
    determining the purpose, 18, 307

Principal parts of verbs, 3–4, 141, 143

Proceed, precede, 13, 226

Progressive verbs, defined, 4, 151

Pronouns, defined, 2, 51, 181
    after *than* and *as,* 183
    agreement with, 9, 30–34, 187, 189, 191
    antecedents of, 3, 9, 30–33, 187, 189, 191, 193
    as appositives, 6, 94, 183
    cases of, 2, 8–9, 181, 183
    demonstrative, 2, 53
    gender of, 30, 187
    indefinite, 2, 53, 175
    intensive, 2, 51
    interrogative, 2, 53
    number of, 30–31, 187
    personal, 2, 51, 181
    possessive, 2, 9, 51, 181
    reflexive, 2, 9, 51
    relative, 2, 53
    who, whom, 2, 13, 185

Proofreading, 317

Proper adjectives, 5, 14, 61, 239

Proper nouns, 2, 13–14, 49, 237

Punctuation rules. *See specific types.*

Q

Question marks, 14, 121, 245
    and quotation marks, 16, 273

Quotation marks, 15–16, 271, 273
    with colons or semicolons, 16, 273
    in direct quotations, 15–16, 271
    in indirect quotations, 235, 271
    within a quotation, 15, 271
    with titles of short works, 15, 273
    with unusual expressions, 15, 273

Quotations, capitalizing, 15, 235

R

Raise, rise, 13, 226

Reason is because, avoiding, 13, 226

Reflexive pronouns, 2, 9, 51

Regardless, not *irregardless,* 12, 224

Regular verbs, 3–4, 141

Relative pronouns, 2, 53

Respectfully, respectively, 13, 227

Résumés, 20, 339

Revising, 18, 315
    coherence, 18, 315
    meaning, 315
    unity, 18, 315

Rise, raise, 13, 226

Roots of words, 17, 293

Run-on sentences, defined, 24–25, 125

S

Said, says, 13, 227
Scarcely, in double negatives, 11, 222
Semiblock form of letters, 19, 337
Semicolons, 14–15, 16, 249, 273
  to correct run-on sentences, 24–25, 125
Sentence fragments, 22–23, 123
Sentence patterns, explained, 5–6, 8, 81, 167
Sentence structure
  complex, 7, 105
  compound, 7, 103
  compound-complex, 7, 105
  simple, 7, 103
Sentences, effective, 323
  active voice, 155, 323
  interruption, 323
  parallelism, 323
  unusual patterns, 323
  varied length, 18, 323
  varied structure, 18, 323
Sentences, kinds of
  declarative, 8, 119
  exclamatory, 8, 121
  imperative, 8, 119
  interrogative, 8, 121
Sentences, run-on, 24–25, 125
Series, commas in, 15, 44, 253
  colon before, 247
Set, sit, 13, 227
Simple predicates, defined, 6, 75
Simple sentences, defined, 7, 103
Simple subjects, defined, 5, 75
Singular nouns, 2, 47
Sit, set, 13, 227
Spatial order, 18, 327
Spelling
  adding *-ly* and *-ness,* 18, 299
  doubling the final consonant, 18, 299
  forming compound words, 16, 18, 279, 299
  of *-cede, -ceed,* and *-sede,* 17, 297
  of *ie* and *ei,* 17, 297
  of plural nouns, 18, 300
  of suffixes, 17, 18, 298
  of unstressed vowels, 297
Subject complements, 6, 85
Subject-verb agreement, 8, 26–29, 161, 163, 165, 167, 169, 171, 173, 175
  in adjective clauses, 8
  and collective nouns, 27, 169

  and compound subjects, 8, 28–29, 171
  and indefinite pronouns, 8, 29, 175
  and intervening expressions, 8, 29, 173
  and intervening prepositional phrases, 8, 26, 163
  in inverted sentences, 8, 26–27, 167
  and linking verbs, 26, 165, 167, 169
  and predicate nominatives, 26, 165
  and special subjects, 8, 169
  with titles, 8
Subjects
  agreement of verb with, 8, 26–29, 161, 163, 165, 167, 169, 171, 173, 175
  complete, 6, 77
  compound, 5, 79, 103, 171
  gerunds and infinitives as, 7, 93, 97
  noun clauses as, 7, 115
  simple, 5, 75
Subjunctive mood, verbs, 4
Subordinate (dependent) clauses, 7, 101, 259
Subordinating conjunctions, 5, 71, 101
Suffixes, 17, 18, 295, 297, 298
Superlative form, 9–10, 67, 199, 201

T

Take, bring, 11, 222
Teach, learn, 12, 225
Tenses, defined, 3, 145
  future, 3, 145
  future perfect, 3, 147
  incorrect, 36–37
  past, 3, 145
  past perfect, 3, 147
  present, 3, 145
  present perfect, 3, 147
  shifts in, avoiding, 35, 153
Than, then, 13, 227
That there, this here, avoiding, 13, 227
Theme, writing, 18, 311
Then, than, 13, 227
Thesis statement, writing, 18, 311
This here, that there, avoiding, 13, 227
This kind, these kinds, 225
Topic sentences, 311, 323, 331
Transitive verbs, defined, 3, 55

U

Understood subject, 119

V

Verb phrases, defined, 3, 6, 59
Verbal phrases, 7, 93, 97
Verbals, defined, 7, 93, 95, 97
  See also Gerunds, Infinitives, Participles
Verbs, defined, 3, 55
  action verbs, 3, 55
    intransitive, 3, 55
    transitive, 3, 55
  agreement with subjects, rules, 8, 26–29, 161, 163, 165, 167, 169, 171, 173, 175
  auxiliary (helping), 3, 59
  emphatic, 4, 152
  intransitive, 3, 55
  irregular, regular, 3–4, 141, 143
  linking, 3, 57
  list, 3–4, 59, 141, 143
  moods of, 4
  principal parts of irregular, 3–4, 143
  principal parts of regular, 141
  progressive, 4, 151
  tenses of, 3, 35–37, 145, 147, 149, 151–152
    compatibility, 153
    shifts in, avoiding, 35
    See also Tenses
  transitive, 3, 55
  voice of, active and passive, 4, 155, 323
Vocabulary building, 17–18, 291, 293, 295
  from context, 17, 291
  prefixes and suffixes, 17–18, 295
  word roots, base words, 17, 293
Voice of verbs, defined, 4, 155, 323
  active, 4, 155, 323
  effective use of, 155, 323
  passive, 4, 155, 323

W

Well, good, 12, 205, 224
Where at, avoiding, 227
Who, whom, 13, 185
Writing process. *See specific steps.*
Writing letters, 19–20, 333, 335, 337–339, 342
Writing paragraphs, 18, 327

Y

You, as understood subject, 119